Frommer's® 2000

PORTABLE
Paris

by Darwin Porter & Danforth Prince

Macmillan • USA

ABOUT THE AUTHORS

Veteran travel writers **Darwin Porter** and **Danforth Prince** have written numerous best-selling Frommer guides, notably to England, France, the Caribbean, Italy, and Germany. Porter, a bureau chief for the *Miami Herald* at the age of 21, has lived in Paris periodically and written about the city for many years. Prince also has lived in the city for many years as a member of the Paris bureau for the *New York Times*.

MACMILLAN TRAVEL

Macmillan General Reference USA, Inc.
1633 Broadway
New York, NY 10019

Find us online at **www.frommers.com**.

ISBN 0-02-863548-5
ISSN 1520-5541

Editor: David Gibbs
Production Editor: Carol Sheehan
Photo Editor: Richard Fox
Design by Michele Laseau
Staff Cartographers: John Decamillis, Roberta Stockwell
Page Creation by John Bitter, Linda Quigley, Melissa Auciello-Brogan, and Marie Kristine Parial-Leonardo

SPECIAL SALES

Contents

List of Maps

AN INVITATION TO THE READER

In researching this book, we discovered many wonderful places—hotels, restaurants, shops, and more. We're sure you'll find others. Please tell us about them, so we can share the information with your fellow travelers in upcoming editions. If you were disappointed with a recommendation, we'd love to know that, too. Please write to:

Frommer's Portable Paris 2000
Macmillan Travel
1633 Broadway
New York, NY 10019

AN ADDITIONAL NOTE

Please be advised that travel information is subject to change at any time—and this is especially true of prices. We therefore suggest that you write or call ahead for confirmation when making your travel plans. The authors, editors, and publisher cannot be held responsible for the experiences of readers while traveling. Your safety is important to us, however, so we encourage you to stay alert and be aware of your surroundings. Keep a close eye on cameras, purses, and wallets, all favorite targets of thieves and pickpockets.

WHAT THE SYMBOLS MEAN
✪ Frommer's Favorites

Our favorite places and experiences—outstanding for quality, value, or both.

The following abbreviations are used for credit cards:

AE	American Express	EC	Eurocard
CB	Carte Blanche	JCB	Japan Credit Bank
DC	Diners Club	MC	MasterCard
DISC	Discover	V	Visa
ER	enRoute		

FIND FROMMER'S ONLINE

Arthur Frommer's Budget Travel Online (www.frommers.com) offers more than 6,000 pages of up-to-the-minute travel information—including the latest bargains and candid, personal articles updated daily by Arthur Frommer himself. No other Web site offers such comprehensive and timely coverage of the world of travel.

Planning a Trip to Paris

*P*aris is preparing for an invasion unlike any it has seen before. "We're having a picnic in the year 2000," said Julian Française, a government employee. "We have a better, cleaner, more exciting, and more dynamic city to show the world than we did in the '70s and '80s. 'Y'all come and see us now,' as they'd say in Texas."

Hoping to put aside its economic woes of the 1990s, Paris is facing the 21st century with a bright face. According to polls, the French people, even the traditionally cynical Parisians, are becoming more optimistic. The city looks better than it has in years, with such monumental projects completed as the cleaning of the Louvre, Opéra, and Notre-Dame. Much of the riverfront has been restored, repaired, and spruced up in anticipation of the millennium. And always the City of Light, Paris will be even more dazzling in 2000, with greater illuminations than ever before.

Paris may not be the most happening city in Europe. London, at least in the opinion of Londoners, still retains that position. But Paris remains queen of the continent, with more museums than ever, greater nighttime diversions, better hotels (many of them also rejuvenated for the millennium), better and more varied shops, and the most talented stable of chefs in the world.

Whether you're heading here for the first or the 50th time, the discovery of the City of Light and the experience of making it your own is and always has been the most compelling reason to visit. Neighborhoods such as Montmartre and Montparnasse, St-Germain and the Marais, are waiting to be explored for the first time or to be rediscovered by a returning visitor. In some ways, they remain the same, as if etched in stone, but after a second look it's obvious that they have changed.

If you're a first-timer, everything in Paris, of course, is new. If you've been away for a while, expect changes: Taxi drivers may no longer correct your fractured French, but address you in English— and that's tantamount to a revolution. More Parisians have a rudimentary knowledge of English, and the country, at least at first glance, seems less hysterically xenophobic than in past years. Part of this derives from Parisians' interest in music, videos, and films from foreign countries, and part from France's growing awareness of its role within a united Europe.

Yet France has never been more concerned about the loss of its identity, as it continues to attract an increasing number of immigrants from its former colonies. Many have expressed concern that France will lose the battle to keep its language strong, distinct, and unadulterated by foreign slang or catchwords. But as the country approaches the millennium, foreign tourists spending much-needed cash are no longer perceived as foes or antagonists. *Au contraire:* The rancor of France's collective xenophobia has been increasingly redirected toward the many immigrants seeking better lives in Paris, where the infrastructure has nearly been stretched to its limits.

Though Paris is clearly a city in flux culturally and socially, it still lures travelers for the same reasons it always has. Grand indestructible sights such as the Tour Eiffel are still here, as is the spruced-up Champs-Elysées—and both are as crowded as ever. The beauty of Paris is still overwhelming, especially in the illumination of night. The City of Light, one of the premier tourist destinations in the world, always puts on a memorable show.

This chapter provides most of the nuts-and-bolts information you'll need before setting off for Paris. We've put everything from information sources to the major airlines at your fingertips.

1   Visitor Information

BEFORE YOU GO

Your best source of information before you go is the **French Government Tourist Office,** which can be reached at 444 Madison Ave., 16th Floor, New York, NY 10022 (☎ **212/838-7800**); 676 N. Michigan Ave., Suite 3360, Chicago, IL 60611-2819 (☎ 312/751-7800); or 9454 Wilshire Blvd., Suite 715, Beverly Hills, CA 90212-2967 (☎ 310/271-6665). To request information, you can call **France on Call** at ☎ **202/659-7779.** The Internet address is www.francetourism.com.

IN PARIS

See chapter 2, "Visitor Information," under "Orientation."

2   Entry Requirements & Customs Regulations

PASSPORT/VISAS

All foreign (non-French) nationals need a valid passport to enter France (check its expiration date). The French government no longer requires visas for **U.S. citizens,** providing they're staying in France for less than 90 days. For longer stays, U.S. visitors must apply for a long-term visa, residence card, or temporary-stay visa. Each requires proof of income or a viable means of support in France and a legitimate purpose for remaining in the country. Applications are available from the **Consulate Section of the French Embassy,** 4101 Reservoir Rd. NW, Washington, DC 20007 (☎ **202/944-6000**), or from the **Visa Section of the French Consulate** at 10 E. 74th St., New York, NY 10021 (☎ **212/ 606-3689**). Visas are required for students planning to study in France even if the stay is for less than 90 days.

At the moment, citizens of Australia, Canada, New Zealand, Switzerland, Japan, and European Community countries do not need visas.

South Africans need a visa to enter France. They're available from the **French Consulate,** 2 Dean St. (next to Queen Victoria St.), Cape Town 8001 (☎ **021/23-15-75;** fax 021/24-84-70).

CUSTOMS
WHAT YOU CAN BRING INTO FRANCE

Customs restrictions differ for citizens of the European Community (EC) and for citizens of non-EC countries. **Non-EC nationals** can bring in duty-free 200 cigarettes, 100 cigarillos, 50 cigars, or 250 grams of smoking tobacco. This amount is doubled if you live outside Europe. You can also bring in 2 liters of wine and either 1 liter of alcohol over 22 proof or 2 liters of wine under 22 proof. In addition, you can bring in 50 grams (1.75 ounces) of perfume, one-quarter liter (250 ml) of eau de toilette, 500 grams (1 pound) of coffee, and 200 grams (one-half pound) of tea. Visitors 15 years of age and over may also bring in other goods totaling 300 F ($51); the allowance for those 14 and under is 150 F ($25.50). (Customs officials tend to be lenient about general merchandise, realizing that the limits are unrealistically low.)

Visitors from **European Union (EU)** countries can bring in 300 cigarettes or 150 cigarillos or 75 cigars or 400 grams of smoking tobacco. You can also bring in 2 liters of wine and either 1 liter of alcohol over 38.80 proof or 2 liters of wine under 38.80 proof. In addition, visitors can bring in 75 grams of perfume, three-eighths of a liter of toilet water, 1,000 grams of coffee, and 80 grams of tea. Passengers 15 and over can bring in 2,400 F ($408) worth of merchandise duty-free; those 14 and under can bring in 620 F ($105.40) worth.

IMPORT RESTRICTIONS

Returning **U.S. citizens** who have been away for 48 hours or more are allowed to bring back, once every 30 days, $400 worth of merchandise duty-free. You'll be charged a flat rate of 10% duty on the next $1,000 worth of purchases. Be sure to have your receipts handy. On gifts, the duty-free limit is $100. You cannot bring fresh foodstuffs into the United States; tinned foods, however, are allowed. For more information, contact the **U.S. Customs Service,** 1301 Constitution Ave. (P.O. Box 7407), Washington, DC 20044 (☎ **202/927-6724**), and request the free pamphlet *Know Before You Go.* It's also available on the Web at www.customs.ustreas.gov/travel/kbygo.htm.

3 Money

CURRENCY   French currency is based on the franc (F), which consists of 100 centimes (c). Coins come in units of 5, 10, 20, and 50 centimes; and 1, 2, 5, and 10 francs. Notes come in denominations of 20, 50, 100, 200, 500, and 1,000 francs.

All banks are equipped for foreign exchange, and you will find exchange offices at the airports and airline terminals. Banks are open from 9am to noon and 2 to 4pm Monday through Friday. Major bank branches also open their exchange departments on Saturday between 9am and noon.

When converting your home currency into French francs, be aware that rates vary. Your hotel will probably offer the worst rate of exchange. In general, banks offer the best rate, but even banks charge a commission for the service, often $3, depending on the transaction. Whenever you can, stick to the big banks of Paris, like Crédit Lyonnais, which usually offer the best exchange rates and charge the least commission. Always make sure you have enough francs for the weekend.

THE EURO   The euro, the new single European currency, became the official currency of France and 10 other countries on January 1, 1999, but the French franc will remain the only currency for cash transactions until December 21, 2001. At that time, euro banknotes and coins will be introduced, and French franc banknotes and coins will be withdrawn from circulation during a maximum 6-month transition period. The symbol of the euro is a stylized **E,** which actually looks like an uppercase C with a horizontal double bar through the middle; its official abbreviation is EUR.

TRAVELER'S CHECKS   Traveler's checks are something of an anachronism from the days before the ATM (automated teller machine) made cash accessible at any time. Many banks, however, impose a fee every time a card is used at an ATM in a different city or bank. If you're withdrawing money every day, you might be better off with traveler's checks—provided that you don't mind showing identification every time you want to cash a check.

ATMs   ATMs are linked to a national network that most likely includes your bank at home. **Cirrus** (☎ **800/424-7787;** www.mastercard.com/atm/) and **Plus** (☎ **800/843-7587;** www.visa.com/atms) are the two most popular networks; check the back of your ATM card to see which network your bank belongs to. Use the 800 numbers to locate ATMs in your destination (Cirrus only). Be sure to check the daily withdrawal limit before you depart, and ask whether you need a new personal ID number.

CREDIT CARDS   Credit cards are invaluable when traveling. They are a safe way to carry money and provide a convenient record of all your expenses. You can also withdraw cash advances from your credit cards at any bank (though you'll start paying hefty interest on the advance the moment you receive the cash, and you won't receive frequent-flyer miles on an airline credit card). At most banks, you don't even need to go to a teller; you can get a cash advance at the ATM if you know your PIN number. If you've forgotten your PIN number or didn't even know you had one, call the phone number on the back of your credit card and ask the bank to send it to you. It usually takes 5 to 7 business days, though some banks will provide the number over the phone if you tell them your mother's maiden name or pass some other security clearance.

THEFT   Almost every credit card company has an emergency 800 number that you can call if your wallet or purse is stolen. They may be able to wire you a cash advance off your credit card immediately, and in many places, they can deliver an emergency credit card in a day or two. The issuing bank's 800 number is usually on the back of the credit card—though of course that doesn't help you much if the card was stolen. Citicorp Visa's U.S. emergency number is ☎ **0800-90-2033** (toll-free); 410-581-3836 (collect). American Express cardholders and traveler's check holders should call ☎ **47-77-70-00** for all money emergencies. MasterCard holders should call ☎ **0800-90-1387** (toll-free).

If you opt to carry traveler's checks, be sure to keep a record of their serial numbers, separately from the checks of course, so you're ensured a refund in case of an emergency.

Odds are that if your wallet is gone, the police won't be able to recover it for you. However, after you realize that it's gone and you cancel your credit cards, it is still worth informing them. Your credit-card company or insurer may require a police report number.

4 When to Go

In August, Parisians traditionally leave for their annual holiday and put the city on a skeleton staff to serve visitors. July has also become a popular vacation month, with many a restaurateur shuttering up for a monthlong respite.

Hotels, especially first-class and deluxe, are easy to come by in July and August. Budget hotels, on the other hand, are likely to be full during these months of student invasion. You might also try to avoid the first 2 weeks in October, when the annual auto show attracts thousands of automobile enthusiasts.

THE CLIMATE   Balmy weather in Paris has prompted more popular songs and love ballads than weather conditions in any other city in the world. But the weather here is actually quite fickle. Rain is much more common than snow throughout the winter, prompting many longtime residents to complain about the occasional bone-chilling dampness.

In recent years, Paris has had only about 15 snow days a year, and there are only a few oppressively hot days (that is, over 86°F) in mid-summer. What will most likely chill a Parisian heart, however, are blasts of rapidly moving air—wind tunnels sweep along the city's long boulevards, channeled by bordering buildings of uniform height. Other than the occasional winds and rain (which add an undeniable drama to many of the city's panoramas), Paris offers some of the most pleasant weather of any capital in Europe, with a highly tolerable average temperature of 53°F.

HOLIDAYS   Holidays in France are known as *jours fériés*. Shops and banks are closed, as well as many (but not all) restaurants and museums. Major holidays include January 1, Easter, Ascension Day (40 days after Easter), Pentecost (seventh Sunday after Easter), May 1, May 8 (V-E Day), July 14 (Bastille Day), August 15 (Assumption of the Virgin Mary), November 1 (All Saints' Day), November 11 (Armistice Day), and December 25 (Christmas).

Paris at the Millennium

In the spirit of a new century, Paris will launch major exhibitions, and dozens of celebrations will be announced in the year 2000. Paris isn't celebrating the millennium with a grand monument, as it did with the Eiffel Tower or Britain is doing with its Greenwich Millennium Dome. Instead, the city will launch a series of smaller-scale projects, exhibits, and cultural festivals. A "planetary garden" is being carved out of a large space at La Villette. A sundial is to be installed at the Place de la Concorde. Major exhibitions will be announced at the newly renovated Georges Pompidou Center (Beaubourg). And a series of exhibits called Visions of the Future is planned at the Grand Palais for the year 2000. A spectacular "message for peace" is to be installed at the Trocadero across from the Eiffel Tower, in the form of a wailing wall like the one in Jerusalem—visitors can leave their peace messages in the cracks in the wall, taking a message left by another. And in the same spirit, a monumental sculpture representing the world's children hand in hand will be erected in front of UNESCO's headquarters. Concerts, sporting events, and parades are also in the works, with festivities expected to reach their peak on the national holiday of July 14, 2000. And the largest balloon in the world (104 feet) will let passengers view Paris from an altitude of 975 feet.

Check with the tourist offices listed under "Visitor Information" above to find out exactly what millennial celebrations will be taking place at the time of your visit. Better yet, visit France's official millennial Web site at **www.celebration2000.gouv.fr**.

5 Getting There

BY PLANE (FROM NORTH AMERICA)

The flying time to Paris from New York is about 7 hours; from Chicago, 9 hours; from Los Angeles, 11 hours; from Atlanta, about 8 hours; and from Washington, D.C., about 7^1/$_2$ hours.

One of the best choices for passengers flying to Paris from both the southeastern United States and the Midwest is **Delta Airlines** (☎ 800/241-4141; www.delta-air.com). **United Airlines** (☎ 800/538-2929; www.ual.com) offers nonstop flights from Chicago, Washington, D.C. (Dulles), and San Francisco to Paris's Charles de

Gaulle Airport. United also offers discounted fares in the low and shoulder seasons to London's Heathrow from five major North American hubs. From London, it's an easy train and Hovercraft or Chunnel connection to Paris, a fact that tempts many passengers to spend a weekend in London either before or after their visit to Paris.

Another good option is **Continental Airlines** (☎ 800/ 231-0856; www.flycontinental.com), which services the Northeast and much of the Southwest through its busy hubs in Newark and Houston. **TWA** (☎ 800/221-2000; www.twa.com), operates daily nonstop service to Charles de Gaulle Airport from New York's JFK, and in summer, several flights a week from Boston and Washington, D.C.'s Dulles airport. In summer, TWA also flies to Paris from St. Louis several times a week nonstop, and to Paris from Los Angeles three times a week, with connections in St. Louis or New York's JFK. In winter, flights from Los Angeles and Washington, D.C., are suspended, and flights from St. Louis are routed with brief touchdowns en route to Paris in New York or Boston.

The French flag carrier, **Air France** (☎ 800/237-2747; www. airfrance.com), offers daily or several-times-a-week flights between Paris's Charles de Gaulle and Newark, New Jersey; Washington, D.C.'s Dulles; Miami; Chicago; New York's JFK; Houston; San Francisco; Los Angeles; Boston; Cincinnati; Atlanta; Montréal; Toronto; and Mexico City.

American Airlines (☎ 800/433-7300; www.american.air.com), provides daily nonstop flights to Paris (Orly) from Dallas/Fort Worth, Chicago, Miami, Boston, and New York's JFK. **US Airways** (☎ 800/428-4322; www.usairways.com), offers daily nonstop service from Philadelphia International Airport to Paris's Charles de Gaulle Airport.

Canadians usually choose **Air Canada** (☎ 800/776-3000 from the U.S. and Canada; www.aircanada.ca) for flights to Paris from Toronto and Montréal. Nonstop flights from Montréal and Toronto depart every evening for Paris. Two of the nonstop flights from Toronto are shared with Air France and feature Air France aircraft.

PARIS AIRPORTS

Paris has two major international airports: **Orly** (☎ 01-49-75-15-15), 8¹/₂ miles south, and **Charles de Gaulle**, or **Roissy** (☎ 01-48-62-22-80), 14¹/₄ miles northeast of the city. A shuttle operates between the two airports about every 30 minutes, taking 50 to 75 minutes. Tickets are 75 F ($12.75).

CHARLES DE GAULLE AIRPORT (ROISSY)   At Charles de Gaulle Airport, foreign carriers use Aérogare 1, and Air France uses Aérogare 2. From Aérogare 1, you take a moving walkway to the passport checkpoint and the Customs area. The two terminals are linked by a shuttle bus *(navette)*.

The free shuttle bus connecting Aérogare 1 with Aérogare 2 also transports passengers to the Roissy rail station, from which fast **RER trains** leave every 15 minutes for such Métro stations as Gare du Nord, Châtelet, Luxembourg, Port-Royal, and Denfert-Rochereau. The train fare from Roissy to any point within central Paris is 69 F ($11.75) in first class or 47 F ($8) in second class. You can also take an **Air France shuttle bus** to central Paris for 60 F ($10.20). It stops at the Palais des Congrès (Port Maillot), then continues on to the place del'Etoile, where underground lines can carry you further along to any other point within Paris. Depending on traffic, the ride takes between 45 and 55 minutes. The shuttle departs about every 12 minutes between 5:40am and 11pm.

Another option, the **Roissybus** (☎ **01-48-04-18-24**), departs from a point near the corner of the rue Scribe and the place de l'Opéra every 15 minutes from 5:45am to 11pm. The cost for the 45- to 50-minute bus ride is 45 F ($7.65).

Taxis from Roissy into the city will run about 250 F ($42.50) on the meter. At night (from 8pm to 7am), fares are about 40% higher. Long queues of both taxis and passengers form outside each of the airport's terminals in a surprisingly orderly fashion.

ORLY AIRPORT   Orly has two terminals: Orly Sud (south) for international flights and Orly Ouest (west) for domestic flights. A free shuttle bus links them together.

Air France buses leave exit E of Orly Ouest, and from exit F, Platform 5 of Orly Sud, every 12 minutes between 5:45am and 11pm, heading for Gare des Invalides in central Paris at a cost of 45 F ($7.65) one-way. Other buses depart for the place Denfert-Rochereau in the south of Paris. Passage on any of these buses costs 30 F ($5.10).

An alternative method for reaching central Paris involves taking a free shuttle bus that leaves both of Orly's terminals at intervals of approximately every 15 minutes for the nearby **RER train station** (Pont-de-Rungis/Aéroport-d'Orly), from which RER trains take 30 minutes to reach the city center. A trip to Les Invalides, for example, costs 35 F ($5.95).

A **taxi** from Orly to the center of Paris costs about 170 F ($28.90) and is higher at night and on weekends. Don't take a meter-less taxi—it's much safer (and usually cheaper) to hire a metered cab from the taxi queues, which are under the scrutiny of a police officer.

Returning to the airport, **buses** leave from the Invalides terminal to either Orly Sud or Orly Ouest every 15 minutes, taking about 30 minutes.

BY TRAIN

If you're already in Europe, you might decide to travel to Paris by train, especially if you have a Eurailpass. Even if you don't, the cost is relatively low. For example, the one-way fare from London to Paris by Eurostar ranges from $179 to $299 in first class and $109 to $149 in second class. Rail passes or individual rail tickets within Europe are available at most travel agencies, at any office of **Rail Europe** (☎ 800/4-EURAIL in the U.S.; www.raileurope.com) or **Eurostar** (☎ 800/EUROSTAR in the U.S.).

In London, an especially convenient place to buy railway tickets to virtually anywhere is just opposite Platform 2 in **Victoria Station,** London SW1V 1JZ, where Wasteels, Ltd. (☎ 0171/834-6744) provides railway-related services and discusses the pros and cons of various types of fares and rail passes. Occasionally, Wasteels charges a £5 ($8.25) fee for its services, but its information warrants the fee and the company's staff spends a generous amount of time planning itineraries with each client. Some of the most popular passes, including Inter-Rail and EuroYouth, are available only to those under 26 years of age for unlimited second-class travel in 26 European countries.

PARIS TRAIN STATIONS

There are six major train stations in Paris: **Gare d'Austerlitz,** 55 quai d'Austerlitz, 13e (serving the southwest, with trains from the Loire Valley, the Bordeaux country, and the Pyrénées); **Gare de l'Est,** place du 11 Novembre 1918, 10e (serving the east, with trains from Strasbourg, Nancy, Reims, and beyond to Zurich, Basel, Luxembourg, and Austria); **Gare de Lyon,** 20 bd. Diderot, 12e (serving the southeast with trains from the Côte d'Azur, Provence, and beyond to Geneva, Lausanne, and Italy); **Gare Montparnasse,** 17 bd. Vaugirard, 15e (serving the west, with trains from Brittany); **Gare du Nord,** 18 rue de Dunkerque, 15e (serving the north, with trains from Holland, Denmark, Belgium, and northern Germany);

and **Gare St-Lazare,** 13 rue d'Amsterdam, 8e (serving the north-west, with trains from Normandy).

For general train information and to make reservations, call ☎ **08-36-35-35-39** from 7am to 8pm daily. Buses operate between rail stations. Each of these stations has a Métro stop, making the whole city easily accessible. Taxis are also available at designated stands at every station. Look for the sign that says TÊTE DE STATION. Be alert in train stations, especially at night.

BY FERRY FROM ENGLAND

In spite of competiton from the Chunnel, services aboard ferryboats and hydrofoils operate day and night, in all seasons, with the exception of last-minute cancellations during particularly fierce storms. Many channel crossings are carefully timed to coincide with the arrival/departure of major trains (especially those between London and Paris). Trains let you off a short walk from the piers. Most ferries carry cars, trucks, and massive amounts of freight, but some hydrofoils take passengers only. The major routes include at least 12 trips a day between Dover or Folkestone and Calais or Boulogne. Hovercraft and hydrofoils make the trip from Dover to Calais, the shortest distance across the channel, in just 40 minutes during good weather, whereas the slower-moving ferries might take several hours, depending on weather conditions and tides. If you're bringing a car, it's important to make reservations, as space below decks is usually crowded. Timetables can vary depending on weather conditions and many other factors.

The leading operator of ferryboats across the channel is **P&O Stena Lines** (call BritRail for reservations at ☎ **800/677-8585** within North America, or 0870/600-0600 in England). It operates car and passenger ferries between Portsmouth, England, and Cherbourg, France (three departures a day; 4^1/$_4$ hours each way during daylight hours, 7 hours each way at night); between Portsmouth and Le Havre, France (three a day; 5^1/$_2$ hours each way). Most popular of all are the routes it operates between Dover and Calais, France (25 sailings a day; 75 minutes each way), costing £24 ($39.60) one-way for adults or £12 ($19.80) for children.

The shortest and by far the most popular route across the channel is between Calais and Dover. **Hoverspeed** operates at least 12 hovercraft crossings daily; the trip takes 35 minutes. It also runs a SeaCat (a catamaran propelled by jet engines) that takes slightly longer to make the crossing between Boulogne and Folkestone; the SeaCats depart about four times a day on the 55-minute voyage. For reservations and information, call Hoverspeed (☎ **800/677-8585** for reservations in North America, or 08705/240-241 in England). Typical one-way fares are £25 ($41.25) per person.

If you plan to transport a rental car between England and France, check in advance with the rental company about license and insurance requirements and additional drop-off charges. And be aware that many car-rental companies, for insurance reasons, forbid transport of one of their vehicles over the water between England and France. Transport of a car each way begins at £75 ($123.75).

UNDER THE CHANNEL

Eurostar tickets, for train service between London and Paris or Brussels, are available through **Rail Europe** (☎ **800/4-EURAIL;** www.raileurope.com). A one-way first-class nonrefundable ticket costs $179 ($219 if refundable). In second class, a nonrefundable one-way ticket goes for $109 ($149 if refundable). In London, make reservations for Eurostar at ☎ **0990/300003** (accessible in the United Kingdom only); in Paris, at ☎ **01-44-51-06-02;** and in the United States, at ☎ **800/EUROSTAR.** Chunnel train traffic is roughly competitive with air travel, if you calculate door-to-door travel time. Trains leave from London's Waterloo Station and arrive in Paris at the Gare du Nord.

The tunnel also accommodates passenger cars, charter buses, taxis, and motorcycles, transporting them under the English Channel from Folkestone, England, to Calais, France. It operates 24 hours a day, 365 days a year, running every 15 minutes during peak travel times, and at least once an hour at night. Tickets may be purchased at the toll booth at the tunnel's entrance. With "Le Shuttle," gone are the days of weather-related delays, seasickness, and advance reservations.

During the ride, motorists stay in bright, air-conditioned carriages, remaining inside their cars or stepping outside to stretch their legs. When the trip is completed, they simply drive off toward their destinations. Total travel time between the French and English highway systems is about 1 hour. Once on French soil, British drivers must remember to drive on the right-hand side of the road.

Stores selling duty-free goods, restaurants, and service stations are available to travelers on both sides of the channel. A bilingual staff is on hand to assist travelers at both the French and British terminals.

Where should you lay your weary head for the 2 or 3 nights you spend in London? The folks at Eurostar can even set that up for you as part of a rail-and-hotel package at a highly discounted rate. For as little as $317 per person, you can buy a package that includes rail transport, 2 nights (double occupancy) in a convenient hotel, and a city sightseeing tour. The price is hard to beat and the sheer convenience of the routing makes the plan easier and faster than flying.

From North America, these packages can most easily be arranged by calling the **Eurostar** division of RailEurope (☎ **800/ EUROSTAR**). For details about hotel packages, contact **EuroVacations** (☎ **888/281-EURO**). If you're already in Paris, contact any travel agency or talk to your hotel concierge, who should be able to arrange the same basic package, depending on seasonal promotions.

PACKAGE TOURS

If you're interested in a package deal (airfare plus hotel room), the best place to start your search is the travel section of your local Sunday newspaper. Also check the ads in the back of national travel magazines like *Travel & Leisure, National Geographic Traveler,* and *Condé Nast Traveler.* **Liberty Travel** (☎ **888/271-1584** to be connected with the agent closest to you; www.libertytravel.com), one of the biggest packagers in the Northeast, often runs a full-page ad in the Sunday papers. You won't get much in the way of service, but you will get a good deal. **American Express Vacations** (☎ **800/ 241-1700;** www.leisureweb.com) is another option. Check out its **Last Minute Travel Bargains** site, offered in conjunction with **Continental Airlines** (www6.americanexpress.com/travel/ lastminutetravel/default.asp), with deeply discounted vacation packages and reduced airline fares that differ from the E-savers bargains that Continental e-mails weekly to subscribers. **Northwest Airlines** offers a similar service. Posted on Northwest's Web site every Wednesday, its **Cyber Saver Bargain Alerts** offer special hotel rates, package deals, and discounted airline fares.

Another good resource is the airlines themselves, which often package their flights together with accommodations. Fly-by-night packagers are uncommon, but they do exist; when you buy your package through the airline, however, you can be pretty sure that the company will still be in business when your departure date arrives. Among the airline packagers, your options include **American Airlines FlyAway Vacations** (☎ 800/321-2121), **Delta Dream Vacations** (☎ 800/872-7786), and **US Airways Vacations** (☎ 800/455-0123). Pick the airline that services your hometown most often.

Delta Dream Vacations offers a full package called Jolie France, lasting 10 nights and costing $4,097 for two people, taking in not only Paris, but some of the regional highlights of France, including Tours, Bordeaux, Carcassonne, Nice, Nimes, Dijon, and back to Paris. All hotels, tours, and breakfasts are included, plus four dinners.

The **French Experience,** 370 Lexington Ave., Room 812, New York, NY 10017 (☎ **212/986-1115;** fax 212/986-3808), offers inexpensive airline tickets to Paris on most scheduled airlines. They arrange tours and stays in various types and categories of country inns, hotels, private châteaux, and bed-and-breakfasts. They take reservations for about 30 small hotels in Paris and arrange short-term apartment rentals in the city or farmhouse rentals in the countryside. They also offer all-inclusive packages in Paris as well as prearranged package tours of various regions of France. Any tour can be adapted to suit individual needs.

2

Getting to Know Paris

*E*rnest Hemingway referred to the many splendors of Paris as a "moveable feast" and wrote, "There is never any ending to Paris, and the memory of each person who has lived in it differs from that of any other." It is this aura of personal discovery that has always been the most compelling reason to come to Paris. And perhaps that's why France has been called *le deuxième pays de tout le monde,* "everybody's second country."

The Seine not only divides Paris into a Right Bank and a Left Bank, but it also seems to split the city into two vastly different sections and ways of life. Depending on your time, interest, and budget, you may quickly decide which section of Paris suits you best.

1 Orientation

VISITOR INFORMATION

The main Paris tourist information office is at 127 av. des Champs-Elysées, 8e (☎ **01-49-52-53-54**), where you can obtain information about both Paris and the provinces. The office is open daily from 9am to 8pm from April through October, with an annual closing May 1. Between November and March, the office is open daily from 11am to 6pm, with an annual closing December 25. There are additional branches in the base of the Eiffel Tower (open only May through October, Monday to Saturday from 8am to 8pm), and in the arrivals hall of the Gare de Lyon (open year-round, Monday to Saturday from 8am to 8pm). Any of these tourist offices will give you free copies of 50-page English-language leaflets entitled *Time Out* and *Paris User's Guide.*

CITY LAYOUT

Paris is surprisingly compact. Occupying 432 square miles (6 more than San Francisco), it is home to more than 10 million people. The River Seine divides Paris into the **Right Bank** *(Rive Droite)* to the north and the **Left Bank** *(Rive Gauche)* to the south. These designations make sense when you stand on a bridge and face downstream, watching the waters flow out toward the sea—to your right is the north bank, to your left the south. Thirty-two bridges link the banks of the Seine, some providing access to the two small islands at the heart of the city, **Ile de la Cité,** the city's birthplace and site of Notre-Dame, and **Ile St-Louis,** a moat-guarded oasis of sober 17th-century mansions. These islands can cause some confusion to walkers who think they've just crossed a bridge from one bank to the other, only to find themselves caught up in an almost medieval maze of narrow streets and old buildings.

MAIN ARTERIES & STREETS   Between 1860 and 1870, Baron Haussmann forever changed the look of Paris by creating the legendary boulevards: St-Michel, St-Germain, Haussmann, Malesherbes, Sébastopol, Magenta, Voltaire, and Strasbourg.

The "main street" on the Right Bank is, of course, the **Champs-Elysées,** beginning at the Arc de Triomphe and running to place de la Concorde. Haussmann also created avenue de l'Opéra (as well as the Opéra), and the 12 avenues that radiate starlike from the Arc de Triomphe, giving it its original name, place de l'Etoile (renamed place Charles-de-Gaulle following the general's death). Today, it is often referred to as place **Charles-de-Gaulle-Etoile.**

Haussmann also cleared Ile de la Cité of its medieval buildings, transforming it into a showcase for Notre-Dame. Finally, he laid out the two elegant parks on the western and southeastern fringes of the city: the **Bois de Boulogne** and the **Bois de Vincennes.**

FINDING AN ADDRESS   Paris is divided into 20 municipal wards called **arrondissements,** each with its own mayor, city hall, police station, and central post office. Some even have remnants of market squares. Most city maps are divided by arrondissement, and all addresses include the arrondissement number (written in Roman or Arabic numerals and followed by *e* or *er*). Arrondissements are the last two digits in a zip code (the first three are 750-).

Numbers on buildings running parallel to the River Seine usually follow the course of the river—that is, east to west. On north–south streets, numbering begins at the river.

THE ARRONDISSEMENTS IN BRIEF

Each of Paris's 20 arrondissements possesses a unique style and flavor. You will want to decide which district appeals most to you and then find accommodations here. Later on, try to visit as many areas as you can.

1st Arr. (Musée du Louvre/Les Halles)   "I never knew what a palace was until I had a glimpse of the Louvre," wrote Nathaniel Hawthorne. Perhaps the world's greatest art museum, the **Louvre,** a former royal residence, still lures all visitors to Paris to the 1st arrondissement. Walk through the **Jardin des Tuileries,** the most formal garden of Paris (originally laid out by Le Nôtre, gardener to Louis XIV). Pause to take in the classic beauty of the **place Vendôme,** the opulent, wealthy home of the Ritz Hotel. Zola's "belly of Paris" (Les Halles) is no longer the food and meat market of Paris (traders moved to the new, more accessible suburb of Rungis)—today the **Forum des Halles** is a center of shopping, entertainment, and culture.

2nd Arr. (La Bourse)   Home to the **Bourse** (stock exchange), this Right Bank district lies mainly between the Grands Boulevards and the rue Etienne Marcel. From Monday to Friday, the shouts of brokers—J'ai! (I have it!) or Je prends! (I'll take it!)—echo across the place de la Bourse until it's time to break for lunch, when the movers and shakers of French capitalism channel their hysteria into the restaurants of the district. Much of the eastern end of the arrondissement **(Le Sentier)** is devoted to wholesale outlets of the Paris garment district, where thousands of garments are sold (usually in bulk) to buyers from clothing stores throughout Europe. "Everything that exists elsewhere exists in Paris," wrote Victor Hugo in *Les Misérables,* and this district provides ample evidence of that.

3rd Arr. (Le Marais)   This district embraces much of Le Marais (the swamp), one of the best-loved of the old Right Bank neighborhoods. (It extends into the 4th as well.) After decades of seedy decay, Le Marais recently made a comeback, although it may never again enjoy the prosperity of its 17th-century aristocratic heyday. One of the district's chief attractions today is **Musée Picasso,** a kind of pirate's ransom of painting and sculpture that the Picasso estate had to turn over to the French government in lieu of the artist's astronomical death duties. Forced donation or not, it's one of the world's great repositories of 20th-century art.

4th Arr. (Ile de la Cité/Ile St-Louis & Beaubourg)   At times it seems as if the 4th has it all: not only Notre-Dame on Ile de la Cité, but Ile St-Louis and its aristocratic town houses, courtyards, and antique shops. **Ile St-Louis,** a former cow pasture and dueling ground, is home to dozens of 17th-century mansions and 6,000 lucky louisiens, its permanent residents. Seek out Ile de la Cité's two glorious Gothic churches, **La Sainte-Chapelle** and **Notre-Dame,** a

Paris at a Glance

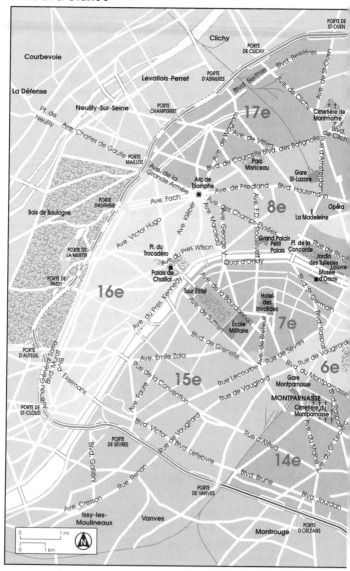

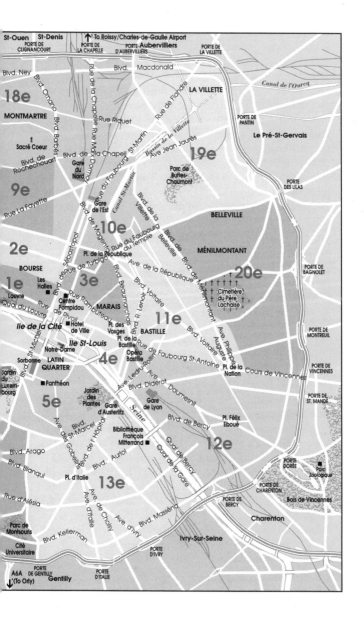

majestic and dignified structure that, according to the poet e.e. cummings, doesn't budge an inch for all the idiocies of this world.

In the 4th, you not only get France's finest bird and flower markets, but the nation's law courts, which Balzac described as a "cathedral of chicanery." It was here that Marie Antoinette was sentenced to death in 1793. The 4th is also home to the **Centre Georges Pompidou,** one of the top three tourist attractions of France. (Sadly, Centre Pompidou will be partially closed for renovations until the millennium tolls on December 31, 1999.) After all this pomp and glory, you can retreat to the **place des Vosges,** a square of perfect harmony and beauty where Victor Hugo lived from 1832 to 1848 and penned many of his famous masterpieces. (His house is now a museum.)

5th Arr. (Latin Quarter)   The Quartier Latin is the intellectual heart and soul of Paris. Bookstores, schools, churches, smoky jazz clubs, student dives, Roman ruins, publishing houses, and, yes, expensive and chic boutiques, characterize the district. Discussions of Artaud or Molière over long cups of coffee may be rarer than in the past, but they aren't at all out of place here. Beginning with the founding of the **Sorbonne** in 1253, the quarter was called Latin because all students and professors spoke the scholarly language.

You'll follow in the footsteps of Descartes, Verlaine, Camus, Sartre, James Thurber, Elliot Paul, and Hemingway as you explore this historic district. Changing times have brought Greek, Moroccan, and Vietnamese immigrants, among others, hustling everything from couscous to fiery-hot spring rolls and souvlaki. The 5th borders the Seine, and you'll want to stroll along quai de Montebello, inspecting the inventories of the bouquinistes who sell everything from antique Daumier prints to yellowing copies of Balzac's *Père Goriot* in the shadow of Notre-Dame. The 5th also has the **Panthéon,** which was constructed by a grateful Louis XV after he'd recovered from the gout and wanted to do something nice for Ste-Geneviève, Paris's patron saint. It's the dank, dark resting place of Rousseau, Gambetta, Emile Zola, Louis Braille, Victor Hugo, Voltaire, and Jean Moulin, the World War II Resistance leader whom the Gestapo tortured to death.

6th Arr. (St-Germain/Luxembourg)   This is the heartland of Paris publishing and, for some, the most colorful quarter of the Left Bank, where waves of earnest young artists still emerge from the famous **Ecole des Beaux-Arts.** The secret of the district lies in discovering its narrow streets, hidden squares, and magnificent gardens. To be really authentic, you'll stroll these streets with an unwrapped loaf of country sourdough bread from the wood-fired ovens of **Poilâne,** the world's most famous baker, at 8 rue du Cherche-Midi.

Everywhere you turn in the district, you encounter famous historical and literary associations, none more so than on **rue Jacob.** At #7, Racine lived with his uncle as a teenager; Richard Wagner resided at #14 from 1841 to 1842; Ingres once lived at #27 (now it's the offices of the French publishing house Editions du Seuil); and Hemingway once occupied a tiny upstairs room at #44. Today's big name is likely to be filmmaker Spike Lee checking into his favorite hotel, **La Villa,** 29 rue Jacob. The 6th takes in the **Jardin du Luxembourg,** a 60-acre playground where Isadora Duncan went dancing in the predawn hours and a destitute writer, Ernest Hemingway, went looking for pigeons for lunch, carrying them in a baby carriage back to his humble flat for cooking.

7th Arr. (Eiffel Tower/Musée d'Orsay)   Paris's most famous symbol, the **Eiffel Tower,** dominates Paris and especially the 7th, a Left Bank district of respectable residences and government offices. The tower is now one of the most recognizable landmarks in the world, despite the fact that many Parisians (especially its nearest neighbors) hated it when it was unveiled in 1889. Many of Paris's most imposing monuments are in the 7th, including the **Hôtel des Invalides,** which contains both Napoléon's Tomb and the Musée de l'Armée. But there is much hidden charm here as well.

Rue du Bac was home to the swashbuckling heroes of Dumas's *The Three Musketeers,* and to James McNeill Whistler, who moved to #110 after selling his *Mother.* Auguste Rodin lived at what is now the **Musée Rodin,** 77 rue de Varenne, until his death in 1917.

Even visitors with little time should rush to the **Musée d'Orsay,** the world's premier showcase of 19th-century French art and culture. The museum is housed in the old Gare d'Orsay, which Orson Welles used in 1962 as a setting for his film *The Trial,* based on the book by Franz Kafka.

8th Arr. (Champs-Elysées/Madeleine)   The prime showcase of the 8th is the **Champs-Elysées,** which stretches grandly from the **Arc de Triomphe** to the purloined Egyptian obelisk on **place de la Concorde.** Here you'll find the fashion houses, the most elegant hotels, expensive restaurants and shops, and the most fashionably attired Parisians. By the 1980s, the Champs-Elysées had become a garish strip, with too much traffic, too many fast-food joints, and too many panhandlers. In the 1990s, Jacques Chirac, then the Gaullist mayor of Paris, launched a massive cleanup, broadening sidewalks and planting new rows of trees.

Everything in the 8th is the city's "best, grandest, and most impressive": It has the best restaurant in Paris **(Taillevent)**; the sexiest strip joint **(Crazy Horse Saloon)**; the most splendid square in all of France **(place de la Concorde)**; the best rooftop cafe **(La Samaritaine)**; the grandest hotel in France **(The Crillon)**; the most impressive triumphal arch on the planet **(L'Arc de Triomphe)**; the world's most expensive residential street **(avenue Montaigne)**; the world's oldest subway station **(Franklin-D-Roosevelt)**; and the most ancient monument in Paris (the 3,300-year-old **Obelisk of Luxor**).

9th Arr. (Opéra Garnier/Pigalle)   From the Quartier de l'Opéra to the strip joints of Pigalle (the infamous "Pig Alley" for World War II GIs), the 9th endures, even if fickle fashion prefers other addresses. Over the decades, the 9th has been celebrated in literature and song for the music halls that brought gaiety to the city. The building at 17 bd. de la Madeleine was the death site of Marie Duplessis, who gained fame as the heroine Marguerite Gautier in Alexandre Dumas the younger's *La Dame aux camélias.* (Greta Garbo later redoubled Marie's legend by playing her in the film *Camille.*)

At **Place Pigalle,** gone is the cafe La Nouvelle Athènes, where Degas, Pissarro, and Manet used to meet. Today, you're more likely to encounter nightclubs in the area. Other major attractions include the **Folies Bergère,** where cancan dancers have been high-kicking it since 1868. More than anything, it was the **Opéra Garnier** (Paris Opera House) that made the 9th the last hurrah of Second Empire opulence. Renoir hated it, but several generations later, Chagall did the ceilings. Pavlova danced *Swan Lake* here, and Nijinsky took the night off to go cruising.

11th Arr. (Opéra Bastille)   For many years, this quarter seemed to sink lower and lower into poverty and decay, overcrowded by working-class immigrants from the far reaches of the former French Empire. The opening of the **Opéra Bastille,** however, has given the 11th new hope and new life. The facility, called the "people's opera house," stands on the landmark place de la Bastille, where on July 14, 1789, 633 Parisians stormed the fortress and seized the ammunition depot, as the French Revolution swept across the city. Over the years, the prison held Voltaire, the Marquis de Sade, and the mysterious "Man in the Iron Mask."

The 11th has its charms, but they exist only for those who seek them out. **Le Marché** at place d'Aligre, for example, is surrounded by a Middle Eastern food market and is a good place to hunt for secondhand bargains: Everything is cheap, and although you must search hard for treasures, they often appear.

14th Arr. (Montparnasse)   The northern end of this large arrondissement is devoted to **Montparnasse,** home of the "lost generation" and former stamping ground of Stein, Toklas, Hemingway, and other American expatriates of the 1920s. After World War II, it ceased to be the center of intellectual life in Paris, but the memory lingers in its cafes. One of the monuments that sets the tone of the neighborhood is **Rodin's statue of Balzac** at the junction of boulevard Montparnasse and boulevard Raspail. At this corner are some of the world's most famous **literary cafes,** including La Rotonde, Le Select, La Dôme, and La Coupole. Though Gertrude Stein avoided them (she loathed cafes), all the other American expatriates, including Hemingway and Fitzgerald, had no qualms about enjoying a drink here (or quite a few of them, for that matter). Stein stayed at home (27 rue de Fleurus) with Alice B. Toklas, collecting paintings, including those of Picasso, and entertaining the likes of Max Jacob, Apollinaire, T. S. Eliot, and Matisse.

16th Arr. (Trocadéro/Bois de Boulogne)   Originally the village of Passy, where Benjamin Franklin lived during most of his time in Paris, this district is still reminiscent of Proust's world. Highlights include the **Bois de Boulogne;** the **Jardin du Trocadéro;** the **Maison de Balzac;** the **Musée Guimet** (famous for its Asian collections); and the **Cimetière de Passy,** resting place of Manet, Talleyrand, Giraudoux, and Debussy. One of the largest of the city's arrondissements, it's known today for its well-heeled bourgeoisie, its upscale rents, and some rather posh (and, according to its critics, rather smug) residential boulevards. The arrondissement also has the best vantage of the Eiffel Tower, the **place du Trocadéro.**

18th Arr. (Montmartre)   The 18th is the most famous outer quartier of Paris, containing **Montmartre,** the **Moulin Rouge,** the **Basilica of Sacré-Coeur,** and the **place du Tertre.** Utrillo was its native son, Renoir lived here, and Toulouse-Lautrec adopted the area as his own. The most famous enclave of artists in Paris's history, the **Bateau-Lavoir,** of Picasso fame, gathered here. Max Jacob, Matisse, and Braque were all frequent visitors. Today, place Blanche is known for its prostitutes, and Montmartre is filled with honky-tonks, too many souvenir shops, and terrible restaurants. You can still find pockets of quiet beauty, though. The city's most famous flea market, the **Marché aux Puces de Clignancourt,** is another landmark.

2 Getting Around

Paris is a city for strollers whose greatest joy in life is rambling through unexpected alleyways and squares. Only when you're dead tired and can't walk another step—or have to go all the way across town in a hurry—should you consider using the swift and dull means of urban transport.

DISCOUNT PASSES   You can purchase a **Paris-Visite pass,** a tourist pass valid for 1 to 5 days on the public transportation system, including the Métro, city buses, RER (regional express) trains within Paris city limits, and even the funicular ride to the top of Montmartre. (The RER has both first- and second-class compartments, and the pass lets you travel in first class.) The cost is 55 F ($9.35) for 1 day, 90 F ($15.30) for 2 days, 120 F ($20.40) for 3 days, or 175 F ($29.75) for 5 days. The card is available at **RATP** (Régie Autonome des Transports Parisiens; ☎ 08-36-69-77-14), tourist offices, or at the main Métro stations; call ☎ 01-44-68-20-20 for information.

Another pass available to temporary visitors is **Carte Mobilis,** allowing unlimited travel on all bus, subway, and RER lines in Paris during a 1-day period for 30 F to 70 F ($5.10 to $11.90), depending on the zone. The pass can be purchased at any Métro station.

BY SUBWAY/RER

The **Métro** (☎ 08-36-68-77-14 for information) is the easiest and most efficient way to get around Paris. Most stations display a map of the system at the entrance; you'll find a copy of this map on the back cover of this book. Within Paris, you can transfer between the subway and the RER regional trains for no additional cost. To make sure you catch the right train, find your destination, then visually follow the line it's on to the end of the route and note its name. This is the sign you look for in the stations and the name you'll see on the train. Transfer stations are known as *correspondances.* (Note that some require long walks—Châtelet/Les Halles is the most notorious.)

Few trips will require more than one transfer. Some stations have maps with push-button indicators that will help you plot your route by lighting up automatically when you press the button for your destination. A ride on the urban lines costs 8 F ($1.35) to any point within the 20 arrondissements of Paris, as well as to many of its near suburbs. A bulk purchase of 10 tickets (which are bound together into what the French refer to as a *carnet*) costs 52 F ($8.85). Métro fares to far-flung, outlying suburbs on the Sceaux, the Noissy-St-Léger, and St-Germain-en-Laye lines cost more, and are sold on an individual basis depending on the distance you travel.

At the entrance to the Métro station, insert your ticket into the turnstile and pass through. Take the ticket back, since it may be checked by uniformed police officers when you leave the subway. There are also occasional ticket checks on the trains, platforms, and passageways.

If you are changing trains, get out and determine which direction (final destination) on the next line you want, and follow the bright orange CORRESPONDANCE signs until you reach the proper platform. Don't follow a SORTIE sign, which means "exit." If you exit, you'll have to pay another fare to resume your journey.

The Paris Métro runs daily from 5:30am to around 1:15am, at which time all underground trains reach their final terminus at the end of each of their respective lines. Be alert that the last train may pass through central Paris as much as an hour before that time. The subways are reasonably safe at any hour, but beware of pickpockets.

BY BUS

Bus travel is much slower than the subway. Most buses run from 7am to 8:30pm (a few operate until 12:30am, and 10 operate during the early morning hours). Service is limited on Sunday and holidays. Bus and Métro fares are the same and you can use the same carnet tickets on both.

At certain bus stops, signs list the destinations and numbers of the buses serving that point. Destinations are usually listed north to south and east to west. Most stops along the way are also posted on the sides of the buses. To catch a bus, wait in line at the bus stop. Signal the driver to stop the bus and board.

Most bus rides (including any that begin and end within the 20 arrondissements of Paris) require one ticket, but there are some destinations in the suburbs that require up to, but never more than, two. If you intend to use the buses a lot, pick up an **RATP bus map** at their office on Place de la Madeleine, 8e, at any tourist information office, or at RATP headquarters, 52-54 quai de la Rapée, 12e (☎ **01-44-68-20-20**). For detailed information on bus and Métro routes, call **08-36-68-41-14.**

BY TAXI

It's nearly impossible to get a taxi at rush hour. Taxi drivers are organized into an effective lobby to keep their number limited to 14,300.

Watch out for the common ripoffs. Always check the meter to make sure you're not paying the previous passenger's fare. Beware of cabs without meters, which often try to snare tipsy patrons outside nightclubs—always settle the tab in advance. Regular cabs can be hailed on the street when their signs read LIBRE. Taxis are easier to find at the many stands near Métro stations.

The flag drops at 14 F ($2.40), and you pay 3.36 F (55¢) per kilometer. At night, expect to pay 5.45 F (95¢) per kilometer. On airport trips you're not required to pay for the driver's empty return ride. You're allowed several small pieces of luggage free if they're transported inside and don't weigh more than 5 kg (11 pounds). Heavier suitcases carried in the trunk cost 6 F ($1) apiece. Tip 12% to 15%—the latter usually elicits a *merci*. To radio cabs, call ☎ **01-45-85-85-85,** 01-42-70-41-41, or 01-42-70-00-42—note that you'll be charged from the point where the taxi begins the drive to pick you up.

BY BOAT

The **Batobus** (☎ **01-44-11-33-44**), a series of 150-passenger ferryboats with big windows suitable for viewing the passing riverfronts, operates at 15-minute intervals from 10am to 7pm every day between April and mid-October. Boats chug along between the quays at the base of the Eiffel Tower and the quays at the base of the Louvre, stopping at the Musée d'Orsay, St-Germain-des-Prés, Notre-Dame, and the Hôtel de Ville. Transit between each stop costs 20 F ($3.40), although most participants opt to pay a flat rate (good all day) of 60 F ($10.20) per adult, 30 F ($5.10) for children under 12, and then settle back and watch the monuments from a prime seat on one of the most historically evocative rivers in Europe. Camera opportunities are endless aboard this leisurely but intensely panoramic "floating observation platform."

FAST FACTS: Paris

American Express   The largest travel service in the world operates a 24-hour-a-day hotline from its administrative headquarters in the Paris suburb of Reuil-Malmaison (☎ **01-47-77-70-00**). Day-to-day services, such as tours and money exchange, are available at 11 rue Scribe, 9e (☎ **01-47-77-47-61;** Métro: Opéra), or the smaller branch at 38 Av. Wagram, 8e (☎ **01-42-27-58-80;** Métro: Ternes). Both of the branches are open Monday through Friday from 9am to 5pm, with money-changing services ending at 4pm. The rue Scribe office is open Saturday from 9am to 5:30pm (no mail pickup).

Area Code There isn't one. The area code for Paris and Ile-de-France, 1, ceased to exist in 1996. Instead, the prefix 01- should be added to all existing 8-digit numbers in Paris and Ile-de-France. Areas of mainland France outside of the Paris region use any of four other area codes (02, 03, 04, or 05, according to their location within France). The international access code from France is now 00.

Banks American Express may be able to meet most of your banking needs. If not, banks in Paris are open from 9am to 4:30pm Monday through Friday. A few are open on Saturday. Ask at your hotel for the location of the bank nearest you. Shops and most hotels will cash your traveler's checks, but not at the advantageous rate a bank or foreign-exchange office will give you, so make sure you've allowed enough funds for the weekend.

Business Hours Opening hours in France are erratic, as befits a nation of individualists. Most museums close 1 day a week (often Tuesday) and on national holidays; hours tend to be from 9:30am to 5pm. Some museums, particularly the smaller ones, close for lunch from noon to 2pm. Most French museums are open Saturday, but many close Sunday morning and reopen in the afternoon. (See chapter 5 for specific times.) Generally, offices are open Monday through Friday from 9am to 5pm, but don't count on it. Always call first. Large stores and chain stores are open from 9 or 9:30am (often 10am) to 6 or 7pm without a break for lunch. Some shops, particularly those operated by foreigners, open at 8am and close at 8 or 9pm. In some small stores, the lunch break can last 3 hours, beginning at 1pm.

Drugstores (Late-Night) After regular hours, ask at your hotel where the nearest 24-hour *pharmacie* is. You'll also find the address posted on the doors or windows of other drugstores in the neighborhood. One all-night drugstore is the **Pharmacy les Champs,** in La Galerie Les Champs, 84 av. des Champs-Elysées, 8e (☎ **01-45-62-02-41;** Métro: George V).

Electricity In general, expect 200 volts AC (60 cycles), although you'll encounter 110 and 115 volts in some older establishments. Adapters are needed to fit sockets. Many hotels have two-pin (in some cases, three-pin) sockets for electric razors. It's best to ask at your hotel before plugging in any electrical appliance.

Embassies/Consulates   If you have a passport, immigration, legal, or other problem, contact your consulate. Call before you go, as they often keep strange hours and observe both French and home-country holidays.

The Embassy of the **United States,** at 2 av. Gabriel, 8e (☎ 01-43-12-22-22; Métro: Concorde), is open Monday through Friday from 9am to 6pm. Passports are issued at its consulate at 2 rue St-Florentin (☎ 01-43-12-22-22; Métro: Concorde). Getting a passport replaced costs $55.

The Embassy of **Canada** is at 35 av. Montaigne, 8e (☎ 01-44-43-29-00; Métro: F.-D.-Roosevelt or Alma-Marceau), open Monday through Friday from 9am to noon and 2 to 5pm. The Canadian consulate is at the embassy.

The Embassy of the **United Kingdom** is at 35 rue Faubourg St-Honoré, 8e (☎ 01-44-51-31-00; Métro: Concorde or Madeleine), open Monday through Friday from 9:30am to 1pm and 2:30 to 5pm. The consulate is at 16 rue d'Anjou, 8e (☎ 01-44-66-29-79), and is open Monday through Friday from 9:30am to 12:30pm and 2:30 to 5pm.

The Embassy of **Australia** is at 4 rue Jean-Rey, 15e (☎ 01-40-59-33-00; Métro:Bir-Hakeim), open Monday through Friday from 9:15am to noon and 2:30 to 4:30pm. The embassy of **New Zealand** is at 7 ter rue Léonard-de-Vinci, 75116 Paris (☎ 01-45-00-24-11; Métro: Victor Hugo), open Monday through Friday from 9am to 1pm and 2:30 to 6pm.

The Embassy of **Ireland** is at 12 ave. Foch, 16e, 75116 Paris (☎ 01-44-17-67-00; Métro: Argentine). Hours are Monday through Friday from 9:30am to noon.

The **Embassy of South Africa** is at 59 quai d'Orsay (☎ 01-53-59-23-23; Métro: Invalides). Hours are Monday through Friday from 8:45 to 11am.

Emergencies   For the police, call ☎ **17;** to report a fire, call ☎ **18.** For an ambulance, call the fire department at ☎ **01-45-78-74-52;** a fire vehicle rushes patients to the nearest emergency room. For **S.A.M.U.,** an independently operated, privately owned ambulance company, call ☎ **15.** For less urgent matters, you can reach the police at 9 bd. du Palais, 4e (☎ **01-53-71-53-71** or 01-53-73-53-73; Métro: Cité).

Hospitals **Central Médical Europe,** 44 rue d'Amsterdam, 9e
(☎ **01-42-81-93-33;** Métro: Liège), maintains contacts with
medical and dental practitioners in all fields. Appointments are
recommended. Open Monday through Saturday from 8:30am to
7pm. Another choice is the **American Hospital of Paris,** 63 bd.
Victor-Hugo, Neuilly (☎ **01-46-41-25-43;** Métro: Pont-de-
Levallois or Pont-de-Neuilly; Bus: 82), which operates 24-hour
medical and dental service. An additional clinic is the **Centre
Figuier,** 2 rue du Figuier (☎ **01-42-78-55-53;** Métro: St-Paul).
Call before visiting.

Internet Access A centrally located cybercafe, in the Latin
Quarter, is **Cybercafé Latino,** 13 rue de l'Ecole Polytechnique,
5e (☎ **01-40-51-86-94;** www.cybercafelinto.com/). Métro:
Maubert-Mutualité. See also **Le Web Bar** under "Bars, Pubs &
Clubs," in chapter 6.

Mail/Post Offices Most post offices in Paris are open Monday
through Friday from 8am to 7pm and Saturday from 8am to noon.
The **main post office (PTT)** for Paris is at 52 rue du Louvre,
75001 Paris (☎ **01-40-28-20-00;** Métro: Louvre). It's open 24
hours a day for the sale of stamps, phone calls, and expedition of
faxes and telegrams, with more limited hours—8am to 5pm Monday through Friday and 8am to noon on Saturday—for more esoteric financial services that include the sale of money orders. Stamps
can also usually be purchased at your hotel reception desk and at
café-tabacs (tobacconists). You can send faxes at the main post office
in each arrondissement.

Airmail letters within Europe cost 3 F (50¢); to the United States
and Canada, 4.40 F (75¢); and to Australia and New Zealand,
5.10 F (85¢).

You can have mail sent to you *poste restante* (general delivery)
at the main post office for a small fee. Take an ID, such as a passport, if you plan to pick up mail. American Express (see above)
also offers a *poste restante* service, but you may be asked to show
an American Express card or traveler's checks.

Medical Emergencies Seek assistance first at your hotel desk if
language is a problem. If you are ill and need medicine at night or
on Sunday, the local *commissariat de police* can tell you the location of the nearest doctor on duty. The police or fire department
will also summon an ambulance if you need to be rushed to a
hospital. See also "Drugstores" and "Hospitals," above.

Newspapers/Magazines   English-language newspapers are available at nearly every kiosk in Paris. Published Monday through Saturday, the *International Herald-Tribune* is the most popular paper with visiting Americans and Canadians; the *Guardian* provides a British point of view. For those who read in French, the leading domestic newspapers are *Le Monde, Le Figaro,* and *Libération;* the top magazines are *L'Express, Le Point,* and *Le Nouvel Observateur.* Kiosks are generally open daily from 8am to 9pm.

Police   Call ☎ **17** for emergencies. The principal Prefecture is at 9 boulevard du Palais, 4e (☎ **01-53-71-53-71;** Métro: Cité).

Rest Rooms   If you are in dire need, duck into a cafe or brasserie to use the lavatory. It's customary to make some small purchase if you do so. In the street, the domed self-cleaning lavatories are a decent option if you have small change; Métro stations and underground garages usually have public lavatories, but the degree of cleanliness varies.

Safety   In Paris, be especially aware of child pickpockets. They roam the French capital, preying on tourists around attractions such as the Louvre, Eiffel Tower, and Notre-Dame, and they also often strike in the Métro, sometimes blocking a victim from the escalator. A band of these young thieves can clean your pockets even while you try to fend them off. Their method is to get very close to a target, ask for a handout (sometimes), and deftly help themselves to your money or passport.

Although public safety is not as much a problem in Paris as it is in large American cities, concerns are growing. Robbery at gun- or knife-point is uncommon here, but not unknown. Be careful.

Telephone   Public phones are found in cafes, restaurants, Métro stations, post offices, airports, train stations, and occasionally on the streets. Finding a coin-operated telephone in France is an arduous task. A simpler and more widely accepted method of payment is the **télécarte,** a prepaid calling card available at kiosks, post offices, and Métro stations. These debit cards are priced at 41 F to 98 F ($6.95 to $16.65), for 50 and 120 units respectively. A local call costs 1 unit, which provides you with 6 to 18 minutes of conversation, depending on the rate. Avoid making calls from your hotel, which might double or triple the charges.

To call **long distance within France,** dial the 10-digit number (9-digit in some cases outside Paris) of the person or place you're calling. To make a **direct international call,** first dial 00,

Calling Paris from Abroad

To call Paris from abroad, first dial the **international prefix,** then France's **country code (33),** then the local number minus the initial 0 (zero). From the United States or Canada, the international prefix is **011,** from Australia **0011,** from Great Britain, Ireland, or New Zealand **00,** and from South Africa **09.** Thus, to call **Notre-Dame** (☎ **01-42-34-56-10**) from the U.S., you would dial ☎ **011-33-1-42-34-56-10.**

---

listen for the tone, then slowly dial the country code, the area code, and the local number. The country code for the **USA and Canada** is 1; **Great Britain,** 44; **Ireland,** 353; **Australia,** 61; **New Zealand,** 64; **South Africa,** 27.

An easy and relatively inexpensive way to call home is **USA Direct/AT&T WorldConnect.** From within France, dial any of the following numbers: ☎ **0800/99-0011, -1011, -1111, -1211.** Then follow the prompt, which will ask you to punch in the number of either your AT&T credit card or a MasterCard or Visa. Along with the **USA,** the countries that participate in the system— referred to as WorldConnect—include **Canada,** the **UK, Ireland, Australia, New Zealand,** and **South Africa.** By punching in the number of the party you want in any of these countries, you'll avoid the surcharges imposed by the hotel operator. An AT&T operator will be available to help you with complications arising during the process.

Time   France is usually 6 hours ahead of eastern standard time in the United States. French daylight savings time lasts from around April to September, when clocks are set 1 hour ahead of the standard time.

Tipping   By law, all bills show *service compris,* which means the tip is included; additional gratuities are customarily given as follows:

For **hotel staff,** tip the porter 6 F to 10 F ($1.10 to $1.80) per item of baggage and 10 F ($1.80) per day for the chambermaid. You're not obligated to tip the concierge, doorman, or anyone else, unless you use his or her services. In **cafes and restaurants,** waiter service is usually included, although you can leave a couple of francs. Tip **taxi drivers** 10% to 15% of the amount on the meter. In **theaters and restaurants,** give cloakroom attendants at least

5 F (90¢) per item. Give **restroom attendants** in nightclubs and such places about 2 F (35¢). Give **cinema and theater ushers** about 2 F (35¢). Tip the **hairdresser** about 15%, and don't forget to tip the person who gives you a shampoo or a manicure 10 F ($1.80). For **guides** for group visits to museums and monuments, 5 F to 10 F (90¢ to $1.80) is a reasonable tip.

Transit Info   For information on the city's public transportation, call ☎ **08-36-68-77-14.**

Useful Telephone Numbers   Police, ☎ **17;** fire, ☎ **18;** emergency medical assistance, ☎ **15;** directory assistance, ☎ **12.**

3

Accommodations

*I*t is estimated that Paris has some 2,000 hotels—with about 80,000 rooms—spread across its 20 arrondissements. They range from the Ritz to dives so repellent that even George Orwell, author of *Down and Out in Paris and London,* wouldn't have considered checking in. (Of course, none of those are in this guide!) We've included deluxe places for those who want to live like the Sultan of Brunei and a wide range of moderate and inexpensive choices.

Most visitors, at least those from North America, come in July and August. Since many French are on vacation then and trade fairs and conventions come to a halt, there are usually plenty of rooms, even though these months have traditionally been the peak season for European travel. In most hotels, February is just as busy as April or September because of the volume of business travelers and the increasing number of tourists who've learned to take advantage of off-season discount airfares.

Since hot weather never lasts long in Paris, few hotels, except the deluxe ones, provide air-conditioning. If you're trapped in a garret on a hot summer night, you'll have to sweat it out. You can open your window to get some cooler air, but open windows admit a major nuisance: noise pollution. To avoid this, you may wish to request a room in the back when making a reservation. Almost all hotels, except for those in the Inexpensive category, have hair dryers in the rooms.

Hotel breakfasts are fairly uniform and include your choice of coffee, tea, or hot chocolate, a freshly baked croissant and roll, plus limited quantities of butter and jam or jelly. It can be at your door moments after you call for it, and is served at almost any hour requested. (When we mention breakfast charges in our listings, we refer to continental breakfasts only.) Breakfasts with eggs, bacon, ham, or other items must be ordered from the à la carte menu. For a charge, larger hotels serve the full or "English" breakfast, but smaller hotels typically serve only the continental variety.

A NOTE ON PRICE CATEGORIES

Classifying Paris hotels by price is a long day's journey into night. It's possible many times to find a moderately priced room in an otherwise "very expensive" hotel or an "expensive" room in an otherwise "inexpensive" property. That's because most hotel rooms, at least in the older properties, are not standard; therefore, the range of rooms goes from superdeluxe suites to the "maid's pantry," now converted into a small bedroom. At some hotels, in fact, you'll find rooms that are "moderate," "expensive," and "very expensive," all under one roof.

The following price categories are only for a quick general reference. When we've classified a hotel as "moderate," it means that the average room is moderately priced, not necessarily all the rooms. It should also be noted that Paris is one of the most expensive cities in the world for hotels.

1   Right Bank

We'll begin with the most centrally located arrondissements on the Right Bank, then work our way through the more outlying neighborhoods.

1ST ARRONDISSEMENT (LOUVRE/LES HALLES)
VERY EXPENSIVE

✪ **Costes.** 239 rue St-Honoré, 75001 Paris. ☎ **01-42-44-50-50.** Fax 01-42-44-50-01. 83 units. A/C MINIBAR TV TEL. 2,250–3,500 F ($382.50–$595) double; 5,250–5,500 F ($892.50–$935) suite. AE, DC, MC, V. Métro: Tuileries or Concorde.

Grand style and a location close to the headquarters of some of the most upscale shops in Paris seem to attract goodly numbers of high-style fashion types, some of whom work within the nearby editorial offices of *Harper's Bazaar.* The five-story, town house–style premises functioned as a maison bourgeoise for many generations, presenting a severely dignified facade to the prestigious neighborhood around it. In 1996, it was richly adorned with the jewel-toned colors, heavy swag curtains, and lavish accessories of the late 19th century (the Napoléon III style). Today, everything about it evokes the rich days of France's Gilded Age, especially the bedrooms. Although small, they're cozy and ornate, with a CD player and fax machine. Units contain one or two large beds, each with a sumptuous mattress. Bathrooms are fairly spacious, with makeup mirrors, deluxe toiletries, thick towels, and a tub and shower combination.

Dining: Four dining rooms, each with a different decorative theme, and each overlooking the building's Italianate-style inner courtyard, are chock-a-block with chinoiserie, dried and framed flowers, and 19th-century art. Open daily from noon to 1am, they feature delectable dishes such as grilled scallops and a grilled version of steak tartare with all the spicy ingredients of its original (raw) version.

Amenities: Car-rental desk, concierge, room service, dry cleaning, laundry service, baby-sitting, and a gym with a steam room, indoor pool, and masseurs/masseuses.

✪ **Hôtel de Vendôme.** 1 Place Vendôme, 75001 Paris. ☎ **01-42-60-32-84.** Fax 01-49-27-97-89. E-mail: reservations@hoteldevendome.com. 30 units. A/C MINIBAR TV TEL. 2,800–3,200 F ($476–$544) double; 4,500–5,500 F ($765–$935) suite. AE, DC, MC, V. Métro: Concorde or Opéra.

Once the home of the Embassy of Texas when that state was a nation, this is a jewel box of a hotel that opened in the summer of 1998 at one of the world's most prestigious addresses. Although the sumptuous bedrooms are only moderate in size, you live in opulent comfort here. Most of the bedrooms are decorated in a classic Second Empire style with luxurious beds and mattresses, tasteful fabrics, and well-upholstered, hand-carved furnishings. Bathrooms are equally sumptuous, with a tub and shower combination, robes, thick towels, and Guerlain toiletries. The security is fantastic, with TV intercoms. This new version of the hotel replaces a lackluster one that stood here for a century. Both its facade and roof are classified as historic monuments by the French government. The building dates from 1723, when it was the home of the secretary to Louis XIV.

Dining: The hotel restaurant, **Café de Vedôme,** is directed by Gérard Sallé, who has worked at some of the premier addresses of Paris, including the Bristol and the Plaza Athénée. The cuisine is imaginative, the setting rather austere but elegant.

Amenities: Room service, laundry, concierge.

Hôtel du Louvre. Place André Malraux, 75001 Paris. ☎ **800/888-4747** in the U.S. and Canada, or 01-44-58-38-38. Fax 01-44-58-38-01. www.hoteldulouvre.com. 195 units. A/C MINIBAR TV TEL. 1,850–2,500 F ($314.50–$425) double; from 3,000 F ($510) suite. AE, DC, MC, V. Ask about midwinter discounts. Parking 100 F ($17). Métro: Palais-Royal.

When Napoléon III inaugurated this hotel in 1855, French journalists described it as "a palace of the people, rising adjacent to the palace of kings." In 1897, Camille Pissarro moved into a room with a view that inspired many of his Parisian landscapes.

Hotels in the Heart of the Right Bank

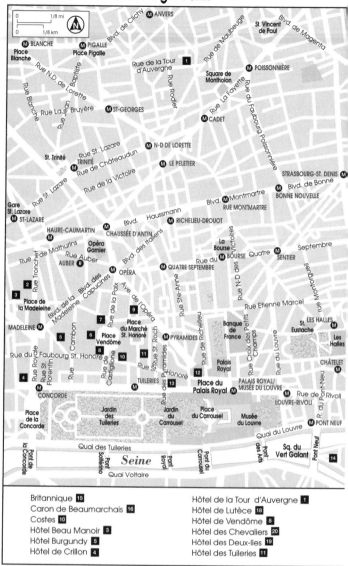

Britannique **15**
Caron de Beaumarchais **16**
Costes **10**
Hôtel Beau Manoir **3**
Hôtel Burgundy **5**
Hôtel de Crillon **4**

Hôtel de la Tour d'Auvergne **1**
Hôtel de Lutèce **18**
Hôtel de Vendôme **8**
Hôtel des Chevaliers **20**
Hôtel des Deux-Iles **19**
Hôtel des Tuileries **11**

Hôtel du Louvre **12**
Hôtel Henri IV **14**
Hôtel Mansart **7**
Hôtel Opal **2**
Hôtel Regina **13**

Hôtel St-Louis **17**
Le Pavillon Bastille **22**
Le Ritz **6**
Le Stendahl **9**
Pavillon de la Reine **21**

Set between the Musée du Louvre and the Palais Royal, the hotel has a decor of soaring marble, bronze, and gilt. The rooms are quintessentially Parisian—cozy, soundproof, and filled with souvenirs of the belle epoque. Most were renovated between 1996 and 1998. Some of the bedrooms are small, but most of them are medium in size—with elegant fabrics and upholstery, excellent wool carpeting, double-glazed windows, plush and comfortable beds with fine linens and quality mattresses, and traditional wood furniture. Bathrooms are medium in size. Extras include robes and trouser presses. The newer rooms have shower stalls, but the older rooms are fitted with large bathtubs.

Dining: Le Bar "Defender" is a cozy hideaway, with mahogany trim, Scottish overtones, and a collection of single-malt whiskies; a pianist plays after dusk. There's also the **French Empire Brasserie du Louvre,** whose tables extend to the terrace in fine weather.

Amenities: Concierge, room service (24 hours), baby-sitting, laundry, dry cleaning, valet, business center.

Hôtel Regina. 2 place des Pyramides, 75001 Paris. ☎ **01-42-60-31-10.** Fax 01-40-15-95-16. tel.comtel.comwww.regina-hotel.com. E-mail: reservation@regina-hotel.com. 135 units. A/C MINIBAR TV TEL. 1,990–2,300 F ($338.30–$391) double; 2,800–4,100 F ($476–$697) suite. AE, DC, MC, V. Métro: Pyramides or Tuileries.

Until a radical renovation upgraded its old-fashioned grandeur in 1995, this hotel slumbered in central Paris, adjacent to rue de Rivoli's equestrian statue of Joan of Arc. The management has poured lots of money into the renovation, retaining the patina and beeswax of the art nouveau interior and making historically appropriate improvements. The rooms that overlook the Tuileries enjoy panoramic views as far away as the Eiffel Tower. The public areas have every period of Louis furniture imaginable, Oriental carpets, 18th-century paintings, and bowls of flowers. Fountains play in a flagstone-covered courtyard, site of alfresco cafe tables and an extension of the hotel's restaurant. Bedrooms are richly decorated, all with comfortable mattresses.

Dining: In the well-managed **Le Pluvinel,** conservative French cuisine is served in an art-deco atmosphere. Pluvinel is closed on weekends, when there's only a less appealing but more affordable bistro-style snack bar.

Amenities: Concierge, 24-hour room service, twice-daily maid service, baby-sitting, laundry/dry cleaning, valet parking 85 F ($14.45), secretarial service, in-room massage, conference room; visits to a nearby health club can be arranged upon request.

✪ **Le Ritz.** 15 place Vendôme, 75001 Paris. ☎ **800/223-6800** in the U.S. and Canada, or 01-43-16-30-30. Fax 01-43-16-31-78. E-mail: resa@ritzparis.com. 187 units. A/C MINIBAR TV TEL. 3,600–4,400 F ($612–$748) double; from 6,200 F ($1,054) suite. AE, DC, MC, V. Parking 220 F ($37.40). Métro: Opéra.

The Ritz is Europe's greatest hotel. This enduring symbol of elegance stands on one of Paris's most beautiful and historic squares. César Ritz, the "little shepherd boy from Niederwald," converted the private Hôtel de Lazun into a luxury hotel that he opened in 1898. With the help of the culinary master Escoffier, he made the Ritz a miracle of luxury living.

In 1979, the Ritz family sold the hotel to the Egyptian business-man Mohamed Al Fayed (Dodi's father), who refurbished it and added a cooking school. (Dodi Al Fayed and Princess Diana were staying here when they set out on their fateful drive through Paris.) Two town houses were annexed, joined by a long arcade lined with miniature display cases representing 125 of the leading boutiques of Paris. The salons are furnished with museum-caliber antiques. The spacious marble bathrooms are among the city's most luxurious, filled with deluxe toiletries, scales, a private phone, cords to summon maids and valets, fluffy towels and robes, full-length and makeup mirrors, and dual basins. Ever since Edward VII got stuck in a too-narrow bathtub with his lover of the evening, bathtubs at the Ritz have been deep and big. The hotel has its own workshop to repair and reproduce the plumbing.

Dining/Diversions: The **Espadon** grill room is one of the fin-est in Paris. The **Ritz Supper Club** includes a bar, a salon with a fireplace, a restaurant, and a dance floor. You can order drinks in either the **Bar Vendôme** or the **Bar Hemingway.**

Amenities: Concierge, 24-hour room service, laundry, valet, health club with pool and massage parlor, florist, shops, squash court.

EXPENSIVE

Hôtel des Tuileries. 10 rue St-Hyacinthe, 75001 Paris. ☎ **01-42-61-04-17.** Fax 01-49-27-91-56. www.members.aol.com/htuileri/. E-mail: htuileri.aol.com. 26 units. A/C MINIBAR TV TEL. 890–1,400 F ($151.30–$238) double. AE, DC, MC, V. Parking 100 F ($17). Métro: Tuileries or Pyramides.

On a narrow, quiet street, this hotel occupies a 17th-century town house that's remembered as the minipalace Marie Antoinette used when she left Versailles for an unofficial visit to Paris. Don't expect mementos of the queen, as all the frippery of her era was long ago stripped away. But in honor of royal antecedents, the hotel's public areas and guest rooms are filled with copies of Louis XV furniture—a bit dowdy but still comfortable. The baths contain whirlpool tubs, separate toilets, and touches of marble. Rooms provide safe, comfortable, cozy getaways from the urban congestion in this busy neighborhood—a welcome and comfortable refuge.

Amenities: Room service 7am to 11pm, newspaper delivery upon request.

MODERATE

Hôtel Britannique. 20 av. Victoria, 75001 Paris. ☎ **01-42-33-74-59.** Fax 01-42-33-82-65. www.hotel-britannique.fr. E-mail: mailbox@hotel-britannique.fr. 40 units. MINIBAR TV TEL. 697–998 F ($118.50–$169.65) double. AE, DC, MC, V. Parking 100 F ($17). Métro: Châtelet.

Cozy, conservatively modern, and plush-looking, this much-renovated 19th-century hotel was re-rated with three stars after a complete renovation in the mid-1980s. The place is not only British in name but seems also to have cultivated an English style of graciousness. It's in the heart of Paris, near Les Halles, the Pompidou Centre, and Notre-Dame. The rooms may be small, but they're spick-and-span, comfortable, soundproof, with comfortable beds and a safety deposit box. A satellite receiver gets U.S. and U.K. TV shows. The reading room is a cozy retreat.

✪ **Hôtel Burgundy.** 8 rue Duphot, 75001 Paris. ☎ **01-42-60-34-12.** Fax 01-47-03-95-20. www.perso.wanadoo.fr/hotel.burgundy. E-mail: hotel.burgundy@iname.com. 89 units. MINIBAR TV TEL. 960 F ($163.20) double; 1,600 F ($272) suite. AE, DC, MC, V. Métro: Madeleine.

The Burgundy is one of the best values in an outrageously expensive neighborhood. This frequently renovated building is a former pension, where Baudelaire wrote some of his eerie poetry in the 1860s. What you'll see today was conceived as two side-by-side town houses in the 1830s. One flourished as a bordello before they were linked by British-born managers, who insisted on using the English name. Radically renovated in 1992, the hotel often hosts many North and South Americans. It features conservatively decorated and very comfortable rooms with cozy-looking decor, efficient, modestly sized bathrooms, and comfortable beds. The **Charles Baudelaire** restaurant is open for lunch and dinner Monday through Friday. There's no bar, but drinks are served in the lobby during restaurant hours. Amenities include limited concierge services, room service from 6:30am to 9:30pm, laundry/dry cleaning, and a conference room.

Hôtel Mansart. 5 rue des Capucines, 75001 Paris. ☎ **01-42-61-50-28.** Fax 01-49-27-97-44. www.hotels.eslprit.de.france.com. E-mail: espranc@micronet.fr. 57 units. MINIBAR TV TEL. 600–900 F ($102–$153) double; 1,600 F ($272) suite. AE, DC, MC, V. Métro: Opéra or Madeleine.

After operating as a glorious wreck for many decades, this hotel—designed by its namesake—was radically renovated in 1991 and now offers some of the lowest rates in this pricey neighborhood. The public areas contain Louis-inspired reproductions and startling floor-to-ceiling geometric designs inspired by inlaid marble floors (or formal gardens) of the French Renaissance. The small to medium-sized guest rooms are subtly formal and comfortable, though only half a dozen of the suites and most expensive rooms actually overlook the famous square. Twenty of the rooms are air-conditioned; all have beds with firm mattresses. The compact bathrooms have a shower stall. Breakfast, the only meal offered, is served one floor above lobby level.

INEXPENSIVE

Hôtel Henri IV. 25 place Dauphine, 75001 Paris. ☎ **01-43-54-44-53.** 21 units (3 with shower). 185–205 F ($31.45–$34.85) double without shower; 240–265 F ($40.80–$45.05) double with shower. Rates include breakfast. No credit cards. Métro: Pont-Neuf.

Four hundred years ago, this narrow, decrepit building housed the printing presses used for the edicts of Henri IV. Today, one of the most famous and most consistently crowded budget hotels in Europe sits in a dramatic location at the westernmost tip of the Ile de la Cité, beside a formal and unexpected park lined with orderly rows of trees. The clientele is mostly bargain-conscious academics, journalists, and francophiles, many of whom reserve rooms as early as 2 months in advance. The low-ceilinged lobby, a flight above street level, is cramped and bleak; the creaky stairway leading to the bedrooms is almost impossibly narrow. Rooms are considered romantically threadbare by many, and run-down and substandard by others. Each contains a sink, but not even the trio of rooms with showers have toilets.

2ND ARRONDISSEMENT (LA BOURSE)
EXPENSIVE

Le Stendhal. 22 rue Danielle Casanova, 75002 Paris. ☎ **01-44-58-52-52.** Fax 01-44-58-52-00. 20 units. A/C MINIBAR TV TEL. 1,440–1,630 F ($244.80–$277.10) double; from 1,800 F ($306) suite. AE, DC, MC, V. Parking 100 F ($17). Métro: Opéra.

Established in 1992, this hotel mixes a young and hip style with a sense of tradition. Its location, close to the glamorous jewelry stores on the place Vendôme, couldn't be grander. Overall, the effect is that of a small, boutique-style *hôtel de luxe* that in some ways seems like an urban and very Parisian version of an upscale English B&B. Bedrooms, accessible via a tiny elevator, have vivid color schemes.

Most bedrooms are small but not without their charm; each comes with fine linen and a quality mattress, plus a tidily maintained and elegant private bath. The red-and-black Stendhal Suite pays homage to the author, who made this his private home for many years and died here in 1842.

Dining: Breakfast is served in a stone cellar with a vaulted ceiling. A small bar adjoins the lobby, but offers little in size or allure. Simple meals can be ordered and are served in the bedrooms or at the bar, 24 hours a day.

Amenities: A receptionist/concierge is able to arrange babysitting, dry cleaning, secretarial services, and car rentals.

3RD ARRONDISSEMENT (LE MARAIS)
VERY EXPENSIVE

✪ **Pavillon de la Reine.** 28 place des Vosges, 75003 Paris. ☎ **01-40-29-19-19.** Fax 01-40-29-19-20. E-mail: pavillon@clubinternet.fr. 55 units. A/C MINIBAR TV TEL. 1,900–2,100 F ($323–$357) double; 2,050–2,500 F ($348.50–$425) duplex; 2,550–3,900 F ($433.50–$663) suite. AE, DC, MC, V. Free parking. Métro: Bastille.

Built in 1986, this cream-colored neoclassical villa blends in seamlessly with the rest of the square. You enter through an arcade that opens onto a small formal garden. The Louis XIII decor evokes the heyday of the place des Vosges, and wing chairs with flame-stitched upholstery combine with iron-banded Spanish antiques to create a rustic feel. Each guest room is unique; some are duplexes with sleeping lofts above cozy salons. All have a warm decor of weathered beams, reproductions of famous oil paintings, and roomy marble baths with thick towels. Most rooms are of good size. The better rooms come with private safes. The preferred rooms are on the upper floors opening onto the romantic square. Quality mattresses and fine linens are used on all the excellent French beds.

Dining: The hotel has an "honesty bar" and a limited 24-hour room-service menu.

Amenities: A receptionist/concierge can arrange massage, dry cleaning, car rentals, and tickets for shows, concerts, and the theater.

MODERATE

Hôtel des Chevaliers. 30 rue de Turenne, 75003 Paris. ☎ **01-42-72-73-47.** Fax 01-42-72-54-10. 24 units. MINIBAR TV TEL. 640–680 F ($108.80–$115.60) double; 854 F ($145.20) triple. Métro: Chemin-Vert or St-Paul.

Half a block from the northwestern edge of the place des Vosges, this carefully renovated hotel occupies a dramatic corner building whose 17th-century vestiges have been elevated into high art. These include the remnants of a stone-sided well in the cellar, a sweeping stone barrel vault that covers the breakfast area, half-timbering that's artfully exposed in the stairwell, and Louis XIII accessories that'll remind you of the hotel's origins. Each room is comfortable and well maintained. Bathrooms are compact, with just a shower stall.

4TH ARRONDISSEMENT (ILE DE LA CITÉ/ ILE ST-LOUIS & BEAUBOURG)
MODERATE

✪ **Hôtel Caron de Beaumarchais.** 12 rue Vieille-du-Temple, 75004 Paris. ☎ **01-42-72-34-12.** Fax 01-42-72-34-63. www.carondebeaumarchais.com. 19 units. A/C MINIBAR TV TEL. 730–810 F ($124.10–$137.70) double. AE, DC, MC, V. Métro: St-Paul or Hôtel-de-Ville.

Built in the 18th century and gracefully renovated and upgraded in 1998, this good-value choice features floors of artfully worn gray stone, antique reproductions, and elaborate fabrics based on antique patterns. Most of the rooms retain their original ceiling beams, and though they're compact, they're comfortable and soundproof. Hotelier Alain Bigeard likes his primrose-colored rooms to evoke the taste of 18th-century French gentry when the Marais was the scene of high society dances or even duels. The smallest units overlook the interior courtyard, and the top floor rooms are also tiny, but they have panoramic balcony views across the Right Bank. Rooms on the lower five levels are more spacious, but contain balconies only on the second and fifth floors. Bathrooms are exceedingly compact but well maintained, most often with a tub and shower combination.

✪ **Hôtel de Lutèce.** 65 rue St-Louis-en-l'Ile, 75004 Paris. ☎ **01-43-26-23-52.** Fax 01-43-29-60-25. www.france-hotel-guide.com/h75004lutece.htm. 23 units. A/C TV TEL. 860 F ($146.20) double; 1,100 F ($187) triple. AE, MC,V. Parking 80 F ($13.60). Métro: Pont-Marie or Cité.

This hotel feels like a country house in Brittany. The lounge, with its old fireplace, is graciously furnished with antiques and contemporary paintings. Each of the individualized guest rooms boasts antiques, adding to a refined atmosphere that attracts celebrities, like the duke and duchess of Bedford. Many of the accommodations, ranging in size from small to medium, were renovated in 1998, with new mattresses added. Each room is well maintained, traditional, and comfortable, with wool carpeting and upholstered chairs. Bathrooms are small but tidy. The hotel is comparable in style and amenities to the Hôtel des Deux-Iles (see below), under the same ownership.

Hôtel des Deux-Iles. 59 rue St-Louis-en-l'Ile, 75004 Paris. ☎ **01-43-26-13-35.** Fax 01-43-29-60-25. 17 units. TV TEL. 860 F ($146.20) double. AE, MC, V. Métro: Pont-Marie.

This much-restored 17th-century town house was an inexpensive hotel until 1976, when an elaborate decor with lots of bamboo and reed furniture and French provincial touches was added. The result is an unpretentious but charming hotel with a great location. Bedrooms and bathrooms are on the small side. A garden of plants and flowers off the lobby leads to a basement breakfast room with a fireplace. Amenities include room service from 7:30am to 8pm and laundry/dry cleaning.

✪ **Hôtel Saint-Louis.** 75 rue St-Louis-en-l'Ile, 75004 Paris. ☎ **01-46-34-04-80.** Fax 01-46-34-02-13. hotel.www.paris-hotel.tm.fr/saint-louis–marais. 21 units. TEL. 775–875 F ($131.75–$148.75) double. MC, V. Métro: Pont-Marie.

Proprietor Guy Record and his wife, Andrée, maintain a charming family atmosphere (which is becoming harder and harder to find in Paris) at this antique-filled small hotel in a 17th-century town house. Despite a full renovation completed in 1998, it still represents an incredible value considering its prime location on the highly desirable, crowded island of Saint-Louis. With mansard roofs and old-fashioned moldings, top-floor rooms sport a tiny balcony with sweeping views over the rooftops of Paris. Expect cozy, slightly cramped rooms. All the bathrooms were renovated in 1998. The breakfast room is in the cellar, whose stone vaulting dates from the 17th century.

8TH ARRONDISSEMENT (CHAMPS-ELYSÉES/ MADELEINE)
VERY EXPENSIVE

✪ **Hôtel de Crillon.** 10 place de la Concorde, 75008 Paris. ☎ **800/241-3333** in the U.S. and Canada, or 01-44-71-15-00. Fax 01-44-71-15-04. www.crillon-paris.com. E-mail: crillon@crillon-paris.com. 163 units. A/C MINIBAR TV TEL. 3,500–4,300 F ($595–$731) double; from 4,950 F ($841.50) suite. AE, DC, MC, V. Parking 150 F ($25.50). Métro: Concorde.

One of Europe's greatest hotels, the Crillon sits across from the U.S. Embassy. The 200-year-old building, once the palace of the duc de Crillon, has been a hotel since the early 1900s and is now owned by Jean Taittinger of the champagne family. Inside are many preserved architectural details as well as museum-quality antiques and reproductions. The salons boast 17th- and 18th-century tapestries, gilt-and-brocade furniture, chandeliers, fine sculpture, and Louis XVI

Hotels & Restaurants near Place Charles-de-Gaulle

Hotels
Alexander **1**
Le Bristol **7**
Plaza Athénée **13**

Restaurants
Alain Ducasse **2**
Café Indochine **8**
Copenhague/Flora Danica **5**
Fouquet's **11**
Jamin **3**
Laudurée **12**

Lasserre **14**
Le Bistro de l'Étoile **4**
Pierre Gagnaire **6**
Spoon, Food, & Wine **12**
Taillevent **9**

M Métro Stop
R RER Stop

chests and chairs. Guest rooms are large and luxurious. Some of the accommodations are spectacular, such as the Leonard Bernstein Suite, which has one of the maestro's pianos and one of the grandest views of any hotel room in Paris. Baths are sumptuous as well, with deluxe toiletries, marble, dual sinks, robes, thick towels, and, in some, thermal taps.

Dining: You can dine at the elegant **Les Ambassadeurs** or the more informal **L'Obélisque,** where menu choices are less experimental. Les Ambassadeurs offers a businessperson's lunch Monday through Friday only. A menu dégustation is served at lunch on weekends and every evening.

Amenities: 24-hour room service, secretarial/translation service, laundry, valet, meeting and conference rooms, garden-style court-yard with restaurant service, shops.

Hôtel Plaza Athénée. 27 av. Montaigne, 75008 Paris. ☎ **800/223-6800** in the U.S. and Canada, or 01-53-67-66-65. Fax 01-53-67-66-66. E-mail: email@hotel-plaza-athenee-fr. 185 units. A/C MINIBAR TV TEL. 3,500–4,000 F ($595–$680) double; 7,600–13,000 F ($1,292–$2,210) suite. AE, MC, V. Parking 150 F ($25.50). Métro: F. D. Roosevelt or Alma Marceau.

Plaza Athénée, a grand art nouveau marvel from 1889, is a landmark of discretion and style. About half the celebrities visiting Paris have been pampered here; in the old days, Mata Hari used to frequent the place. Decors throughout are sumptuous. The finest public room is the Montaigne Salon, paneled in grained wood and dominated by a marble fireplace. The quietest guest rooms overlook a courtyard with awnings and parasol-shaded tables; they have ample closet space, and their large tiled baths have double basins and a tub and shower. Some rooms overlooking the avenue Montaigne have views of the Eiffel Tower. In 1999, the hotel completed a radical overhaul, creating larger rooms out of some of the smaller, less desirable rooms.

Dining/Diversions: La Régence offers superb food—try the lobster soufflé. For lunch, **Grill Relais Plaza** is the meeting place of dress designers and personalities from the worlds of publishing, cinema, and art. The **Bar Anglais** is a favorite spot for a late-night drink.

Amenities: Concierge, 24-hour room service, laundry, conference rooms, beauty salon, massage, fitness club.

Le Bristol. 112 rue du Faubourg St-Honoré, 75008 Paris. ☎ **01-53-43-43-00.** Fax 01-53-43-43-26. www.hotel-bristol.com. E-mail: resa@hotel-bristol.com. 3,250–4,000 F ($552.50–$680) double; 4,600–36,000 F ($782–$6,120) suite. AE, DC, MC, V. Free parking. Métro: Miromesnil.

This medium-size palace is near the Palais d'Elysée (home of the French president), on the shopping street that runs parallel to the Champs-Elysées. Personalized old-world service is rigidly and meticulously maintained in a venue that some guests find stiff and forbidding, and others absolutely adore. The classic 18th-century Parisian facade has a glass-and-wrought-iron entryway, where guests are greeted by uniformed English-speaking attendants. Hippolyte Jammet founded the Bristol in 1924, installing many valuable antiques and furnishings from the Louis XV and Louis XVI eras. Bedrooms are opulently furnished, either with antiques or well-made reproductions, inlaid wood, bronze, and crystal, Oriental carpets, and original oil paintings. Each room is renovated and freshened every 3 years.

Dining/Diversions: The Restaurant d'Eté (Summer Restaurant), set within a greenhouse-style room overlooking the garden, is open from April through October, and the richly paneled Restaurant d'Hiver (Winter Restaurant) is open the rest of the year. Tea and drinks are served either at the hushed and sometimes irritatingly reverent Bristol Bar or in the garden.

Amenities: 24-hour room service, business center with translation services, hairdressing salon, massage parlor, sauna, conference rooms, lobby bar and cocktail lounge, heated indoor swimming pool, rooftop solarium with a view of Sacré Coeur (open daily from 6:30am to 10:30pm.)

EXPENSIVE

Hôtel Beau Manoir. 6 rue de l'Arcade, 75008 Paris. ☎ **800/528-1234** in the U.S. and Canada, or 01-42-66-03-07. Fax 01-42-68-03-00. www. paris-hotels-charm.com. E-mail: bm@paris-hotels-charm.com. 32 units. A/C MINIBAR TV TEL. 1,200 F ($204) double; 1,600 F ($272) suite. Rates include breakfast. AE, DC, MC, V. Métro: Madeleine.

Open since 1994, this four-star hotel has a 19th-century feel. The lobby is like a private living room, with walnut reproductions of 18th- and 19th-century antiques, Aubusson tapestries, and fresh flowers. Breakfast is served beneath the chiseled vaults of a very old stone cellar. The guest rooms are charming and well accessorized, ranging in size from small to spacious. Each is soundproof, with a safe for valuables. Baths are in marble, with thick towels. The suites often have exposed beams or sloping garret-style ceilings.

Amenities: Limited room service from 7am to 7pm. A receptionist/concierge can arrange most things within reason.

INEXPENSIVE

Hôtel Opal. 19 rue Tronchet, 75008 Paris. ☎ **01-42-65-77-97.** Fax 01-49-24-06-58. www.hotels.fr/opal. E-mail: h_opal@club-internet.fr. 36 units. A/C MINIBAR TV TEL. 590–730 F ($100.30–$124.10) double. Extra bed 100 F ($18). AE, DC, V. Parking 120 F ($20.40) nearby. Métro: Madeleine.

This rejuvenated hotel is a real find in the heart of Paris, behind the Madeleine and near the Opéra Garnier. The guest rooms are somewhat cramped but very clean and comfortable, and many of them are air-conditioned. Those on the top floor are reached by a narrow staircase; some have skylights. Most rooms have twin brass beds with decent mattresses. Compact bathrooms have shower stalls and hair dryers. Reception will make arrangements for parking at a nearby garage.

9TH & 10TH ARRONDISSEMENTS (OPÉRA GARNIER/ GARE DU NORD)
INEXPENSIVE

Hôtel de la Tour d'Auvergne. 10 rue de la Tour d'Auvergne. 75009 Paris.
☎ **01-48-78-61-60.** Fax 01-49-95-99-00. 24 units. TV TEL. 550–750 F
($93.50–$127.50) double. AE, DC, MC, V. Parking 100 F ($17). Métro: Cadet
or Gare du Nord.

You wouldn't know it from the exterior, but the building that contains this hotel was erected before Baron Haussmann reconfigured the avenues of Paris around 1870. Later, Modigliani rented a room here for 6 months, and the staff will tell you that both Victor Hugo and Rodin lived on this street for brief periods before moving on to greater glory. The interior was long ago modernized into a glossy internationalism, with touches of paneling and marble. The comfortable bedrooms are meticulously coordinated, though the small decorative canopies over the headboards make them feel cluttered, particularly after you put down all your luggage and travel gear. Although the views over the courtyard in back are uninspired, even gloomy, some clients request a rear-view room for its relative quiet. Every year five rooms are renovated, so the comfort level is kept at a high standard. The small bathrooms have a tub and shower combination and a hair dryer.

11TH & 12TH ARRONDISSEMENTS (OPÉRA BASTILLE/ BOIS DE VINCENNES)
MODERATE

Le Pavillon Bastille. 65 rue de Lyon, 75012 Paris. ☎ **01-43-43-65-65.**
Fax 01-43-43-96-52. www.france-paris.com. E-mail: hotel-pavillon@
akamail.com. 24 units. A/C MINIBAR TV TEL. 815–955 F ($138.55–$162.35)
double; 1,375 F ($233.75) suite. AE, DC, V. Parking 85 F ($14.45).
Métro: Bastille.

For those who want to stay in this increasingly fashionable district, this is the finest choice. Hardly your cozy little backstreet Paris digs, it's a bold, brassy, and innovative hotel. The 1991-vintage town house is situated across from the Bastille Opera House and about a block south of place de la Bastille. A 17th-century fountain graces the courtyard between the hotel and the street. The rooms provide twin or double beds with firm mattresses, partially mirrored walls, and comfortable, contemporary built-in furniture. The English-speaking staff is friendly and efficient, offering room service, baby-sitting, and laundry and valet service. Breakfast is served below the ceiling vaults of the cellar. Partly because of its location near Paris's hottest new classical music venue and partly because it emphasizes middle-bracket comfort and practicality, the hotel derives at least 70% of its business from foreign visitors, especially Americans, Australians, and Japanese. If you're looking for a bargain, the cheapest rooms at 815 F ($138.55) have the same size and configuration as the more expensive *chambres privilegées,* priced at 955 F ($162.35). The extra cost gets you added amenities such as slippers, better cosmetics in the bathrooms, fruit baskets, and a complimentary bottle of wine upon arrival. Nice extras, but not at that price. Bathrooms are efficiently organized and well equipped.

16TH ARRONDISSEMENT (TROCADÉRO/ BOIS DE BOULOGNE)
EXPENSIVE

Alexander. 102 av. Victor Hugo, 75116 Paris. ☎ **800/888-4747** or 212/ 752-3900 in the U.S. and Canada, or 01-45-53-64-65. Fax 01-45-53-12-51. 62 units. MINIBAR TV TEL. 890–1,490 F ($151.30–$253.30) double; 1,800–2,200 F ($306–$374) suite. AE, DC, MC, V. Parking 100 F ($17) across the street. Métro: Victor Hugo.

Though it functioned as a simple pension throughout the 1950s, the hotel was radically upgraded in the 1970s and became the four-star property you'll see today. Rich paneling in the reception hall immediately assures guests they will be met with luxury, and bedrooms cement the deal with fabric stretched over the walls for added ambience, warmth, and soundproofing. Half of the rooms face a well-planted, quiet courtyard. About a dozen bedrooms are renovated every year, and comfort is of a very high standard. Most beds are twins. Bathrooms are beautifully maintained, with thick towels and a tub and shower combination.

Dining/Diversions: A hotel bar open daily from 7am to 9:30pm serves sandwiches and light snacks. Room service is available from 7am to 10pm.

Amenities: One-day laundry service. A receptionist/concierge can help meet most needs.

18TH ARRONDISSEMENT (MONTMARTRE)
VERY EXPENSIVE

✪ **Terrass Hôtel.** 12-14 rue Joseph de Maistre, 75018 Paris. ☎ **800/ 344-1212** in the U.S. and Canada, or 01-46-06-72-85. Fax 01-42-52-29-11. E-mail: terrass@francenet.fr. 101 units. MINIBAR TV TEL. 1,320–1,470 F ($224.40–$249.90) double; 1,710 F ($290.70) suite. Rates include breakfast. AE, DC, MC, V. Métro: Place de Clichy or Blanche.

Built in 1913, and richly renovated into a plush but traditional style in 1991, this is the only four-star hotel on the Butte Montmartre. In an area filled with some of the seediest hotels in Paris, this place is easily in a class of its own. Its main advantage is its location amid Montmartre's bohemian atmosphere (or what's left of it). Staffed with English-speaking employees, it has a large marble-floored lobby ringed with blond oak paneling and accented with 18th-century antiques and even older tapestries. The bedrooms are high-ceilinged, cozy, and well upholstered, and often have views.

Dining/Diversions: An elegant street-level restaurant and a seventh-floor summer-only garden terrace with bar and food service and sweeping views of many of Paris's most important monuments. In colder weather, the hotel's **Lobby Bar** offers live piano music and a working fireplace.

Amenities: Foreign exchange, car rentals, tour desk, laundry/dry cleaning, conference facilities.

INEXPENSIVE

Hôtel Ermitage. 24 rue Lamarck, 75018 Paris. ☎ **01-42-64-79-22.** Fax 01-42-64-10-33. 12 units. TEL. 440–500 F ($74.80–$85) double. No credit cards. Parking 60 F ($10.20). Métro: Lamarck-Caulaincourt.

Erected in 1870 of chiseled limestone in the Napoléon III style, this hotel's facade might remind you of a perfectly proportioned, small-scale villa. It's set in a calm and quiet area—just a brief uphill stroll from the Basilica of Sacré-Coeur—where all the neighbors seem to have known each other for generations. Views extend out over Paris, and there's a verdant garden in the back courtyard. The small bedrooms evoke a countryside auberge with exposed ceiling beams, flowered wallpaper, and casement windows that open onto the garden or onto a street seemingly airlifted from the respectable provinces. Mattresses are reasonably comfortable. Only breakfast is served.

2 Left Bank

We'll begin with the most centrally located arrondissements on the Left Bank, then work our way through the more outlying neighborhoods.

5TH ARRONDISSEMENT (LATIN QUARTER)
MODERATE

Hôtel Abbatial St-Germain. 46 bd. St-Germain. 75005 Paris. ☎ **01-46-34-02-12.** Fax 01-43-25-47-73. www.abbatial.com. E-mail: abbatial@hotellerie.net. 43 units. A/C MINIBAR TV TEL. 750–850 F ($127.50–$144.50) double. AE, MC, V. Parking 100 F ($17). Métro: Maubert-Mutualité.

The origins of this hotel run deep: Interior renovations have revealed such 17th-century touches as dovecotes and massive oak beams. In the early 1990s, a radical restoration brought the six stories of rooms up to modern and smallish but comfortable standards. The public areas are especially appealing. The guest rooms are furnished in faux Louis XVI. Bathrooms are small. All windows are double glazed, and the fifth- and sixth-floor rooms enjoy views over Notre-Dame. Breakfast is served beneath the vaulted ceilings of the stone-sided cellar.

Hôtel Agora St-Germain. 42 rue des Bernardins, 75005 Paris. ☎ **01-46-34-13-00.** Fax 01-46-34-75-05. 39 units. A/C MINIBAR TV TEL. 720–820 F ($122.40–$139.40) double; 960 F ($163.20) triple. AE, DC, MC, V. Parking 120 F ($20.40). Métro: Maubert-Mutualité.

One of the best of the neighborhood's moderately priced choices, this hotel occupies a building constructed in the early 1600s, probably to house a group of guardsmen protecting the brother of the king at his lodgings nearby. It's in the heart of the artistic and historic section of Paris and offers compact, soundproof guest rooms, each comfortably, although not particularly fashionably, furnished. Towels are relatively small and thin, and mattresses are adequately comfortable. Room service is provided daily from 7:30 to 10:30am.

Hôtel des Arènes. 51 rue Monge, 75005 Paris. ☎ **01-43-25-09-26.** Fax 01-43-25-79-56. 52 units. MINIBAR TV TEL. 450–700 F ($76.50–$119) double. AE, MC, V. Parking 80 F ($13.60). Métro: Monge or Cardinal-Lemoine.

Set within a 19th-century structure whose chiseled stone facade evokes fine old traditions, this hotel offers well-maintained modern bedrooms. Many in back overlook the tree-dotted ruins of Paris's ancient Roman arena, unearthed in 1865 during the construction of the surrounding labyrinth of streets. Breakfast is served in a simple, windowless room in the hotel's cellar. The staff is overworked and somewhat distracted, and the place a bit anonymous, but the location is appealing and the rooms are practical and comfortable. Bedrooms range from small to medium in size. Each unit has a compact private bath with a shower stall and adequate shelf space.

Hôtel des Grands Hommes. 17 place du Panthéon, 75005 Paris. ☎ **01-46-34-19-60.** Fax 01-43-26-67-32. 32 units. A/C MINIBAR TV TEL. 700–600 F ($119–$102) double; 1,200 F ($204) suite. AE, DC, MC, V. Parking 80 F ($13.60). Métro: Cardinal-Lemoine or Luxembourg.

Built in the 18th century and renovated in the early 1990s, this six-story hotel offers direct profile views (from many rooms) of the Panthéon. All but a handful of the accommodations have exposed ceiling beams and pleasantly old-fashioned furnishings that sometimes include brass beds. The rooms on the second and fifth floors have small balconies; those on the fifth and sixth floors have the

Hotels in the Heart of the Left Bank

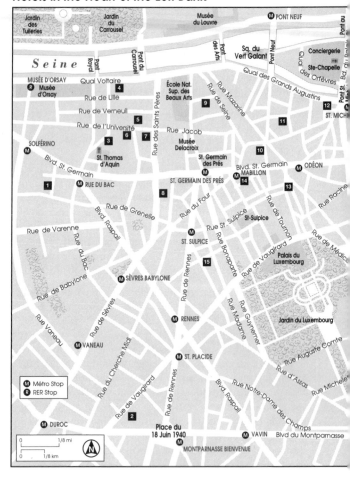

best views; and those with the most space are on the ground floor. Towels are small and thin, and mattresses are comfortable but not plush. The welcome is charming, and the staff speaks English.

Hôtel des Jardins du Luxembourg. 5 impasse Royer-Collard, 75005 Paris. ☎ **01-40-46-08-88.** Fax 01-40-46-02-28. www.globe-market. com/w/75005jardlux.htm. 25 units. A/C MINIBAR TV TEL. 795–840 F ($135.15–$142.80) double. AE, DC, MC, V. Parking 85 F ($14.45). Métro: Cluny–La Sorbonne. RER: Luxembourg.

Agora St-Germain **19**
Delhy's Hotel **12**
Familia-Hôtel **20**
Hôtel Abbatial St-Germain **16**
Hôtel Aviatic **2**
Hôtel Clément **14**
Hôtel de Fleurie **10**
Hôtel de l'Abbaye
  St-Germain **15**
Hôtel de l'Académie **7**
Hôtel de l'Université **5**
Hôtel des Arènes **23**
Hôtel des Grandes Écoles **24**
Hôtel des Grands Hommes **21**
Hôtel des Jardins de
  Luxembourg **18**
Hôtel des Saints-Pères **8**
Hôtel du Quai Voltaire **4**
Hôtel le Home Latin **17**
Hôtel Lenox **6**
Hôtel Montalembert **3**
Hôtel-Résidence
  St-Christophe **22**
L'Hôtel **9**
Le Duc de St-Simon **1**
Odéon-Hôtel **13**
Relais Christine **11**

Built during Baron Haussmann's 19th-century overhaul of Paris, this hotel boasts an imposing facade of honey-colored stone accented with ornate iron balconies. The interior is outfitted in strong, clean lines, often with groupings of vintage art-deco furnishings. The high-ceilinged guest rooms, some with Provençal tiles and ornate moldings, are well maintained, the size in general ranging from small to medium. Best of all, they overlook a quiet dead-end alley, ensuring relatively peaceful nights. Some have balconies overlooking the rooftops. Mattresses are comfortable but not plush.

Hôtel-Résidence St-Christophe. 17 rue Lacépède, 75005 Paris. ☎ **01-43-31-81-54.** Fax 01-43-31-12-54. E-mail: hotelstchristophe@compuserve.com. 31 units. MINIBAR TV TEL. 600 F ($102) double. AE, DC, MC, V. Parking 100 F ($17). Métro: Place-Monge.

This hotel, in one of the Latin Quarter's undiscovered but charming districts, has a gracious English-speaking staff. It was created in 1987 when a derelict hotel was connected to a butcher shop. All the small to medium-sized rooms were successfully renovated in 1998. Millions of francs later, the St-Christophe is inviting and comfortable, with Louis XV–style furniture, wall-to-wall carpeting, and comfortably firm mattresses. The compact bathrooms have adequate shelf space. Breakfast is the only meal served, but the staff offers advice about neighborhood bistros.

INEXPENSIVE

✪ **Familia-Hôtel.** 11 rue des Ecoles, 75005. ☎ **01-43-54-55-27.** Fax 01-43-29-61-77. 30 units. MINIBAR TV TEL. 380–580 F ($64.60–$98.60) double. AE, DC, MC, V. Métro: Jussieu or Maubert-Mutualité.

As the name implies, this is a hotel that has been family run for decades. Many personal touches make the place unique, and it was lavishly renovated in 1998. The walls of 14 rooms are graced with finely executed sepia-colored frescoes of Parisian scenes. Eight rooms have restored stone walls and seven rooms have balconies with delightful views over the Latin Quarter. All rooms have cable TV (with CNN), hair dryers, and high-quality mattresses, making the hotel more comfortable than most in this price category.

Hotel des Grandes Écoles. 75 rue de Cardinal Lemoine, 75005 Paris. ☎ **01-43-26-79-23.** Fax 01-43-25-28-15. 51 units. TEL. 490–670 F ($83.30–$113.90) double. MC, V. Parking 100 F ($17). Metro: Cardinal-Lemoine, Monge.

Few other hotels in the neighborhood offer so much low-key charm at such reasonable prices. It's composed of a trio of high-ceilinged buildings, each interconnected via a sheltered courtyard where singing birds provide a worthy substitute for the TVs deliberately missing from the rooms. Rooms are artfully old-fashioned, with feminine touches that include Laura Ashley–inspired flowered upholsteries and ruffles. Many offer views of a bucolic-looking garden whose trellises and flower beds evoke the countryside. Bathrooms are small but exceedingly well organized, with adequate shelf space, shower stalls, and hair dryers. Thanks to dozens of restaurants in the surrounding rue Mouffetard neighborhood, no one seems to mind the hotel's lack of a restaurant, and when the weather cooperates, breakfast is served in the garden.

✪ **Hôtel Le Home Latin.** 15–17 rue du Sommerard, 75005 Paris. ☎ **01-43-26-25-21.** Fax 01-43-29-87-04. 55 units. TV TEL. 550–650 F ($93.50–$110.50) double. AE, V. Parking 85 F ($14.45). Métro: St-Michel or Maubert-Mutualité.

This is one of the most famous budget hotels in Paris, known since the 1970s for clean and simple lodgings. The blandly functional rooms—streamlined without a lot of frills—were renovated in 1999; some of them have small balconies overlooking the street. The rooms facing the courtyard are quieter than those fronting the street. The elevator doesn't reach beyond the fifth floor, but to make up for the stair climb, the sixth floor's *chambres mansardées* offer a romantic location under the eaves and panoramic views over the rooftops. Bathrooms are sterile-looking and efficient, with thin towels.

6TH ARRONDISSEMENT (ST-GERMAIN/LUXEMBOURG)
VERY EXPENSIVE

Relais Christine. 3 rue Christine, 75006 Paris. ☎ **01-40-51-60-80.** Fax 01-40-51-60-81. E-mail: relaisch@club-internet.fr. 51 units. A/C MINIBAR TV TEL. 1,800–2,300 F ($306–$391) double; 2,400–4,200 F ($408–$714) duplex or suite. AE, DC, MC, V. Free parking. Métro: Odéon.

Relais Christine welcomes you into what was a 16th-century Augustinian cloister. You enter from a narrow cobblestone street into first a symmetrical courtyard and then an elegant reception area with baroque sculpture and Renaissance antiques. Each guest room is uniquely decorated with wooden beams and Louis XIII–style furnishings. The rooms come in a wide range of styles and shapes, and some are among the most spacious on the Left Bank, with such extras as mirrored closets, plush carpets, thermostats, and in some cases balconies facing the outer courtyard. The least attractive, smallest, and dimmest rooms are those in the interior.

Dining: Off the reception area is a paneled sitting room/bar area ringed with 19th-century portraits and comfortable leather chairs. The breakfast room is in a vaulted cellar; the ancient well and massive central stone column are part of the cloister's former kitchen.

Amenities: 24-hour room service, laundry, baby-sitting.

EXPENSIVE

Hôtel de Fleurie. 32–34 rue Grégoire-de-Tours, 75006 Paris. ☎ **01-53-73-70-00.** Fax 01-53-73-70-20. www.hotel-de-fleurie.tm.fr. E-mail: bonjour@hotel-de-fleurie.tm.fr. 29 units. A/C MINIBAR TV TEL. 930–1,200 F ($158.10–$204) double; 1,550–1,650 F ($263.50–$280.50) family room. Children 12 and under stay free in parents' room. AE, DC, MC, V. Métro: Odéon.

Just off boulevard St-Germain on a colorful little street, the Fleurie is one of the best of the "new" old hotels. About half the rooms and bathrooms were renovated in 1999. The hotel has a facade that's studded with spotlit statuary, recapturing a 17th-century elegance. The stone walls have been exposed in the reception salon, where you check in at a refectory desk. An elevator takes you to well-furnished bedrooms, each with a comfortable bed and a safe. Many of them have elaborate curtains, reproductions of antiques, and a sense of late 19th-century charm. This hotel has long been a family favorite because of the interconnecting doors that open between certain pairs of its rooms, thereby creating safe havens the hotel refers to as *chambres familiales.*

Dining: Only breakfast is served, although there is a small bar.

Amenities: Car rentals arranged, room service, dry cleaning, laundry.

Hôtel de l'Abbaye St-Germain. 10 rue Cassette, 75006 Paris. ☎ **01-45-44-38-11.** Fax 01-45-48-07-86. www.hotel-abbaye.com. E-mail: hotel.abbaye@wanadoo.fr. 46 units. A/C TV TEL. 1,080–1,600 F ($183.60–$272) double; 1,950–2,000 F ($331.50–$340) suite. Rates include continental breakfast. AE, MC, V. Métro: St-Sulpice.

Built early in the 18th century as a convent for the Eglise St-Germain, this place later became a cheap youth hostel. It's since been transformed into a charming boutique hotel whose brightly colored rooms have traditional furniture like you'd find in a private club, and touches of sophisticated flair. In front is a small garden, and in back is a verdant courtyard featuring a fountain, raised flower beds, and masses of ivy and climbing vines. If you don't mind the expense, one of the most charming rooms has a terrace overlooking the upper floors of neighboring buildings.

Dining: Only breakfast is served, but the public areas include a trio of salons and a bar.

Amenities: Car rentals arranged, concierge, room service, dry cleaning, laundry.

✪ **L'Hôtel.** 13 rue des Beaux-Arts, 75006 Paris. ☎ **01-44-41-99-00.** Fax 01-43-25-64-81. www.l-hotel.com. E-mail: reservation@l-hotel.com. 26 units. A/C MINIBAR TV TEL. 800–2,800 F ($136–$476) double; from 3,000 F ($510) suite. AE, DC, MC, V. Métro: St-Germain-des-Prés.

This boutique hotel was once a 19th-century fleabag called the Hôtel d'Alsace, whose major distinction was that Oscar Wilde died here, broke and in despair. But today's guests aren't anywhere near poverty row: Show-business and fashion celebrities march through the lobby. L'Hôtel was the creation of the late French actor Guy-Louis Duboucheron, who established an atmosphere of supersophistication. You'll feel like a movie star while bathing in your rosy-pink marble tub. An eclectic collection of antiques pops up throughout the hotel. The spacious 2,800 F ($476) room contains the original furnishings and memorabilia of Mistinguette, France's legendary stage star, a frequent performer with Maurice Chevalier and his on-again, off-again lover. Her pedestal bed is set in the middle of the room, surrounded everywhere by mirrors, as she liked to see how she looked or "performed" at all times of the day and night! Rooms vary widely in size, style, and price, from quite small to deluxe. (Elizabeth Taylor found all the rooms too small for her trunks). All rooms have nonworking fireplaces, private safes, and fabric-covered walls. The relatively small marble baths are well equipped, with thick towels and a bidet; however, about half of them are tiny tubless nooks.

Dining: Other than breakfast, afternoon tea, and room service, there's no conventional dining within the hotel. Breakfast and tea are served in a greenhouse-style room loaded with plants.

Amenities: Concierge, room service daily from 6:30am to 11pm, baby-sitting, laundry, and valet services.

Odéon-Hôtel. 3 rue de l'Odéon, 75006 Paris. ☎ **01-43-25-90-67.** Fax 01-43-25-55-98. 33 units. A/C TV TEL. 800–1,412 F ($136–$240.05) double. AE, DC, MC, V. Parking 80 F ($13.60). Métro: Odéon.

Reminiscent of a modernized Norman country inn, the Odéon offers charming rustic touches such as exposed beams, rough stone walls, high crooked ceilings, and tapestries mixed with contemporary fabrics, mirrored ceilings, and black leather furnishings. Conveniently located near both the Théâtre de l'Odéon and boulevard St-Germain, the Odéon stands on the first street in Paris to have pavements (1779) and gutters. By the turn of the century, this area, which had drawn the original Shakespeare & Co. bookshop to no. 12 rue de l'Odéon, began attracting such writers as Gertrude Stein and her coterie. Rooms are small to medium sized, with comfortable mattresses.

MODERATE

Hôtel Aviatic. 105 rue de Vaugirard, 75006 Paris. ☎ **01-45-44-38-21.** Fax 01-45-49-35-83. www.aviatic.fr. E-mail: parishotel@aol.com. 43 units. A/C MINIBAR TV TEL. 680–1,180 F ($115.60–$200.60) double. AE, DC, MC, V. Parking 140 F ($23.80). Métro: Montparnasse-Bienvenue.

This is a bit of old Paris, with a modest inner courtyard and a vine-covered lattice on the walls. It has been a family-run hotel for a century. The reception lounge, with marble columns, brass chandeliers, antiques, and a petit salon, provides an attractive setting. It doesn't have the decorative flair of some of the other 6th arrondissement hotels we've listed, but it offers good comfort and a warm ambience. Completely remodeled, it's in an interesting section of Montparnasse, surrounded by cafes frequented by artists, writers, and jazz musicians. Rooms were renovated in stages throughout the 1990s, and each has a safe and comfortable beds. The staff speaks English.

Hôtel des Saints-Pères. 65 rue des Sts-Pères, 75006 Paris. ☎ **01-45-44-50-00.** Fax 01-45-44-90-83. www.hotelsts.peres@wanadoo.fr. 39 units. MINIBAR TV TEL. 650–1,150 F ($110.50–$195.50) double; 1,700 F ($289) suite. AE, MC, V. Métro: St-Germain-des-Prés or Sèvres-Babylone.

This hotel just off boulevard St-Germain is comparable to the Odéon, attracting people who love Paris or, more specifically, love traditional Left Bank hotels. There is no better recommendation for this old favorite than the long list of guests who return again and again. The late Edna St. Vincent Millay enjoyed the camellia-trimmed garden. The hotel, designed in the 17th century by Louis XIV's architect Jacques Gabriel, is decorated in part with antique paintings, tapestries, and mirrors. Many of the bedrooms face a quiet courtyard accented in summer with potted plants. The most sought-after room is the *chambre à la fresque,* which has a 17th-century painted ceiling. The hotel has installed new plumbing and has replastered and repainted the rooms. Whenever weather permits, breakfast is served in the courtyard.

Hôtel St-Germain-des-Prés. 36 rue Bonaparte, 75006 Paris. ☎ **01-43-26-00-19.** Fax 01-40-46-83-63. 30 units. MINIBAR TV TEL. 980–1,350 F ($166.60–$229.50) double; from 1,700 F ($289) suite. Rates include breakfast. MC, V. Métro: St-Germain-des-Prés.

Most of this hotel's attraction comes from its enviable location in the Latin Quarter—behind a well-known Left Bank street near many shops. Janet Flanner, the legendary correspondent for the *New Yorker* in the 1920s, lived here for a while. Each room is small but charming, with antique ceiling beams, a safe, and reasonably comfortable beds. Each has been renovated within the past few years. The public areas are severely elegant. Air-conditioning is available in most of the rooms.

INEXPENSIVE

Delhy's Hotel. 22 rue de l'Hirondelle, 75006 Paris. ☎ **01-43-26-58-25.** Fax 01-43-26-51-06. 21 units, 7 with private bathroom (shower only). TV TEL. 356 F ($60.50) double without bathroom, 446 F ($75.80) double with shower; 586 F ($99.60) triple with shower. Rates include breakfast. AE, DC, MC, V. Métro: St-Michel.

This building was built around 1400 and later acquired by François I as a home for one of his mistresses. It's on a narrow and crooked alley in the heart of the densest part of the Latin Quarter. Don't expect luxury, but look for certain touches of charm that help compensate for the lack of an elevator. If you get a room without a shower, you'll have to go down to the ground floor for access to the public facilities. The building's staircase is listed as a national relic, and most of the compact rooms still have the original, almost fossilized, timbers and beams. Rooms were for the most part renovated in the late 1990s. Mattresses are reasonably comfortable; bath linens are acceptable but not plush.

Hôtel Clément. 6 rue Clément, 75006 Paris. ☎ **01-43-26-53-60.** Fax 01-44-07-06-83. E-mail: hotelment@worldnet.fr. 31 units. A/C TV TEL. 530–580 F ($90.10–$98.60) double; 750 F ($127.50) suite. AE, DC, V. Métro: Mabillon.

This hotel sits on a quiet, narrow street, within sight of the twin towers of the Église St-Sulpice. Built in the 1700s, the six-story structure that houses the hotel was stripped down and renovated several years ago into a bright, uncomplicated design. Don't expect deluxe bedrooms; they're simple and small, in some cases not much bigger than the beds they contain. Mattresses are medium quality, but not luxurious, and towels are thin. On the premises is a simple bistro with specialties from the Auvergne.

7TH ARRONDISSEMENT (EIFFEL TOWER/ MUSÉE D'ORSAY)
VERY EXPENSIVE

✪ **Hôtel Montalembert.** 3 rue de Montalembert, 75007 Paris. ☎ **800/447-7462** in the U.S. and Canada, or 01-45-49-68-68. Fax 01-45-49-69-49. www.montalembert.com. E-mail: welcome@hotel-montalembert.fr. 56 units. A/C MINIBAR TV TEL. 1,750–2,300 F ($297.50–$391) double; 2,850 F ($484.50) junior suite; 4,400 F ($748) suite. AE, DC, MC, V. Parking 120 F ($20.40). Métro: Rue-du-Bac.

Unusually elegant for the Left Bank, the Montalembert was built in 1926 in beaux-arts style. It was restored between 1989 and 1992 and was hailed as a smashing success, borrowing sophisticated elements of Bauhaus and postmodern design in honey beiges, creams, and golds. Bedrooms are spacious, except for some standard doubles, which are quite small unless you're a very thin model. All rooms have VCRs and safes. Embroidered linens and quality mattresses adorn the large beds, and the bathrooms are elegant, with marble vanities, generous shelf space, and thick towels.

Dining/Diversions: Le Montalembert is favored by area artists, writers, publishers, and antique dealers. The stylish dining room provides excellent service and exceptionally good food based on market-fresh ingredients. Dishes include traditional veal chops slathered with wild mushrooms, along with more inventive fare from the relatively young kitchen staff. Expect crowds for weekday lunches; it thins out at other times. In summer, dining is offered on the terrace. The hotel also has a full-fledged bar and 24-hour room service.

Amenities: The concierge can arrange for practically anything under the sun. Hotel clients receive privileges at a nearby health club.

EXPENSIVE

Hôtel de l'Université. 22 rue de l'Université, 75007 Paris. ☎ **01-42-61-09-39.** Fax 01-42-60-40-84. www.paris-hotel.tm.fr/fr/saintgermain.04/universite.html. 27 units. A/C TV TEL. 850–1,300 F ($144.50–$221) double. AE, MC, V. Métro: St-Germain-des-Prés.

Long favored by well-heeled parents of North American students studying in Paris, this 300-year-old town house filled with fine antiques enjoys a location in a discreetly upscale neighborhood. Number 54 is a favorite room, with a rattan bed, period pieces, and a marble bath. Another charmer is no. 35, opening onto a courtyard and with a fireplace. The most expensive accommodation, at 1,300 F ($234), has a small terrace overlooking the surrounding rooftops. Most of the compact bathrooms have a tub and shower combination and adequate shelf space. The bistro-style breakfast room opens onto a courtyard with a fountain.

Le Duc de Saint-Simon. 14 rue de St-Simon, 75007 Paris. ☎ **01-44-39-20-20.** Fax 01-45-48-68-25. 34 units. TEL. 1,050–1,450 F ($178.50–$246.50) double; from 1,900 F ($323) suite. AE, MC, V. Métro: Rue-du-Bac.

Set on a quiet residential street on the Left Bank, this is the only hotel in the 7th arrondissement to pose a serious challenge to the Montalembert. Two immortal cafes, Les Deux Magots and Le Flore, are a few steps away. The small villa has a tiny front garden and an 1830s decor with *faux-marbre* trompe-l'oeil panels, a frescoed elevator, and climbing wisteria gracing the courtyard. Each bedroom is unique and sure to include at least one antique. A few of the rooms are ridiculously small, but most offer adequate space. Baths are tiny, with just shower stalls, but have adequate shelf space. The service reflects the owner's extensive training in the art of pampering guests.

Dining: Room service is offered daily from 7am to 10:30pm.

Amenities: The concierge can arrange for just about anything, discreetly; and the hotel supplies televisions for clients who request them.

Hotels & Restaurants near the Eiffel Tower & Invalides

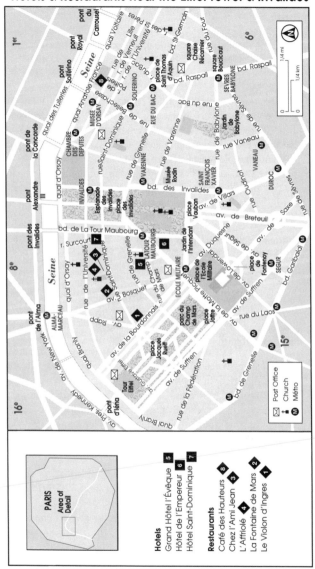

PARIS Area of Detail

Hotels
5 Grand Hôtel l'Évêque
6 Hôtel de l'Empereur
7 Hôtel Saint-Dominique

Restaurants
8 Café des Hauteurs
3 Chez l'Ami Jean
4 L'Affriolé
2 La Fontaine de Mars
1 Le Violon d'Ingres

MODERATE

Hôtel de l'Académie. 32 rue des Saints-Pères, 75007 Paris. ☎ **800/ 246-0041** in the U.S. and Canada, or 01-45-49-80-00. Fax 01-45-49-80-10. E-mail: academie@aol.com. 34 units. A/C MINIBAR TV TEL. 690–990 F ($117.30–$168.30) double; 1,290–1,590 F ($219.30–$270.30) suite. AE, DC, MC, V. Parking 150 F ($25.50). Métro: St-Germain-des-Prés.

The exterior walls and old ceiling beams are all that remain of this 17th-century residence of the private guards of the duc de Rohan. In 1999, the hotel was completely renovated to include an elegant reception area. The up-to-date guest rooms have duvets on the beds and comfortable mattresses, an Ile-de-France decor, and views over the 18th- and 19th-century buildings of the neighborhood. By American standards the rooms are small, but they're average for Paris. Baths are attractive and functional. The staff speaks English.

✪ **Hôtel du Quai-Voltaire.** 19 quai Voltaire, 75007 Paris. ☎ **01-42-61- 50-91.** Fax 01-42-61-62-26. 33 units. TV TEL. 670–720 F ($113.90–$122.40) double; 850 F ($144.50) triple. AE, DC, MC, V. Parking 110 F ($18.70) nearby. Métro: Musée d'Orsay.

Built in the 1600s as an abbey, then transformed into a hotel in 1856, Quai-Voltaire is best known for its illustrious guests, including Wilde, Baudelaire, and Wagner, who occupied rooms 47, 56, and 55, respectively. Camille Pissarro painted Le Pont Royal from the window of his room on the 4th floor. Many rooms in this modest inn have been renovated, and most overlook the bookstalls and boats of the Seine. In 1999, the facade of the hotel was painted, as were most of the bedrooms. Mattresses are comfortable and firm, with rarely, if ever, any complaints from the guests, and bathrooms are well designed. You can have drinks in the bar or small salon, and simple meals (like omelets and salads) can be prepared for those who prefer to eat in.

Hôtel Lenox. 9 rue de l'Université, 75007 Paris. ☎ **01-42-96-10-95.** Fax 01-42-61-52-83. 34 units. TV TEL. 740–1,100 F ($125.80–$187) double; 1,500 F ($255) duplex suite. AE, DC, MC, V. Métro: Rue-du-Bac.

The Lenox is a favorite for those seeking reasonably priced accommodations in St-Germain-des-Prés. In 1910, T. S. Eliot spent a summer here "on the old man's money" when the hotel was just a basic pension. Today, this much-improved establishment offers a helpful staff and cramped but comfortable rooms. Radically and expensively upgraded in 1996, the rooms evoke the chintzes and traditional furniture of an English country house. Many returning guests request the attic duplex with its tiny balcony and skylight. Most of the rooms are small to medium in size, each with a firm mattress. Bathrooms are tiny but have adequate shelf space.

INEXPENSIVE

Grand Hôtel L'Éveque. 29 rue Cler, 75007 Paris. ☎ **01-47-05-49-15.** Fax 01-45-50-49-36. www.interresa.ca/hotel/leveque/fr. E-mail: leveque@ hotellerie.net. 50 units. TV TEL. 380–400 F ($64.60–$68) double. AE, MC, V. Métro: École Militaire.

Built in the 1930s, with pastel-colored bedrooms that retain a vague art-deco inspiration, this five-story hotel is loaded with English-speaking clients, many of whom appreciate its proximity to the Eiffel Tower. Each bedroom contains a hair dryer, a small lockbox for valuables, just enough space to be comfortable, and double-insulated windows that overlook either a courtyard in back or the street in front. In 1998, the hotel's interior was completely renovated and repainted, although the older, very comfortable mattresses were left in place. Clients rarely, if ever, complain about them. There's an elevator.

Hôtel de l'Empereur. 2 rue Chevert, 75007 Paris. ☎ **01-45-55-88-02.** Fax 01-45-51-88-54. www.franc.hotel.guide.com/h75007empereur.htm. E-mail: globeman@easynet.fr. 38 units. MINIBAR TV TEL. 470–530 F ($79.90–$90.10) double. AE, DC, MC, V. Parking 110–150 F ($18.70–$25.50) across the street. Métro: Latour-Maubourg.

This inexpensive and convenient six-story hotel was built in the early 1700s and enjoys a loyal group of repeat visitors. There's an elevator inside to haul you and your luggage to one of the smallish but attractively decorated bedrooms. In 1998, the two top floors were renovated. There's no restaurant or bar, but a nearby restaurant will send up platters of food upon request.

Hôtel Saint-Dominique. 62 rue Saint-Dominique, 75007 Paris. ☎ **01-47-05-51-44.** Fax 01-47-05-81-28. 34 units. MINIBAR TV TEL. 500–580 F ($85–$98.60) double. AE, DC, MC, V. Métro: Latour-Maubourg or Invalides.

Part of the charm of this establishment derives from its division into three separate buildings interconnected through an open-air courtyard. The most visible of these was a convent in the 18th century; you can still see its battered ceiling beams and structural timbers in the reception area. The rooms aren't large, but each is warm, simply decorated, and comfortable. Many have patterned wallpaper in nostalgic patterns. Beds usually have wooden headboards and comfortable mattresses. Bathrooms are cramped, but they have hair dryers.

3 Near the Airports

ORLY

Hilton International Orly. Aéroport Orly, 267 Orly Sud, 94544 Val-de-Marne. ☎ **800/445-8667** in the U.S. and Canada, or 01-45-12-45-12. Fax 01-45-12-45-00. www.hilton.com. 356 units. A/C MINIBAR TV TEL. 1,020–1,510 F ($173.40–$256.70) double; 1,570–2,290 F ($266.90–$389.30) suite. AE, DC, MC, V. Parking 88 F ($14.95). Free shuttle bus between the hotel and both Orly terminals; 40-minute taxi ride from central Paris, except during rush hours.

Boxy and bland, the Hilton International at Orly remains a solid and well-maintained, but not particularly imaginative, hotel that business travelers appreciate for its convenience. Try as they might, incoming jets can't penetrate the bedrooms' sound barriers, guaranteeing you a decent shot at a night's sleep. (And unlike the 24-hour Charles de Gaulle Airport, Orly is closed to arriving flights between midnight and 6am.) Bedrooms are standard chain-hotel, with most of the mattresses replaced in 1998.

Dining: The hotel has two restaurants: an upscale restaurant open Monday through Friday for lunch and dinner, and a less expensive bistro that serves lunch and dinner 7 days a week.

Amenities: 24-hour room service, laundry, exercise room and sauna, nearby tennis courts.

ROISSY/CHARLES DE GAULLE

Hôtel Sofitel Paris Aéroport CDG. Aéroport Charles de Gaulle, Zone Central, B.P. 20248, 95713 Roissy. ☎ **800/221-4542** in the U.S. and Canada, or 01-49-19-29-29. Fax 01-49-19-29-00. www.accor.com. 352 units. A/C MINIBAR TV TEL. 980–1,550 F ($166.60–$263.50) double; from 1,900 F ($323) suite. AE, DC, MC, V. Parking 160 F ($27.20). Free shuttle bus service to and from the airport.

Many international travelers shuttle happily through this bustling but somewhat anonymous member of the nationwide French chain. Rising nine floors above a gray, industrial landscape, it employs a multilingual staff that's accustomed to accommodating constantly arriving and departing international business travelers. The monochromatic, conservatively international bedrooms are soundproof havens against the all-night roar of jets. Each was renovated in 1998, and many of the older mattresses were replaced with newer models. Bathrooms have oversized mirrors.

Dining: International food with a French slant is served at a comfortable restaurant and a bar on the hotel's ground floor.

Amenities: 24-hour room service, business center, video movies in several different languages, swimming pool and sauna.

4

Dining

$I\!V$elcome to the city that prides itself on being the culinary capital of the world. Only in Paris can you turn onto the nearest side street, enter the first place you see, sit down at the bare and wobbly table, glance at an illegibly hand-scrawled menu, and get a memorable meal.

1 Right Bank

We'll begin with the most centrally located arrondissements on the Right Bank, then work our way through the more outlying neighborhoods.

1ST ARRONDISSEMENT (MUSÉE DU LOUVRE/ LES HALLES)
VERY EXPENSIVE

Carré des Feuillants. 14 rue de Castiglione (near place Vendôme and the Tuileries), 1er. ☎ **01-42-86-82-82.** Fax 01-42-86-07-71. Reservations required. Main courses 240–280 F ($40.80–$47.60); fixed-price menu 295 F ($50.15) at lunch, 780 F ($132.60) at dinner. AE, DC, MC, V. Mon–Fri noon–2:30pm; Mon–Sat 7:30–10:30pm. Closed first 3 weeks in Aug. Métro: Tuileries, Concorde, Opéra, or Madeleine. FRENCH.

When leading chef Alain Dutournier converted this 17th-century convent into a restaurant, it was an overnight success. The interior is like a turn-of-the-century bourgeois house with several small salons opening onto a skylit courtyard, across from which is a glass-enclosed kitchen. Much of the inspiration here derives from a sophisticated reinterpretation of cuisine from France's southwest, using seasonally fresh ingredients and lots of know-how. Examples include roasted veal kidneys cooked in their own fat; grilled wood pigeon served with chutney and polenta; fillet of rabbit in a bitter chocolate sauce with quince; and roasted leg of suckling lamb from the Pyrénées with autumn vegetables. Lighter dishes include scallops in a crispy coat of parsley-infused puff pastry served with cabbage and truffles, and mullet-studded risotto with lettuce. Dessert might include a slice of something many grandmothers in the southwest of France remember from their childhoods: pistachio cream cake with candied tangerines.

Restaurants in the Heart of the Right Bank

Angélina ⑦
Aquarius ㉘
Au Clair de Lune ⑱
Au Gourmet de l'Ile ㉛
Au Petit Riche ⑪
Au Pied de Cochon ⑳

Au Rendezvous
  des Camionneurs ㉒
Au Trou Gascon ㊱
Babylone ⑲
Blue Elephant ㊲
Bofinger ㊳

Buddha Bar ①
Café Beaubourg ㉔
Café de la Paix ⑨
Carré des Feuillants ⑥
Chartier ⑬
Chez Georges ⑰

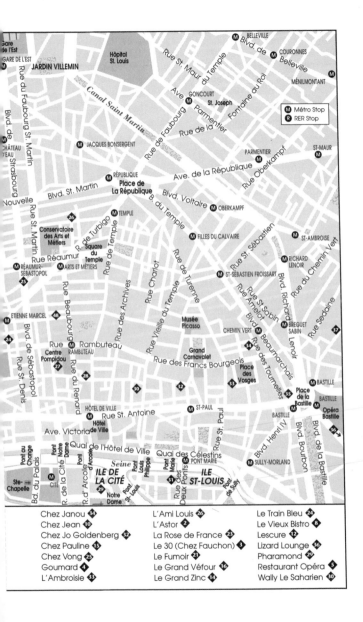

Chez Janou 🟤	L'Ami Louis 🟤	Le Train Bleu 🟤
Chez Jean 🔟	L'Astor ❷	Le Vieux Bistro 🟤
Chez Jo Goldenberg 🟤	La Rose de France 🟤	Lescure 🟤
Chez Pauline 🟤	Le 30 (Chez Fauchon) ❸	Lizard Lounge 🟤
Chez Vong 🟤	Le Fumoir 🟤	Pharamond 🟤
Goumard ❹	Le Grand Véfour 🟤	Restaurant Opéra ❺
L'Ambroisie 🟤	Le Grand Zinc 🟤	Wally Le Saharien 🟤

Goumard. 9 rue Duphot, 1er. ☎ **01-42-60-36-07.** Fax 01-42-60-04-54. Reservations recommended. Main courses 190–380 F ($32.30–$64.60); fixed-price lunch 390 F ($66.30); *menu gastronomique* (tasting menu) 780 F ($132.60). AE, DC, MC, V. Tues–Sat 12:30–2:30pm and 7:30–10:30pm. Closed 2 weeks in Aug. Métro: Madeleine or Concorde. SEAFOOD.

Opened in 1872, this landmark is one of the leading seafood restaurants in Paris. It's so devoted to the fine art of preparing fish that other food is strictly banned from the menu, although if someone who dislikes fish wanders in by accident, a limited roster of meat dishes will be orally presented by the cooperative staff. The decor consists of an unusual collection of Lalique crystal fish displayed in artificial aquariums lining the walls. Even more unusual are the men's and women's rest rooms, now classified as historical monuments by the French government. The commodes were designed by the art-nouveau master cabinetmaker Majorelle around the turn of the century.

Much of the seafood is flown in direct from Brittany every day. Examples include a craquant of crayfish in its own herb salad; lobster soup with coconut; a *parmentier* of crabmeat served with a mousseline of potatoes; fillet of grilled seawolf served with a fricassée of artichokes and Provençal *pistou;* and a salad of grilled turbot on a bed of artichokes with tarragon. Especially appealing is poached turbot with hollandaise sauce, served with leeks in vinaigrette. In all these dishes nothing (no excess butter, spices, or salt) is allowed to interfere with the natural flavor of the sea. Be prepared for some very unusual food—the staff will help translate the menu items for you.

✪ **Le Grand Véfour.** 17 rue de Beaujolais, 1er. ☎ **01-42-96-56-27.** Fax 01-42-86-80-71. Reservations required. Main courses 230–380 F ($39.10–$64.60); fixed-price menu 360–780 F ($61.20–$132.60) at lunch, 780 F ($132.60) at dinner. AE, DC, MC, V. Mon–Fri 12:30–2pm and 7:30–10:15pm. Métro: Louvre. FRENCH.

This restaurant has been around since the reign of Louis XV, though not under the same name. Napoléon, Danton, Hugo, Colette, and Cocteau have dined here—as the brass plaques on the tables testify—and it's still a great gastronomic experience. Guy Martin, chef here for the past 8 years, bases many dishes on recipes from the French Alps. His best dish is roast lamb in a juice of herbs. And have you ever had cabbage sorbet in a dark chocolate sauce? Other specialties include noisettes of lamb with star anise and Breton lobster. The desserts are often grand, like the gourmandises au chocolat, a richness of chocolate served with chocolate sorbet.

MODERATE

♻ Au Pied de Cochon. 6 rue Coquillière, 1er. ☎ **01-40-13-77-00.** Reservations recommended for conventional lunch and dinner hours. Main courses 86–148 F ($14.60–$25.15). AE, DC, MC, V. Daily 24 hours. Métro: Les Halles. FRENCH/LATE-NIGHT.

Although the great market that used to surround this restaurant has moved to Rungis, by the distant expanses of Orly, traditions die hard. Au Pied de Cochon's famous onion soup still lures visitors, and besides, where else in Paris can you be assured of getting a good meal at 3am? The house specialty is the restaurant's namesake: pig's feet grilled and served with béarnaise sauce. Both dishes are as good—or, in the view of some, as bad—as they always were. Along the same lines is the *tentation* ("temptation") platter, including a grilled version of pig's tail, pig's snout, and a half pig's foot served with béarnaise sauce and *frites*. (The French get all nostalgic about this dish, which reminds them of their childhood.) *Andouillette* (chitterling sausages) with béarnaise sauce is another speciality. Two particularly flavorful dishes that North Americans might prefer include a *jarret* of pork, caramelized in honey and served on a bed of sauerkraut; and grilled pork ribs served with sage sauce.

On the street outside, you can buy some of the freshest oysters in town. The attendants will give you slices of lemons to accompany them, and you can down them on the spot.

Chez Pauline. 5 rue Villedo, 1er. ☎ **01-42-96-20-70.** Reservations recommended. Main courses 190–400 F ($32.30–$68); fixed-price menu 220 F ($37.40). AE, DC, MC, V. Mon–Fri 12:15–2:30pm and 7:30–10:30pm; Sat 7:30–10:30pm. Closed Sat–Sun between May and early Sept. Métro: Palais-Royal. BURGUNDIAN/FRENCH.

Loyal fans say that this "bistrot de luxe" is a less expensive, less majestic version of Le Grand Véfour. The early 20th-century setting is grand enough to impress a business client and lighthearted enough to attract an impressive roster of VIPs. You'll be ushered to a table on one of two levels, amid polished mirrors, red leather banquettes, and the memorabilia of long-ago Paris. The emphasis is on the cuisine of central France, especially Burgundy, as shown by the liberal use of wines in time-honored favorites like cassoulet of Burgundian snails with bacon and tomatoes; a terrine of parslied ham; sweetbreads in puff pastry; fillet of wild duckling with seasonal berries; old-fashioned beef bourguignonne with tagliatelle; salmon steak with green peppercorns; and a ragout of wild hare in an aspic of Pouilly. If you're at all in doubt about the composition of any of these, you'll do well with the roasted Bresse chicken with dauphinois potatoes, or any of the stews that swim with savory morsels of duck, wild boar, and venison. Dessert might include a clafoutis of apricots and raspberries lightly sautéed in sugar, or a caramelized version of rice pudding. Owner and chef André Genin is a noteworthy author of children's books, some of them instructional volumes for children on the value and techniques of French cuisine.

Le Fumoir. 6 rue de l'Amiral Coligny, 1er. ☎ **01-42-92-00-24.** Reservations recommended. Main courses 105–120 F ($17.85–$20.40). Daily for salads, pastries, and snacks 11am–1am; complete menu daily noon–3pm and 7–11:30pm. AE, DC, MC, V. Métro: Louvre. INTERNATIONAL.

Stylish and breezy, and set in an antique building a few steps from the Louvre, this is an upscale brasserie with ample opportunities for watching the denizens of Paris's arts scene come and go. Currently, it is the most fashionable place in Paris to be seen eating or drinking. In a high-ceilinged ambience of warm but somber browns and indirect lighting, you can order salads, pastries, and drinks during off-hours, and platters of more substantial food during conventional mealtimes. Examples include fillet of codfish with onions and herbs; sliced rack of veal simmered in its own juices with tarragon; calf's liver with onions; a combination platter of lamb chops with grilled tuna steak; and herring in a mustard-flavored cream sauce.

✪ **Pharamond.** 24 rue de la Grande-Truanderie, 1er. ☎ **01-42-33-06-72.** Reservations required. Main courses 90–150 F ($15.30–$25.50); fixed-price menu 200 F ($34) at lunch (with wine), 310 F ($52.70) at dinner (with wine). AE, DC, MC, V. Tues–Sat noon–2:30pm; Mon–Sat 7:30–10:45pm. Métro: Les Halles or Châtelet. FRENCH/NORMAN.

Part of an 1832 neo-Norman structure that's classified as a national landmark, Pharamond sits on a Les Halles street once frequented by the vagabonds of Paris. For an appetizer, work your way through half a dozen Breton oysters (October to April). But the dish to order is *tripes à la mode de Caen,* served over a charcoal burner. Tripe is a delicacy, and if you're at all experimental, you'll find no better introduction to it. Try the *coquilles St-Jacques au cidre* (scallops in cider) if you're not up to tripe.

INEXPENSIVE

✪ **Angélina.** 226 rue de Rivoli, 1er. ☎ **01-42-60-82-00.** Reservations accepted for lunch, not for teatime. Pot of tea for one 34–36 F ($5.80–$6.10); sandwiches and salads 58–98 F ($9.85–$16.65); main courses 68–135 F ($11.55–$22.95). AE, V. Daily 9am–7pm (lunch served 11:45am–3pm). Métro: Tuileries. TEA/LIGHT FARE.

In the high-rent district near the Hôtel Inter-Continental, this *salon de thé* combines fashion-industry glitter and bourgeois respectability. The carpets are plush, the ceilings are high, and the gilded accessories have the right amount of patina. For a view (over tea and delicate sandwiches) of the lionesses of haute couture, this place has no equal. Overwrought waitresses bear silver trays with light platters, pastries, drinks, and tea or coffee to tiny marbletop tables. Lunch usually offers a salad and a plat du jour like chicken salad, steak tartare, sole meunière, or poached salmon. The house specialty, designed to go well with a cup of tea, is a Mont Blanc, a combination of chestnut cream and meringue. There are two drawbacks: The tearoom is in a section of rue de Rivoli that's getting scuzzy, and the service tends to be a bit snooty.

Au Rendezvous des Camionneurs. 72 quai des Orfèvres, 1er. ☎ **01-43-54-88-74.** Reservations recommended on weekends. Main courses 88–98 F ($14.95–$16.65); fixed-price menu 78–138 F ($13.25–$23.45). AE, MC, V. Daily noon–2:30pm and 7–11:30pm (last order). Métro: Pont-Neuf. FRENCH.

Set adjacent to the Pont-Neuf on the Ile de la Cité, this restaurant that draws a gay crowd has the look, feel, and service of a traditional Lyonnais bistro. It was founded in 1870, and many of its original mirrors and banquettes remain, even the burgundy, olive, and khaki color scheme. Its traditional fare is reasonably priced and well prepared. Dishes include terrine of rabbit, *crottin de chevignol* (a traditional appetizer layered with goat's cheese), noisettes of lamb with tarragon, snails with garlic cream sauce, and a ragout of mussels and shrimp on a bed of leeks. Particularly delicious is St-Jacques with Dieppoise sauce—a stew of scallops garnished with mussels, shrimp, white wine, herbs, and cream. The staff is intelligent and charming.

Chez Vong. 10 rue de la Grande-Truanderie, 1er. ☎ **01-40-26-09-36.** Reservations recommended. Main courses 100–185 F ($17–$31.45). AE, DC, MC, V. Mon–Sat noon–2:30pm and 7pm–midnight. Métro: Étienne-Marcel. CANTONESE.

This is the kind of Les Halles restaurant you head for when you've had your fill of grand French cuisine and grander culinary pretensions. The decor is a soothing mixture of green and browns, steeped in a Chinese colonial ambience that evokes turn-of-the-century Shanghai. Menu items feature shrimps and scallops served as spicy as you like, including a superheated version with garlic and red peppers; "joyous beef" that mingles sliced fillet with pepper sauce; chicken in puff pastry with ginger; and a tempting array of fresh fish dishes. No run-of-the-mill setting, the whims of fashion have decreed this as one of the hipster-restaurants-of-the-moment, and as such, it's full of folk from the worlds of entertainment and the arts.

La Rose de France. 24 place Dauphine, 1er. ☎ **01-43-54-10-12.** Reservations recommended. Main courses 80–100 F ($13.60–$17); menu du jour 140 F ($23.80). AE, V. Mon–Fri noon–2pm and 7–10pm. Closed last 3 weeks in Aug and 15 days at end of Dec. Métro: Cité or Pont-Neuf. FRENCH.

This restaurant is located in the old section of Ile de la Cité near Notre-Dame, just around the corner from the old Pont-Neuf. You'll dine with a crowd of young Parisians who know they can expect a good meal here at reasonable prices. Founded more than 30 years ago by its present owner, Mr. Cointepas, this place can be relied on for fresh food at affordable prices served in a warm and friendly atmosphere. In warm weather the sidewalk tables overlooking the Palais de Justice are most popular.

Main dishes include sweetbreads, veal chop flambéed with Calvados and served with apples, fillet of beef en croûte, and lamb chops seasoned with the herbs of Provence and served with gratin of potatoes. For dessert, try the fruit tart of the day or the sorbet of the month.

✪ **Lescure.** 7 rue de Mondovi, 1er. ☎ **01-42-60-18-91.** Reservations not accepted. Main courses 26–84 F ($4.40–$14.30); four-course fixed-price menu 105 F ($17.85). V. Mon–Fri noon–2:15pm and 7–11pm. Closed 3 weeks in Aug. Métro: Concorde. FRENCH.

This minibistro is a major find—it's one of the few reasonably priced restaurants near place de la Concorde. It's animated, fun, irreverent, and very appealing. You'll get a lot for your franc here. The tables on the sidewalk are tiny and there isn't much room inside, but what this place does have is rustic charm. The kitchen is wide open and the aroma of drying bay leaves, salami, and garlic pigtails hanging from the ceiling fills the room. Expect *cuisine bourgeoise*—nothing that innovative, just substantial, hearty fare. Perhaps begin with *pâté en croûte* (pâté encased in pastry). Main-course house specialties include *confit de canard* (duckling) and cabbage stuffed with salmon. The chef's fruit tarts are a favorite dessert. In autumn and winter, expect a savory repertoire of game dishes such as venison and pheasant.

2ND ARRONDISSEMENT (LA BOURSE)
MODERATE

Chez Georges. 1 rue du Mail, 2e. ☎ **01-42-60-07-11.** Reservations required. Main courses 140–160 F ($23.80–$27.20). AE, MC, V. Mon–Sat noon–2:15pm and 7–9:45pm. Closed 3 weeks in Aug. Métro: Bourse. FRENCH.

This bistro is something of a local landmark, opened in 1964 near the Bourse, and run by three generations of the same family. Naturally, at lunch it's packed with stock-exchange members.

The owners serve what they call *la cuisine bourgeoise,* or comfort food. Waiters bring around bowls of appetizers, such as celery rémoulade, to get you started. You can follow with sweetbreads with morels, duck breast with cêpe mushrooms, a classic cassoulet, or a pot-au-feu (beef simmered with vegetables). A delight is fillet of sole with a sauce made from Pouilly wine and crème fraîche. Beaujolais goes great with this hearty food.

INEXPENSIVE

Au Clair de Lune. 13 rue Française, 2e. ☎ **01-42-33-59-10.** Main courses 54–70 F ($9.20–$11.90); fixed-price menu 68 F ($11.55). DC, MC, V. Daily noon–2:30pm and 7:30–11pm. Métro: Etienne-Marcel or Sentier. ALGERIAN/FRENCH.

This neighborhood staple has flourished in the heart of Paris's wholesale garment district since the 1930s, when Algeria was a distinct part of the French-speaking world. Today you'll dine in a long, narrow room whose walls are hung with colorful Berber carpets and whose patrons are likely to include many shop workers from the nearby wholesale clothiers. There's always the Algerian staple of couscous on the menu, as well as an array of such oftchanging daily specials as veal stew, shoulder or rack of lamb, grilled fish, and roast chicken. The portions are so large you should take along a ravenous appetite. The wines are from throughout France and North Africa.

Babylone. 34 rue Tiquetonne, 2e. ☎ **01-42-33-48-35.** Main courses 75–125 F ($12.75–$21.25). V. Daily 8pm–7am. Métro: Etienne-Marcel or Sentier. CREOLE/LATE-NIGHT.

This place honors the French Caribbean island of Guadeloupe with culinary specialties of accras of codfish and Creole *boudin* (blood sausage), which usually preface such main courses as fricassee of shrimp or chicken or a *colombo* (stew) of baby goat. Look for African masks, touches of zebra skin, and photos of the divas and celebrities (like Stevie Wonder and Jesse Jackson) who have dined here. Some (Diana Ross) you might know; others are celebrated French sports stars and fashion models. Don't think of coming before dark. After 2am or so, the focus shifts away from the hearty Caribbean soul food toward reggae, jazz, and cocktails.

3RD ARRONDISSEMENT (LE MARAIS)
EXPENSIVE

L'Ami Louis. 32 rue du Vertbois, 3e. ☎ **01-48-87-77-48.** Reservations required. Main courses 195–320 F ($33.15–$54.40). AE, DC, MC, V. Wed–Sun noon–2pm and 8–11pm. Closed July 19–Aug 25. Métro: Temple. FRENCH.

L'Ami Louis is in one of the least fashionable neighborhoods of central Paris, far removed from the part of the Marais that has become chic, and its facade has seen better days. Nonetheless, this bistro preserves something magical from the prewar years. It's always luring in politicians and moguls, who could be accused of slumming if it were any cheaper.

L'Ami Louis became one of the most famous brasseries in all of Paris in the 1930s, thanks to excellent food served in copious portions and its ostentatiously old-fashioned décor. Its traditions are fervently maintained today. Amid a "brown gravy" decor (the walls retain a smoky patina from the old days), dishes such as roasted suckling lamb, pheasant, venison, confit of duckling, and endless slices of foie gras may commune atop your marble table. Though some whisper that the restaurant's ingredients aren't as select as they were in its heyday, its sauces are as thick as they were between the wars. Don't save room for dessert, which isn't very good.

INEXPENSIVE

Chez Janou. 2 rue Roger-Verlomme, 3e. ☎ **01-42-72-28-41.** Reservations recommended. Main courses 68–98 F ($11.55–$16.65). No credit cards. Daily noon–3pm and 7:30pm–midnight. Métro: Chemin-Vert. PROVENÇAL.

On one of the narrow 17th-century streets behind place des Vosges, this unpretentious bistro operates from a pair of cramped but cozy dining rooms filled with memorabilia from Provence. Service is brusque and sometimes hectic. The menu items include such dishes as large shrimp with pastis sauce, *brouillade des pleurotes* (baked eggs with oyster mushrooms), *velouté* of frog's legs, fondue of ratatouille, a gratin of mussels, and a simple but savory version of *daube provençale*, which is sometimes compared to pot roast. There's a covered terrace.

4TH ARRONDISSEMENT (ILE DE LA CITÉ/ ILE ST-LOUIS & BEAUBOURG)
VERY EXPENSIVE

✪ **L'Ambroisie.** 9 place des Vosges, 4e. ☎ **01-42-78-51-45.** Reservations required. Main courses 350–530 F ($59.50–$90.10). AE, MC, V. Tues–Sat noon–1:30pm and 8–9:30pm. Métro: St-Paul. FRENCH.

One of the most talented chefs in Paris, Bernard Pacaud has drawn world attention with his vivid flavors and expert culinary skill. He trained at the prestigious Le Vivarois before striking out on his own, first on the Left Bank and now at this early 17th-century town house in Le Marais, a former goldsmith's shop converted into two high-ceilinged salons with a decor that vaguely recalls an Italian palazzo. In summer, there's outdoor seating as well.

Pacaud's tables are nearly always filled with satisfied diners who come back again and again to see where his imagination will take him next. The dishes change with the seasons. From time to time, they'll include a fricassee of Breton lobster with a civet/red wine sauce served with a puree of peas; or a fillet of turbot braised with celery, served with a julienne of black truffles; or one of our favorite dishes in all of Paris, *poulard de Bresse demi-deuil hommage à la Mère Brazier*—chicken roasted with black truffles and truffled vegetables in a style invented by a Lyonnais matron (La Mère Brazier) after World War II. An award-winning dessert is a *tarte fine sablée* served with bitter chocolate and vanilla-flavored ice cream.

MODERATE

✪ **Bofinger.** 5-7 rue de la Bastille, 4e. ☎ **01-42-72-87-82.** Reservations recommended. Main courses 86–144 F ($14.60–$24.50); fixed-price menu 178 F ($30.25). AE, DC, MC, V. Mon–Fri noon–3pm and 6:30pm–1am, Sat–Sun noon–1am. Métro: Bastille. ALSATIAN/FRENCH.

Founded in the 1860s, Bofinger is the oldest Alsatian brasserie in town and certainly one of the best. It's a belle-epoque dining palace, resplendent with shiny brass and stained glass. If you prefer, you can dine on an outdoor terrace, weather permitting.

Affiliated today with La Coupole, Julien, and the Brasserie Flo, the restaurant has updated its menu, retaining only the most popular of its traditional dishes, such as sauerkraut and a well-prepared version of sole meunière. Recent additions have included such stylish platters as roasted leg of lamb with a fondant of artichoke hearts and a puree of parsley; grilled turbot served with a brandade of fennel; and fillet of stingray with chives and a burnt butter sauce. Shellfish, including an abundance of fresh oysters and lobster, is almost always available in season.

Le Vieux Bistro. 14 rue du Cloître-Notre-Dame, 4e. ☎ **01-43-54-18-95.** Main courses 90–165 F ($15.30–$28.05). MC, V. Daily noon–2pm and 7:30–11pm. Métro: Cité. FRENCH.

Few other restaurants offer so close-up, and so forbidding, a view of the massive and somber walls of Paris's largest cathedral, visible through lacy curtains from the windows of the front dining room. To reach it, you'll bypass a dozen souvenir stands, then settle into one of two old-time dining rooms for a flavorful meal of standard French staples. In a pair of rooms flanked with mirrors and a jutting zinc-plated bar, you can order snails with garlic butter, filet

mignon roasted in a bag and served with marrow sauce, fillets of
veal, and a dessert that every French child is exposed to early in life,
a *tarte-Tatin,* studded with apples and sugar, drenched with
Calvados, and capped with fresh cream.

INEXPENSIVE

Aquarius. 54 rue Ste-Croix-de-la-Bretonnerie, 4e. ☎ **01-48-87-48-71.**
Reservations not required. Main courses 50–64 F ($8.50–$10.90); fixed-price
menu 64–94 F ($10.90–$16) at lunch, 94 F ($16) at dinner. MC, V. Mon–Sat
noon–10:15pm. Métro: Hôtel-de-Ville. RER: Châtelet—Les Halles. VEGETARIAN.

In a 17th-century building whose original stonework forms part of
the rustic, earthy decor, this is one of the best-known vegetarian restaurants of the Marais. The owners serve only a limited array of
(strictly organic) wine, and smoking is expressly forbidden. Their
flavorful meals are healthfully prepared and come in generous portions. Choose from an array of soups and salads; a galette of wheat
served with crudités and mushroom tarts; or a country plate composed of fried mushrooms and potatoes, garlic, and goat cheese,
served with a salad.

Au Gourmet de l'Ile. 42 rue St-Louis-en-l'Ile, 4e. ☎ **01-43-26-79-27.**
Reservations required. Main courses 70–95 F ($11.90–$16.15); fixed-price menu
100–140 F ($17–$23.80). AE, MC, V. Wed–Sun noon–2pm and 7–10:30pm.
Métro: Pont-Marie. FRENCH.

Local regulars swear by the cuisine at Au Gourmet de l'Ile, whose
fixed-price meals are among the best bargains in Paris. The setting is beautiful, with a beamed ceiling, walls dating from the 1400s,
and candlelit tables. Many Parisian restaurants have attained this
level of decor, but they cannot approach the food on this "Gourmet
Island."

In the window you'll see a sign emblazoned with five A's, which,
roughly translated, stands for the Amiable Association of Amateurs
of the Authentic Andouillette. These chitterling sausages are soul
food to the French. Popular and tasty, too, are *la charbonnée de l'Ile,*
a savory pork with onions, and the stuffed mussels in shallot butter.
The fixed-price menu includes a choice of 15 appetizers, 15 main
courses, salad or cheese, and a choice of 15 desserts.

✪ **Chez Jo Goldenberg.** 7 rue des Rosiers, 4e. ☎ **01-48-87-20-16.**
Reservations recommended. Main courses 75–110 F ($12.75–$18.70). AE, DC,
MC, V. Daily noon–1am. Métro: St-Paul. JEWISH/CENTRAL EUROPEAN.

This is the best-known restaurant on the "Street of the Rose
Bushes." Albert Goldenberg, the doyen of Jewish restaurateurs in
Paris, long ago moved to choicer surroundings (at 69 av. de

Wagram, 17e), but his brother, Joseph, has remained here. Dining is on two levels, one for nonsmokers. Look for the collection of samovars and the white fantail pigeon in a wicker cage. Interesting paintings and strolling musicians add to the ambience. The *carpe farcie* (stuffed carp) is a preferred selection, but the beef goulash is also good. We like the eggplant moussaka and the pastrami. The menu also offers Israeli wines, but Monsieur Goldenberg admits that they're not as good as French wine. Live Israeli music is presented every night beginning at 9pm, and during Jewish holidays, such as Pesach, Rosh Hashana, and Yom Kippur, special menus are presented in honor of the event—but reservations are a must.

8TH ARRONDISSEMENT (CHAMPS-ELYSÉES/ MADELEINE)
VERY EXPENSIVE

Lasserre. 17 av. Franklin D. Roosevelt, 8e. ☎ **01-43-59-53-43.** Fax 01-45-63-72-23. Reservations required. Main courses 150–270 F ($25.50–$45.90) at lunch, 240–340 F ($40.80–$57.80) at dinner. AE, MC, V. Tues–Sat 12:30–2:30pm; Mon–Sat 7:30–10:30pm. Closed Aug. Métro: F. D. Roosevelt. FRENCH.

This elegant restaurant was a simple bistro before World War II, but it's since become a legend that attracts gourmands from around the world. The main salon stretches two stories high, with a mezzanine on each side. Tall arched windows draped with silk frame tables set with fine porcelain, crystal glasses edged in gold, and silver candelabras. Overhead, the ceiling is painted with lamb-white clouds and a cerulean sky, but in good weather the staff slides back the roof to reveal the real sky, letting moonlight or sunshine pour into the room.

Food is a combination of classicism and originality, and count on imagination and high drama in the presentation. Michelin awards this restaurant only two stars, as opposed to three for Lucas-Carton or Taillevent, but we've never understood why.

The appetizers are among the finest in Paris, including a salad of truffles, a three-meat terrine, or Belon oysters flavored with Chablis. The signature main course is fillets of sole *Club de la Casserole,* poached fillets served in puff pastry with asparagus tips and asparagus-flavored cream sauce. When you taste the meat and poultry dishes, such as veal kidneys flambé or pigeon André Malraux, you'd swear Escoffier were still alive. The spectacular desserts include a soufflé Grand Marnier or a selection of three freshly made sorbets of the season. The cellar, with some 180,000 bottles of wine, is among the most remarkable in Paris.

L'Astor. In the Hotel Astor, 11 rue d'Astorg, 8e. ☎ **01-53-05-05-20.**
Fax 01-53-05-05-30. Reservations recommended. Main courses 110–240 F
($18.70–$40.80); fixed-price menu 298–520 F ($50.65–$88.40). AE, DC,
MC, V. Mon–Fri noon–2pm and 7:30–10pm. Métro: St-Augustin. FRENCH.

What happens to great French chefs after they retire? If they're lucky
enough, they maintain their role by defining themselves as "culinary
consultants" and dropping in to keep an eye on what's happening
two or three times a week. That's what happened when guru Joël
Robuchon retired from his citadel on avenue Raymond Poincaré in
favor of a quieter life. His replacement is well-respected Eric Lecerf,
a formidable chef who knows better than anyone else how to match
the tours-de-force of the master. The setting, established early in
1996, is a gray-and-white enclave sheltered by an etched-glass art-
deco ceiling with discreetly luxurious touches inspired by the 1930s
and 1940s.

If you dine here, expect an almost religious devotion to
Robuchon's specialties, and a less overwhelming emphasis on newer
dishes created and fostered by his replacement. Examples of
"classic Robuchon" include caramelized sea urchins in aspic with a
fennel-flavored cream sauce; cannellonis stuffed with eggplant with
fillets of tuna and olive oil; and spit-roasted Bresse chicken roasted
with flap mushrooms. Items created by Lecerf include carpaccio of
Breton lobster with olive oil and confit of tomatoes; roasted and
braised rack of lamb; and supreme of pigeon with cabbage and foie
gras. The old Robuchon standbys have stood the test of time,
although to an increasing degree they're viewed as one would vintage Chanel or Dior, and priced accordingly.

✪ **Pierre Gagnaire.** 6 rue Balzac, 8e. ☎ **01-44-35-18-25.** Fax 01-44-
35-18-37. Reservations are imperative and difficult to make. Main courses
290–450 F ($49.30–$76.50); fixed-price menu 500–900 F ($85–$153) at lunch,
900 F ($153) at dinner. AE, DC, MC, V. Mon–Fri 12:30–2:15pm; Sun–Fri
7–10pm. Métro: George V. FRENCH.

Although the PR here may be the worst in Paris, if you are able to
make a reservation, it's worth the effort. Menus are seasonally adjusted to take advantage of France's rich bounty. The chef has a dazzling way of blending flavors and textures. Every dish is cooked to
order, and Pierre Gagnaire, the famous owner, demands perfection
before the plate is served. One critic wrote, "Picasso stretched the
limits of painting; Gagnaire does it with cooking." Try anything
from a menu that changes every 2 months: Examples of the creative
panache include freshwater crayfish cooked tempura style with
thin-sliced flash-seared vegetables and a sweet-and-sour sauce, or

turbot cooked in a bag and served with fennel and Provençal lemons. Chicken with truffles is part of a two-tiered service: first, featuring the breast in a wine-based aspic, and second, featuring the thighs chopped into roughly textured pieces. Dessert might be a chocolate soufflé served with a frozen parfait and Sicilian pistachios.

✪ **Taillevent.** 15 rue Lamennais, 8e. ☎ **01-44-95-15-01.** Fax 01-42-25-95-18. Reservations required weeks, even months, in advance for both lunch and dinner. Main courses 295–500 F ($50.15–$85). AE, DC, MC, V. Mon–Fri noon–2:30pm and 7–10pm. Closed Aug. Métro: George V. FRENCH.

Taillevent dates from 1946 and has since climbed steadily in the ranks of excellence. Today, it's recognized as the most outstanding all-around restaurant in Paris, challenged only by Lucas-Carton, Pierre Gagnaire, and Lassere in this highly competitive arrondissement.

The setting is a grand 19th-century town house off the Champs-Elysées, with paneled rooms and crystal chandeliers. The restaurant is named after a famous chef of the 14th century (Guillaume Tirel Taillevent) who wrote one of the oldest known books on French cookery. The place is small, as the owner wishes, since it permits him to give personal attention to every facet of the operation and maintain a discreet club atmosphere. You might begin with a *boudin* (sausage) of Breton lobster à la Nage; cream of watercress soup with Sevruga caviar; or duck liver with spice bread and ginger. Main courses include red snapper with black olives; Scottish salmon cooked in sea salt with a sauce of olive oil and lemons; or a cassolette of crayfish from Brittany. Dessert might be a nougatine glacé with pears. The wine list is among the best in Paris.

Although Monsieur Vrinat likes Americans, it isn't always easy for visitors from the States and other countries to book a table, since the owner prefers about 60% of his clients to be French.

EXPENSIVE

✪ **Buddha Bar.** 8 rue Boissy d'Anglas, 8e. ☎ **01-53-05-90-00.** Reservations recommended. Main courses 115–260 F ($19.55–$44.20). AE, MC, V. Mon–Fri noon–3pm; daily 6pm–2am. Métro: Concorde. FRENCH/PACIFIC RIM.

This place is hot, hot, hot—truly the restaurant of the moment in Paris. A location on a chic street near the Champs-Elysées, and allegiance to a fashionable fusion of French, Asian, and Californian cuisine, almost guarantees a clientele devoted to the whims of fashion and trend. That might actually enhance your appreciation of a cutting-edge culinary theme that combines Japanese sashimi, Vietnamese spring rolls, lacquered duck, sautéed shrimp with black bean sauce, grilled chicken skewers with orange sauce, sweet-and-sour spareribs, and crackling squab à l'orange. Many come here just for a drink in the carefully lacquered, hip-looking bar, upstairs from the street-level dining room.

✪ **Copenhague/Flora Danica.** 142 av. des Champs-Elysées, 8e. ☎ **01-44-13-86-26.** Reservations recommended. Main courses 70–180 F ($11.90–$30.60); fixed-price menu 175–260 F ($29.75–$44.20). AE, DC, MC, V. Restaurant Copenhague: Mon–Fri noon–2:30pm; Mon–Sat 7–10:30pm; closed Aug and Jan 1–7. Flora Danica: daily noon–2:30pm and 7–11pm. Métro: George V. DANISH.

The specialties of Denmark are served with flair at the "Maison du Danemark," which functions as a quasi-official Danish goodwill ambassador. In many ways, it's the best restaurant along the Champs-Elysées, with an outside terrace for midsummer dining. There are two dining areas to choose from: the Flora Danica, on the street level, and the somewhat more formal Restaurant Copenhague, upstairs.

To be thoroughly Danish, order an aperitif of aquavit and ignore the wine list in favor of Carlsberg. Menu items include a terrine of reindeer, foie gras, smoked salmon, fresh shrimp, or an elegant array of open-faced sandwiches. The house specialty is a platter of Scandinavian delicacies drawn from the many seafood and dairy specialties that the Danes prepare exceptionally well. Our preferred dish is grilled Norwegian salmon cooked on one side only. The cookery is forever competent here, not "forever boring," as one critic suggested.

Le 30 (Chez Fauchon). 30 place de la Madeleine, 8e. ☎ **01-47-42-56-58.** Reservations recommended, especially for lunch. Main courses 150–310 F ($25.50–$52.70). AE, DC, MC, V. Mon–Sat 12:15–2:30pm and 7:30–10:30pm. Métro: Madeleine. FRENCH.

In 1990, Fauchon, one of Europe's most legendary delicatessens, transformed one of its upper rooms into an airy pastel-colored showplace that caught on immediately as a lunch spot for local bankers, stockbrokers, and merchants. Menu selections employ the freshest ingredients available downstairs, and might include crayfish tails roasted with sweet spices; foie gras with pepper and champagne sauce; warm oysters with a purée of cauliflower and parsley; crayfish roasted with fennel, smoke-flavored salt, and saffron-flavored vinegar; and strips of sole poached in a vanilla-flavored coffee sauce.

Spoon, Food & Wine. In the Marignan-Elysée Hotel, 14 rue Marignan, 8e. ☎ **01-40-76-34-44.** Reservations recommended. Appetizers, main courses, vegetable side dishes each 65–180 F ($11.05–$30.60). Mon–Fri noon–2:30pm and 7–11:30pm. AE, DC, MC, V. Métro: F. D. Roosevelt. INTERNATIONAL.

The newest venture of *wunderkind* chef Alain Ducasse, opened in December 1998, has been both hailed as a "restaurant for the millennium" and condemned by some Parisian food critics. Surreal and a bit absurd, the venue is hypermodern, with a claustrophobic dining room that evokes both stylish Paris and stylish California. The cuisine roams the world for inspiration, with such middlebrow offerings as classic but rather bland American macaroni and cheese, a BLT, barbecued ribs, chicken wings, and pastrami. Other dishes evoke Italy, Latin America, Asia, and India. (Sometimes the wait staff didn't know the national origin of a dish—youm loumg, for example, which is squid and shellfish in a spicy bouillon.) The steamed lobster with mango chutney is a winner. For a "vegetable garden," you can mix and match among 15 ingredients, including iceberg lettuce. Pasta comes with a selection of five different sauces. Although a first glance at the menu makes the restaurant seem moderate in price, tabs zoom up very quickly, especially when wine, service, and VAT are added in.

MODERATE

Laudurée. 75 av. des Champs-Elysées, 8e. ☎ **01-40-75-08-75.** Reservations needed for the restaurant, not for the cafe. Main courses 150–250 F ($25.50–$42.50); pastries from 25 F ($4.25). AE, DC, MC, V. Daily 8am–1am. FRENCH.

Laudurée, acclaimed since 1862 as one of the grand cafes of Paris (in a location near the Madeleine), has invaded the Champs-Elysées, adding an extra touch of class to the neighborhood. This offshoot of one of the city's best-loved tea salons was expanded in 1999 and caters to an international set attired in everything from Givenchy to Gap. The ornate belle-epoque decor is an ideal setting for sampling the magnificent macaroons for which Laudurée has long been celebrated—not the sticky coconut version familiar to Americans, but actually two almond meringue cookies, flavored with vanilla, coffee, strawberry, pistachio, and stuck together with buttercream.

Noting all the fast-food neighbors along the Champs-Elysées, the talented young chef here, Pierre Hermé, claims that the opening of Laudurée is a "return to civility" for the boulevard. Many come here for breakfast, others preferring a late-night dinner. There are no real main dish specialties, as the menu is constantly adjusted to take advantage of the freshest ingredients on any day. Although service is not always efficient, the food is competently prepared and tasty regardless of the hour served. Menu items include a crisp and tender fillet of pork accompanied with a potato-and-parsley purée, and marinated fillets of red mullet on a salad of cold ratatouille. And if you're interested in a midafternoon pick-me-up to accompany your cups of tea, consider a dish of ice cream scented with rose petals and fresh raspberries.

INEXPENSIVE

Café Indochine. 195 rue du Faubourg St-Honoré, 8e. ☎ **01-53-75-15-63.** Reservations recommended. Main courses 80–118 F ($13.60–$20.05); fixed-price menu 175 F ($29.75). AE, MC, V. Mon–Fri noon–2:30pm; Mon–Sat 7–11:30pm. Métro: Etoile or Ternes. INDOCHINESE.

The setting here evokes the French Colonial Empire at its peak, and includes art objects from Laos, Cambodia, and Thailand, artfully outdated maps, and antique photographs of the region and its people. In any of the street-level dining rooms, you can enjoy a cross-section of the cuisines of at least four different nations. Caramelized pork or chicken, cooked with coconut milk, accents an array of shrimp, scallops, and beef dishes prepared with red or green curry, and fiery-hot soups. For a novelty, try the shrimp and scallops with calamari and pepper-flavored basil sauce; steamed fish wrapped in a banana leaf; or a Thai version of Provençal bouillabaisse. Equally appealing are the grilled meats, seared over flames and served with a spicy sauce that goes especially well with wine or, even better, any of the restaurant's medley of international beers.

9TH ARRONDISSEMENT (OPÉRA GARNIER/PIGALLE)
EXPENSIVE

Chez Jean. 8 rue St-Lazare, 9e. ☎ **01-48-78-62-73.** Reservations recommended. Main courses 175–200 F ($29.75–$34); fixed-price menu 185 F ($31.45). MC, V. Daily noon–2:30pm and 7–11pm. Métro: Notre-Dame de Lorette, Opéra, or Cadet. FRENCH.

There's been a brasserie of one sort or another on this site since around 1900, and some specialties remain intact from the days of Clemenceau. You'll dine amid well-oiled pinewood panels and carefully polished copper, on menu items that include some of grandmother's favorites. More modern dishes include risotto with lobster and squid ink; scallops with a fricassee of endive; a "nougat" of oxtails with a balsamic-flavored vinaigrette; lamb roasted with basil; and a pavé of duckling served with honey sauce and a fricassee of exotic mushrooms. The ever-changing menu attracts fans who consider the food a lot more sophisticated than the efforts of other brasseries. Part of this is the result of chefs who gained their prior experience in some surprisingly upscale restaurants.

MODERATE

Au Petit Riche. 25 rue Le Peletier, 9e. ☎ **01-47-70-68-68.** Reservations recommended. Main courses 94–130 F ($16–$22.10); fixed-price menu 165 F ($28.05) at lunch, 140–180 F ($23.80–$30.60) at dinner. AE, MC, V. Mon–Sat noon–2:15pm and 7pm–midnight. Métro: Le Peletier or Richelieu-Drouot. LOIRE VALLEY (ANJOU).

When it opened in 1865, this bistro was conceived as the food outlet for a grandly ornate cafe (Café Riche) that stood next door. Today, you'll find yesterday's grandeur and simple, well-prepared food here. You'll be ushered to one of five different areas, each crafted for maximum intimacy, with red velour banquettes, ceilings painted with allegorical themes, and accents of brass and frosted glass. The wine list favors Loire Valley vintages that go well with such dishes as *rillettes* and *rillons* (potted fish or meat, especially pork) in an aspic of Vouvray wine; a platter of poached fish served with a buttery white wine sauce; old-fashioned blanquette of chicken; and seasonal game dishes that include a civet of rabbit.

Wally Le Saharien. 36 rue Rodier, 9e. ☎ **01-42-85-51-90.** Reservations recommended. Main courses 150 F ($25.50); fixed price dinner menu 240 F ($40.80). MC, V. Tues–Sat noon–2pm; Mon–Sat 7–10pm. Métro: Anvers. ALGERIAN.

Head here for an insight into the spicy, slow-cooked cuisine that fueled the Colonial expansion of France into North Africa. The inspiration is southern Algerian, served within a dining room lined with photographs of the desert and tribal artifacts crafted from ceramics, wood, and weavings. The set-price menu that's featured every evening begins with a trio of starters that include a spicy soup, stuffed and grilled sardines, and a savory *pastilla* of pigeon in puff pastry. This can be followed by any of several kinds of couscous, or a succulent *méchouia* (slow-cooked tart) of lamb dusted with an optional coating of sugar, according to your taste. *Merguez*, the cumin-laden spicy sausage of the North African world, factors importantly into any meal, as does homemade (usually honey-infused) pastries. End your meal with a traditional cup of mint-flavored tea.

INEXPENSIVE

Chartier. 7 rue de Faubourg Montmartre, 9e. ☎ **01-47-70-86-29.** Main courses 38–54 F ($6.45–$9.20). MC, V. Daily 11:30am–3pm and 6–10pm. Métro: Rue Montmartre. FRENCH.

Established in 1896, this unpretentious *fin-de-siècle* restaurant is now an official monument. Chartier has long been a favorite budget restaurant offering good value in surroundings that feature a whimsical mural with trees, a flowering staircase, and an early depiction of an airplane. It was painted in 1929 by a penniless artist who executed his work in exchange for food. Menu items follow conservative brasserie-style traditions, including dishes few foreigners dare to eat—boiled veal's head, tripe, tongue, sweetbreads, chitterling sausages, and lamb's brains—as well as some old-time tempters. The waiter will steer you through dishes such as beef bourguignonne, *pot-au-feu* (one of the best-sellers, combining beef, turnips, cabbage, and carrots into a savory platter), pavé of rump steak, and at least five kinds of fish. Prices are low, even for a three-course meal, a fact that as many as 320 diners appreciate at a time.

✪ **Le Grand Zinc.** 5 Faubourg Montmartre, 9e. ☎ **01-47-70-88-64.** Reservations not required. Main courses 55–142 F ($9.35–$24.15); fixed-price menu 99 F ($16.85). AE, DC, MC, V. Mon–Sat noon–midnight. Métro: Rue Montmartre. FRENCH.

The Paris of the 1880s lives on here. You make your way into the restaurant past baskets of *bélons* (brown-fleshed oysters) from Brittany, a year-round favorite. The specialties of the house are *coq au vin* (chicken in white wine) and savory, old-fashioned staples like rack of lamb, rump steak, veal chops with morels—even a simple form of Provençal bouillabaisse. Nothing ever changes—certainly not the time-tested recipes.

11TH & 12TH ARRONDISSEMENTS (OPÉRA BASTILLE/BOIS DE VINCENNES)
EXPENSIVE

✪ **Au Trou Gascon.** 40 rue Taine, 12e. ☎ **01-43-44-34-26.** Reservations required. Main courses 145–165 F ($24.65–$28.05); fixed-price menu 200 F ($34) at lunch, 320 F ($54.40) at dinner. AE, DC, MC, V. Mon–Fri noon–2pm; Mon–Sat 7:30–10pm. Closed Aug. Métro: Daumesnil. GASCONY.

One of the most acclaimed chefs in Paris today, Alain Dutournier launched his cooking career in the Gascony region of southwest France. His parents mortgaged their own inn to allow Dutournier to open a turn-of-the-century bistro in an unfashionable part of the 12th arrondissement. At first he got little business, but word soon spread of a savant in the kitchen who knew and practiced authentic cuisine moderne. His wife, Nicole, is the welcoming hostess, and the wine steward has distinguished himself for his exciting cave containing several little-known wines along with a fabulous collection of Armagnacs. It is estimated that the wine cellar has some 800 varieties.

You can enjoy the true and authentic cuisine of Gascony. Start with fresh duck foie gras cooked in a terrine, or Gascony cured ham cut from the bone. Main courses include fresh tuna with braised cabbage and the best cassoulet in town. Try the chicken from the Chalosse region of Landes, which Dutournier roasts and serves in its own drippings. We'd compare these hens to the finest birds of Bresse for good quality and flavor.

Blue Elephant. 43 rue de la Roquette, 11e. ☎ **01-47-00-42-00.** Reservations recommended. Main courses 85–160 F ($14.45–$27.20); fixed-price menu 150 F ($25.50) Mon–Fri at lunch, 275 F ($46.75) at dinner. AE, DC, MC, V. Sun–Fri noon–2:30pm; daily 7pm–midnight (Sun until 11pm). Métro: Bastille. THAI.

This is the Paris branch of an international chain of stylish Thai restaurants. The decor evokes an artful version of the jungles of Southeast Asia, interspersed with Thai sculptures and paintings. Menu items are savory, succulent, and infused with lemongrass, curries, and the aromas that make Thai cuisine so distinctive. Examples include a salad made with *pomelo,* a Thai fruit that's larger and more tart than a grapefruit, studded with shrimp and herbs. Other specialties include salmon soufflé served in banana leaves, chicken in green curry sauce, and a delectable grilled fish served with passion fruit.

MODERATE

✪ **Le Train Bleu.** In the Gare de Lyon, 12e. ☎ **01-43-43-09-06.** Reservations recommended. Main courses 100–185 F ($17–$31.45); fixed-price menu 250 F ($42.50), including wine. AE, DC, MC, V. Daily 11:30am–3pm and 7–11pm. Métro: Gare de Lyon. FRENCH.

To reach this restaurant, climb the ornate double staircase that faces the grimy platforms of the Gare de Lyon. Both restaurant and station were built simultaneously with the Grand Palais, the Pont Alexandre III, and the Petit Palais, for the World Exhibition of 1900. As a fitting end to a traveler's long trip, the station's architects designed a restaurant whose decor is classified as a national artistic treasure. Inaugurated by the French president in 1901 and renovated and cleaned at great expense in 1992, the restaurant displays an army of bronze statues, a lavishly frescoed ceiling, mosaics, mirrors, old-fashioned banquettes, and 41 belle-epoque murals. Each of these celebrates the distant corners of the French-speaking world, which join Paris via its rail network.

Service is fast, attentive, and efficient, in case you're about to catch a train. A formally dressed staff will bring steaming platters of soufflé of brill, escargots in Chablis sauce, steak tartare, loin of lamb Provençal, veal kidneys in mustard sauce, rib of beef for two, and rum cake with raisins. The cuisine is well prepared in a classic French Escoffier manner.

16TH ARRONDISSEMENT (TROCADÉRO/ BOIS DE BOULOGNE)
VERY EXPENSIVE

✪ **Alain Ducasse.** In the Le Parc Hotel, 59 av. Raymond Poincaré, 16e.
☎ **01-47-27-12-27.** Fax 01-47-27-31-22. Reservations required 6 weeks in
advance. Main courses 385–590 F ($65.45–$100.30); fixed-price menu 480 F
($81.60) at lunch, 920–1,490 F ($156.40–$253.30) at dinner. AE, DC, MC, V.
Mon–Fri noon–2pm and 7:45–10pm. Métro: Trocadéro. FRENCH.

The celebrated Monte Carlo chef has taken Paris by storm since taking over the reins from the great Joël Robuchon (now semiretired).
This six-star Michelin chef divides his time between Paris and
Monaco, although he insists that he does not repeat himself in the
Paris restaurant. In this restored four-story mansion he seeds his
dishes with produce from every corner of France. He serves rare local
vegetables, fish from the country's coasts, and dishes incorporating
cardoons, turnips, celery, turbot, cuttlefish, and Bresse fowl. His
French cuisine is contemporary and Mediterranean, though not
new. Although many dishes are light, Ducasse isn't afraid of lard, as
he proves by his thick, fatty, oozing slabs of pork grilled to a crisp.
He's kept a single Robuchon dish on the menu as a tribute: the
famed caviar in aspic with cauliflower cream. The food remains
sober in presentation—true, precise, and authentic.

The wine list is based on the fine cellar left by Robuchon; it's
noted for its classic composition, extensiveness, and high quality.
Ducasse has added many new acquisitions from France's vineyards,
but he has also opened his cellar doors to young wine growers of
his generation, including those from Germany, Switzerland, Spain,
and Italy.

✪ **Jamin.** 32 rue de Longchamp, 16e. ☎ **01-45-53-00-07.** Fax 01-45-53-
00-15. Reservations required. Main courses 185–230 F ($31.45–$39.10);
fixed-price menu 280–375 F ($47.60–$63.75) at lunch, 375 F ($63.75)
at dinner. AE, DC, MC, V. Mon–Fri 12:30–2pm and 7:30–10pm. Métro:
Trocadéro. FRENCH.

In the 1980s, Joël Robuchon, the great French chef, became a sen-
sation at this very spot, and all Paris made its way to his door. Now
Benoit Guichard, his longtime second in command, is in charge.
He's clearly inspired by his master, but is an imaginative and inventive chef in his own right. Guichard has chosen pale green panels
and pink banquettes—referred to as "Italo–New Yorkaise"—for a
soothing backdrop to his brief but well-chosen menu. Lunches can
be relatively simple affairs, although each dish, such as a beautifully
seasoned salmon tartare, is done to perfection. Classic technique and

a homage to tradition characterize the cuisine, which is filled with such offerings as John Dory with celery and fresh ginger, or a pigeon sausage with foie gras, pistachios, and mâche lettuce. His beef shoulder was so tender it had obviously been braising for hours. This grand chef makes delectable what is normally thrown away. A particularly earthy dish celebrates various parts of the sow that are usually rejected by most upscale diners, blending the tail and cheeks of the sow on a platter with walnuts and fresh herbs. Finish off with an apple tarte Tatin.

INEXPENSIVE

Le Bistro de L'Étoile. 19 rue Lauriston, 16e. ☎ **01-40-67-11-16.** Reservations recommended. Main courses 96–115 F ($16.30–$19.55); fixed-price lunch 135–165 F ($22.95–$28.05). AE, DC, MC, V. Mon–Fri noon–2:30pm; Mon–Sat 7:30pm–midnight. Métro: Etoile. FRENCH.

This is the most interesting of three separate baby bistros, each with the same name, clustered around place de l'Etoile. They're affordable versions of the grand cuisine featured in superstar Guy Savoy's nearby two-star restaurant. The setting is a warmly contemporary dining room outfitted in shades of butterscotch and caramel. Menu items include a *mijotée*—a dish of pork and sage cooked over low heat for hours, coming out *extremely* tender (almost mushy)—and codfish studded with dabs of lard and prepared with a coconut-lime sauce. A particularly interesting sampler involves three of Savoy's creations on a platter, including a cup of lentil cream soup, a fondant of celery, and a pan-fried slice of foie gras. Equally appealing are fillets of red snapper with caramelized endive and exotic mushrooms. Expect some odd terms on the dessert menu, which only a professional chef can fully describe. An example is spice bread baked in the fashion of *pain perdu* (lost bread) garnished with banana sorbet and pineapple sauce.

2   Left Bank

We'll begin with the most centrally located arrondissements on the Left Bank and then survey the outlying neighborhoods.

5TH ARRONDISSEMENT (LATIN QUARTER)
VERY EXPENSIVE

✪ **La Tour d'Argent.** 15-17 quai de la Tournelle, 5e. ☎ **01-43-54-23-31.** Fax 01-44-07-12-04. Reservations required. Main courses 200-400 F ($34–$68); fixed-price lunch 350 F ($59.50). AE, DC, MC, V. Tues—Sun noon–2:30pm and 7:30–10:30pm. Métro: Maubert-Mutualité or Cardinal-LeMoine. FRENCH.

Restaurants in the Heart of the Left Bank

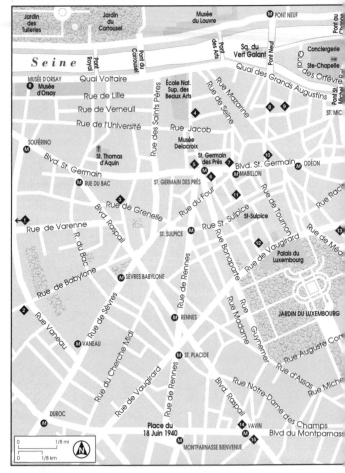

La Tour d'Argent is a national institution. From this penthouse restaurant, the view over the Seine and of the apse of Notre-Dame is panoramic. Although this restaurant's long-established reputation as "the best" in Paris has been eclipsed, to dine here remains unsurpassed as a theatrical event.

A restaurant of some sort has stood on this site since at least 1582. Madame de Sévigné refers to a cafe here in her celebrated letters, and Dumas used it as a setting for one of his novels. The fame of La

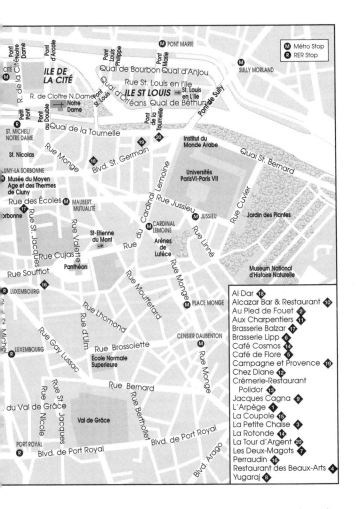

Tour d'Argent spread during its ownership by Frédéric Delair, who bought the fabled wine cellar of Café Anglais to supply his restaurant. It was Delair who started the practice of issuing certificates to diners who ordered the house specialty: *caneton* (pressed duckling). The birds are numbered: the first one was served to Edward VII in 1890, and now they're up to nearly one million.

Under the sharp eye of its current owner, Claude Terrail, the cooking is superb, and the service impeccable. Limoges china adorns each table. Although a good part of the menu is devoted to duck, we assure you that the kitchen does know how to prepare other dishes. We especially recommend the ravioli with foie gras, salmon and turbot *à la Sully*, and, to begin your meal, either the pheasant consommé or the quenelles of pike-perch André Terrail.

MODERATE

Brasserie Balzar. 49 rue des Ecoles, 5e. ☎ **01-43-54-13-67.** Reservations strongly recommended. Main courses 75–124 F ($12.75–$21.10). AE, MC, V. Daily noon–midnight. Métro: Odeon or Cluny–La Sorbonne. FRENCH.

Established in 1898, Brasserie Balzar is battered but cheerful, with some of the friendliest waiters in Paris. The menu makes almost no concessions to nouvelle cuisine, and includes pepper steak, sole meunière, sauerkraut garnished with ham and sausage, pig's feet, and calf's liver fried and served without garnish. The food is decently prepared, and it's clear these dishes still keep people happy. Be warned that if you just want coffee or a drink, you probably won't get a table during meal hours. But the staff will be happy to serve you if you want to have a full dinner in the midafternoon, accustomed as they are to the odd hours of their many clients. You'll be in good company here: Former patrons have included both Sartre and Camus (who often got in arguments), James Thurber, countless professors from the nearby Sorbonne, and a bevy of English and American journalists.

INEXPENSIVE

Al Dar. 8 rue Frédéric Sauton, 5e. ☎ **01-43-25-17-15.** Reservations recommended. Main courses 85–92 F ($14.45–$15.65). AE, DC, MC, V. Daily noon–midnight. Métro: Maubert-Mutualité. LEBANESE.

This is a well-respected restaurant that works hard to popularize the savory cuisine of Lebanon. You'll dine on dishes that might include *taboulé*, a refreshing combination of finely chopped parsley, mint, milk, tomatoes, onions, lemon juice, olive oil, and salt; *baba ganoush*, pulverized and seasoned eggplant; and *hummus*, pulverized chickpeas with herbs. Any of these can be followed with savory roasted chicken; tender minced lamb prepared with mint, cumin, and Mediterranean herbs; and any of several kinds of delectable tangines and couscous.

Campagne et Provence. 25 quai de la Tournelle, 5e. ☎ **01-43-54-05-17.** Reservations recommended. Fixed-price lunch 120 F ($20.40); two-course fixed-price dinner 170 F ($28.90); three-course fixed-price dinner 198 F ($33.65). V. Tues–Fri noon–2pm; Mon–Sat 7:30–11pm. Métro: Maubert-Mutualité. PROVENÇAL.

This modestly priced restaurant is across from the Ile de la Cité beside a quay. Bouquets of dried flowers garnish pale blue walls, and the upholstery hints of Provence's blue sky. The waiters are likely to speak with the modulated accents of southern France. The savory foods served here include a salad of wild Provençal mesclun garnished with Parmesan; a *pissaladière* (Provençal tart) flavored with onions or a combination of sardines and red mullet; and grilled fish served with risotto. A particularly tasty dessert is the anise-flavored crème brûlée.

✪ **Perraudin.** 157 rue St-Jacques, 5e. ☎ **01-46-33-15-75.** Reservations not accepted. Main courses 59 F ($10.05); fixed-price menu 63 F ($10.70) at lunch, 150 F ($25.50) at dinner. No credit cards. Tues–Fri noon–2:15pm; Mon–Sat 7:30–10:15pm. Métro: Cluny–La Sorbonne. RER: Luxembourg. FRENCH.

Everything about this place—decor, cuisine, price, and service—attempts to duplicate the bustling allure of the turn-of-the-century bistro. This one was built in 1870 as an outlet for coal and wine (both sold as remedies against the cold). Eventually, the site evolved into the old-fashioned, wood-paneled bistro you see today, where very little has changed since Émile Zola was buried nearby in the Pantheon. Walls look like they've been marinated in tea; the marbletop tables, old mirrors, and posters of Parisian vaudeville have likely been here forever.

Reservations aren't made in advance: Instead, clients usually drink a glass of kir at the zinc-topped bar as they wait. (Tables turn over quickly.) The old-fashioned dishes include roast leg of lamb served with dauphinois potatoes, beef bourguignonne, or navarin of lamb and grilled salmon with sage sauce. An onion tart, pumpkin soup, snails, or any of several pâtés and terrines precede the main course.

6TH ARRONDISSEMENT (ST-GERMAIN/LUXEMBOURG)
VERY EXPENSIVE

✪ **Jacques Cagna.** 14 rue des Grands-Augustins, 6e. ☎ **01-43-26-49-39.** Fax 01-43-54-54-48. Reservations required. Main courses 180–350 F ($30.60–$59.50); fixed-price menu 260–470 F ($44.20–$79.90) at lunch, 470 F ($79.90) at dinner. AE, DC, MC, V. Tues–Fri noon–2pm; Mon–Sat 7:30–10:30pm. Closed 3 weeks in Aug. Métro: St-Michel. FRENCH.

St. Germain knows no finer dining than at Jacques Cagna, a sophisticated restaurant set in a 17th-century town house with massive timbers, burnished paneling, and 17th-century Dutch paintings. The main dining room is located one flight above street level.

Jacques Cagna is one of the best classically trained chefs in Paris, though he's become a half-apostle to the cuisine moderne. This is evident in his delectable carpaccio of pearly sea bream with a caviar-lavished *céleric rémoulade* (celery root in a mayonnaise sauce tinged with capers, parsley, gherkins, spring onions, chervil, chopped tarragon, and anchovy essence). Other dishes, such as rack of suckling veal with ginger and lime sauce, Challons duckling in a red burgundy sauce, or fried scallops served with celery and potatoes in a truffle sauce, are equally sublime. The menu is forever changing, according to the season and momentary inspirations, but if you're lucky, he'll be offering his line-caught sea bass served with caviar in a potato shell when you visit.

MODERATE

Alcazar Bar & Restaurant. 62 rue Mazarine, 6e. ☎ **01-53-10-19-99.** Reservations recommended. Main courses 90–190 F ($15.30–$32.30); fixed-price lunch 140–180 F ($23.80–$30.60). AE, DC, MC, V. Daily noon–5:30pm and 7pm–1am. Métro: Odéon. FRENCH.

One of Paris's newest high-profile, stylish *brasseries de luxe* is this artfully hi-tech establishment funded by British restaurateur and *wunderkind* Sir Terence Conran. (His chain of well-publicized restaurants in London has succeeded in captivating a tough audience of terminally jaded European foodies.) Set within what functioned for many years as the headquarters of a publishing house, it features an all-white futuristic decor within a large street-level dining room, a busy and hyperstylish bar one floor above street level, and a menu that stresses the establishment's role as an upscale bistro and brasserie. Examples of justifiably popular dishes include grilled entrecôte with béarnaise sauce and fried potatoes; Charolais duckling with honey and spices; sashimi and sushi with lime; fillet of monkfish with saffron in puff pastry; and a comprehensive collection of shellfish and oysters from the waters of Brittany. Wines are as stylish and diverse as you'd expect, and the trendy clientele tends to wear a lot of black.

Yugaraj. 14 rue Dauphine, 6e. ☎ **01-43-26-44-91.** Reservations recommended. Main courses 98–165 F ($16.65–$28.05); fixed-price menu 130–280 F ($22.10–$47.60) at lunch, 180–280 F ($30.60–$47.60) at dinner. AE, DC, MC, V. Tues–Sun noon–2:15pm; daily 7–11pm. Métro: Odeon. INDIAN.

Set within two floors of an old building in the Latin Quarter, this restaurant serves flavorful, moderately priced food based on the recipes of northern and, to a lesser degree, southern India. In rooms outfitted in vivid shades of "Indian pink," with formally dressed staff and lots of intricately carved Kashmiri panels and statues, you can sample the spicy, aromatic tandoori dishes that are becoming all the rage in France. Seafood specialties are usually concocted from warm-water fish imported from the Seychelles, including species such as thiof, capitaine, and bourgeois, prepared as they would be in Calcutta, with tomatoes, onions, cumin, coriander, ginger, and garlic. Flavors are spicy and earthy, rich with mint and touches of yogurt. Curried lamb with coriander is a particular favorite.

INEXPENSIVE

Aux Charpentiers. 10 rue Mabillon, 6e. ☎ **01-43-26-30-05.** Reservations required. Main courses 90–125 F ($15.30–$21.25); fixed-price menu 120 F ($20.40) at lunch, 158 F ($26.85) at dinner. AE, DC, MC, V. Daily noon–3pm and 7:30–11:30pm. Métro: Mabillon. FRENCH.

This bistro, established more than 130 years ago, was once the rendezvous of the master carpenters, whose guild was next door. Nowadays it's where young men take their dates. Although the food is not especially imaginative, it is well prepared in the best tradition of cuisine bourgeoise: hearty but not refined. Appetizers include pâté of duck and rabbit terrine. Especially recommended as a main course is the roast duck with olives. The plats du jour recall French home cooking: salt pork with lentils, pot-au-feu, or stuffed cabbage. The wine list has a large selection of Bordeaux direct from the châteaus, including Château Gaussens.

✪ **Chez Diane.** 25 rue Servandoni, 6e. ☎ **01-46-33-12-06.** Reservations recommended for groups of 4 or more. Main courses 100–140 F ($17–$23.80); fixed-price menu 160 F ($27.20). V. Mon–Fri noon–2pm; Mon–Sat 8–11:30pm. Métro: St-Sulpice. FRENCH.

Fashionable restaurant food at simple bistro prices. Designed to accommodate only 40 diners at a time, this place is illuminated with Venetian glass chandeliers and paved with old-fashioned floor tiles. Inside, deep ochres and terra-cottas are redolent of the landscapes and villas of Provence. Chez Diane's offerings acknowledge the seasons, perishable ingredients, and their owners' inspirations. Recently we enjoyed sweetbreads in a sauce of flap mushrooms; nuggets of wild boar in honey sauce; minced salmon prepared as a terrine with green peppercorns; and a modern, light-textured adaptation of *hachis Parmentier*, an elegant meat loaf lightened with parsley, chopped onions, and herbs.

✪ **Crémerie-Restaurant Polidor.** 41 rue Monsieur-le-Prince, 6e. ☎ **01-43-26-95-34.** Reservations not accepted. Main courses 40–76 F ($6.80–$12.90); fixed-price menu (Mon–Fri) 55 F ($9.35) at lunch, 100 F ($17) at dinner. No credit cards. Daily noon–2:30pm; Mon–Sat 7pm–12:30am, Sun 7–11pm. Métro: Odéon. FRENCH.

Crémerie Polidor is the most traditional bistro in the Odeon area, serving *cuisine familiale*. Its name dates from the early part of the century, when the restaurant specialized in frosted cream desserts, but the restaurant itself can trace its history back to 1845.

The Crémerie is one of the Left Bank's oldest and most established literary bistros. It was André Gide's favorite, and Hemingway, Valéry, Artaud, Joyce, and Kerouac also dined here. The place is still frequented largely by students and artists, who head for the rear. Peer beyond the lace curtains and polished brass hat racks to see drawers in the back where repeat customers lock up their cloth napkins. Smiling, overworked waitresses with frilly aprons and T-shirts bearing the likeness of old mère Polidor serve a 19th-century cuisine. Try the old-fashioned pumpkin soup followed by hearty portions of beef bourguignonne or veal in white sauce. Equally satisfying is the Basque-style chicken. For dessert, get a chocolate, raspberry, or lemon tart—the best in all of Paris.

Restaurant des Beaux-Arts. 11 rue Bonaparte, 6e. ☎ **01-43-26-92-64.** Reservations recommended. Main courses 65–115 F ($11.05–$19.55); fixed-price menu 95 F ($16.15). MC, V. Daily noon–2:15pm and 7–10:45pm. Métro: St-Germain-des-Prés. FRENCH.

Located across from Paris's School of Fine Arts, this is the most famous budget restaurant in Paris. Does it please everyone? Hardly. Are there complaints about bad food and service? Some. Is it packed every day with hungry patrons? Inevitably. That means it must please thousands of diners every year, drawn to its cheap prices, large portions, and stick-to-the-ribs dishes, all featured on a set menu. The place still captivates the starving students of the Latin Quarter.

The best tables are upstairs, but on the main floor you can see the steaming pots in the open kitchen. This is what a provincial French family might cook at home—*bourguignon navarin d'agneau* (lamb chops cooked with carrots, onions, and tomatoes), grilled pig's foot, trout with saffron sauce, rabbit leg with mustard sauce, and codfish fillet with garlic sauce.

7TH ARRONDISSEMENT (EIFFEL TOWER/ MUSÉE D'ORSAY)
VERY EXPENSIVE

L'Arpège. 84 rue de Varenne, 7e. ☎ **01-47-05-09-06.** Fax. 01-44-18-98-39. Reservations required. Main courses 320–560 F ($54.40–$95.20); fixed-price lunch 390 F ($66.30); menu dégustation (tasting menu) 1,200 F ($204). AE, DC, V. Mon–Fri 12:30–2pm and 7:30–10pm. Métro: Varenne. FRENCH.

One of the least expensive of Paris's three-star restaurants, L'Arpège is best known for Alain Passard's adventurous and divine specialties. No restaurant in the 7th serves better food. Set across from the Rodin Museum in a prosperous residential neighborhood, L'Arpège has claimed the site of what for years was the world-famous L'Archestrate, where Passard worked in the kitchens.

Amid an intensely cultivated modern decor of etched glass, burnished steel, monochromatic oil paintings, and pearwood paneling, you can enjoy specialties heralded as among the most innovative to emerge in recent culinary history. Some of Passard's latest creations include Breton lobster in a sweet-and-sour rosemary sauce, scallops prepared with cauliflower and a lime-flavored grape sauce, and pan-fried duck with juniper and lime sauce, followed by the signature dessert, a candied tomato stuffed with 12 kinds of dried and fresh fruit and served with anise-flavored ice cream.

EXPENSIVE

L'Affriolé. 17 rue Malar, 7e. ☎ **01-44-18-31-33.** Reservations required. Fixed-price menu 120–190 F ($20.40–$32.30). MC, V. Mon–Sat noon–2:30pm and 7:30–11:30pm. Métro: Invalides. FRENCH.

Fine food, reasonable prices, and simplicity have guaranteed this upscale bistro's burgeoning business. Loyal clients line up by the dozen for a table within a long and narrow, deliberately old-fashioned art-deco dining room. The house staple is the fixed-price menu—they refer to it as a "menu-carte." It includes an "amuse-bouche" (a kind of preappetizer), a starter (often concocted with some derivation of foie gras), a main course (worthy choices include a jarret of glazed and roasted pork or scallops with lime juice), a cheese, a "predessert" (pear tarte, caramelized banana), and a dessert (crêpes stuffed with quince marmalade, chocolate soup, or clafoutis with grapes were all available during our recent visit). For most of these courses, seven options are available, each changing at frequent intervals. The vast majority opt for the six-course medley, but if you're not feeling particularly hungry, you can order a two-course menu (starter and main course) for 120 F ($22).

✪ **Le Violon d'Ingres.** 135 rue St-Dominique, 7e. ✪ **01-45-55-15-05.** Fax 01-45-55-48-42. Reservations required. Main courses 130–190 F ($22.10–$32.30); fixed-price menu 240–400 F ($40.80–$68) at lunch, 400 F ($68) at dinner. AE, MC, V. Tues–Sat noon–2:30pm and 7–10:30pm. Métro: École Militaire. FRENCH.

This restaurant is quickly becoming Paris's pièce de résistance. For a chance to experience chef/owner Christian Constant's gastronomic masterpieces, you have to reserve a table a minimum of 3 to 4 days in advance. There is talk that Monsieur Constant will be "the new Robuchon," although many Parisian chefs are vying for that lofty position. Those who are fortunate enough to dine in the Violin's warm atmosphere of rose-colored wood, soft cream walls, and elegant chintz fabrics patterned with old English tea roses always rave about the cleverly artistic dishes. They range from a starter of pan-fried foie gras with gingerbread and spinach salad to more elegant main courses such as lobster ravioli with crushed vine-ripened tomatoes, roasted veal in a light and creamy milk sauce served with tender spring vegetables, or even a selection from the popular rôtisserie, like spit-roasted leg of lamb rubbed with fresh garlic and thyme. Even his familiar dishes seem new at each tasting. Chef Constant keeps a copious and well-chosen selection of wine to accompany his overwhelmingly satisfying meals. The service is charming and discreet.

MODERATE

La Petite Chaise. 36-38 rue de Grenelle, 7e. ☎ **01-42-22-13-35.** Reservations required. Fixed-price menu 125–190 F ($21.25–$32.30). AE, V. Daily noon–2pm and 7–11pm. Métro: Sèvres-Babylone. FRENCH.

This is the oldest restaurant in Paris, established as an inn in 1680 by the Baron de la Chaise at the edge of what was a large hunting preserve. (According to popular lore, the baron used the upstairs bedrooms for midafternoon dalliances, between fox and pheasant hunts.) Very Parisian, the "Little Chair" invites you into a world of cramped but attractive tables, very old wood paneling, and ornate wall sconces. Guests choose from a four-course set menu with a large choice of dishes in each category.

A vigorous chef has brought renewed taste and flavor to this long-time favorite. Samplings from the menu might include salad with strips of duck breast on a bed of fresh lettuce; a seafood and scallop ragout with saffron; fillet of beef prepared with green peppercorns; and poached fish with steamed vegetables served in a sauce of fish and vegetable stock and cream.

INEXPENSIVE

Au Pied de Fouet. 45 rue de Babylone, 7e. ☎ **01-47-05-12-27.** Reservations not necessary. Main courses 50–70 F ($8.50–$11.90). No credit cards. Mon–Sat noon–2:30pm; Mon–Fri 7–9:30pm. Closed Aug. Métro: Vaneau. FRENCH.

Au Pied de Fouet is one of the smallest, oldest, and most reasonably priced restaurants in the neighborhood. In the 1700s, it was a stopover for carriages en route to Paris from other parts of Europe, offering wine, food, and stables. Don't expect a leisurely or attentive meal: Food and drink will disappear quickly from your table, under the gaze of others waiting their turn. Dishes are solid and unpretentious, and include veal in white sauce, *petit salé* (a savory stew made from pork and vegetables), and such fish dishes as sole meunière, a warhorse of French cuisine but always good.

Chez l'Ami Jean. 27 rue Malar, 7e. ☎ **01-47-05-86-89.** Reservations recommended. Main courses 75–105 F ($12.75–$17.85). V. Mon–Sat noon–3pm and 7–10:30pm. Métro: Invalides. BASQUE/SOUTHWESTERN FRENCH.

Its ardent fans claim that its Basque cuisine and setting are the most authentic and uncompromising on the Left Bank. Established by a Basque nationalist in 1931, details include wood panels, memorabilia from pelote (a Basque game much like jai alai) and soccer, and red and white woven tablecloths like the ones sold in Bayonne, along with a bent bargoer or two sporting the Basque nation's headwarmer of choice, the beret. Menu items include cured Bayonne ham; earthy and herb-laden Béarn-influenced vegetable soups; a succulent omelet with peppers, tomatoes, and onions; squid stewed in its own ink and served with tomatoes and herbs; and the poultry dish of the Basque world, *poulet basquaise,* cooked with spicy sausage, onions, peppers, and very strong red wine. In springtime, look for a truly esoteric specialty rarely available from nearby competitors: *saumon de l'Adour* (Adour river salmon) served with béarnaise sauce.

La Fontaine de Mars. 129 rue St-Dominique, 7e. ☎ **01-47-05-46-44.** Reservations recommended. Main courses 75–140 F ($12.75–$23.80). AE, MC, V. Daily noon–2:30pm and 7:30–11pm. Métro: École-Militaire. PYRENÉE/SOUTHWESTERN FRANCE.

The name of this restaurant doesn't derive from its location near the Champ de Mars, but from the ornate, historic stone fountain that sits on its tree-lined terrace. You'll find an animated, sometimes boisterous dining room on the street level, plus two cozier and calmer upstairs rooms whose round tables and wooden floors make you feel like you're in a private home. An additional 70 or so seats become available by the fountain whenever weather permits. Much of the cuisine here derives from the Pyrénées and southwestern France, bearing rich, heady flavors that go well with robust red wines. Examples include a confit of duckling with parsley potatoes; a cassoulet inspired by the traditions of Toulouse; veal chops with morels;

fillets of red mullet or monkfish with herb-flavored butter; and other typical Parisian bistro food. Our favorite dessert is a thin tart filled with a sugared purée of apples, capped with more apple, and garnished with Calvados and cream.

3 The Best Cafes

Parisians use cafes as combination club/tavern/snack bars, almost as extensions of their living rooms. Coffee, of course, is the chief drink. It comes black in a small cup, unless you specifically order it *au lait* (with milk). Tea (*thé*, pronounced tay) is also fairly popular, but is generally not of a high quality.

If you prefer beer, we advise you to pay a bit more for the imported German, Dutch, or Danish brands, which are much better than the local brew. If you insist on a French beer, at least order it *à pression* (draft), which is superior. There is also a vast variety of fruit drinks, as well as Coca-Cola, which can be rather expensive.

✪ **Brasserie Lipp.** 151 bd. St-Germain, 6e. ☎ **01-45-48-53-91.** Full meals average 280 F ($47.60); café au lait 18 F ($3.05). Daily 9am–2am; restaurant service 11am–1am. Métro: St-Germain-des-Prés.

On the day of Paris's liberation in 1944, former owner Roger Cazes (now deceased) spotted Hemingway, the first man to drop in for a drink. Then as now, famous people often drop by the Lipp for its beer, wine, and conversation. Cazes's nephew, Michel-Jacques Perrochon, now runs this quintessential Parisian brasserie. The food is secondary, yet quite good, providing you can get a seat (an hour and a half waiting time is customary if you're not familiar to the management). The specialty is *choucroute garni,* the best sauerkraut in Paris. You not only get sauerkraut, but a thick layer of ham and braised pork as well, which can all be downed with the house Riesling (a white wine) or beer. Even if you don't go inside for a drink, you can sit at a sidewalk cafe table to enjoy a cognac and people-watch.

Café Beaubourg. 100 rue St-Martin, 4e. ☎ **01-48-87-63-96.** Glass of wine 23–40 F ($3.90–$6.80); beer 26–45 F ($4.40–$7.65); American breakfast 110 F ($18.70); sandwiches and platters 30–120 F ($5.10–$20.40). Sun–Thurs 8am–1am, Fri–Sat 8am–2am. Métro: Rambuteau or Hôtel-de-Ville.

Located next to the all-pedestrian plaza of the Centre Pompidou, this is a trendy, avant-garde cafe with soaring concrete columns and a minimalist decor. Many of the regulars work in the neighborhood's eclectic shops and galleries. In warm weather, tables are set up on the sprawling outdoor terrace, providing a great place to watch the young and the restless go by.

Café Cosmos. 101 bd. du Montparnasse, 6e. ☎ **01-43-26-74-36.** Café espresso 25 F ($4.25); platters 42-85 F ($7.15–$14.45); fixed-price lunch 69 F ($11.75). MC, V. Daily 8am–3am. Métro: Vavin.

Does today's generation have a cafe to equal the Lost Generation's Select or Coupole? Perhaps it's the ultramodern Cosmos. Today, you might rub elbows with a French film star or executive ("no one writes novels anymore"). The cafe features wooden tables, black leather chairs, and black clothing in winter—the perfect backdrop for smoked salmon with toast.

Café de Flore. 172 bd. St-Germain, 6e. ☎ **01-45-48-55-26.** Café espresso 23 F ($3.90); glass of beer 39–41 F ($6.65–$6.95). Daily 7am–2am. Métro: St-Germain-des-Prés.

Sartre—the granddaddy of existentialism, a key figure in the Resistance movement, and a renowned cafe-sitter—often came here during World War II. Wearing a leather jacket and beret, he sat at his table and wrote his trilogy, *Les Chemins de la Liberté (The Roads to Freedom)*. Camus, Picasso, and Apollinaire also frequented the Flore. The cafe is still going strong, although the famous patrons have moved on, and tourists have taken up all the tables.

✪ **Café de la Paix.** Place de l'Opéra, 9e. ☎ **01-40-07-30-20.** Café espresso 19 F ($3.25); fixed-price menu 139 F ($23.65) for two courses, 180 F ($30.60) for three courses; daily specials from 105 F ($17.85). Daily noon–midnight. Métro: Opéra.

This hub of the tourist world rules the place de l'Opéra, and the legend goes that if you sit here long enough, you'll see someone you know passing by. Huge, grandiose, frighteningly fashionable, and sometimes brusque and anonymous, it harbors not only Parisians, but, at one time or another, nearly every visiting American—a tradition dating from the end of World War I. Once Émile Zola sat on the terrace; later, Hemingway and Fitzgerald frequented it. The best news for tourists who stop in for a bite is that prices have recently been lowered because of stiff competition in the area.

Café des Hauteurs. In the Musée d'Orsay, 1 rue de Bellechasse, 7e. ☎ **01-45-49-47-03.** Reservations not accepted. "Suggestions du Jour" 30–65 F ($5.10–$11.05). AE, MC, V. Tues–Wed and Fri–Sun 10am–5pm, Thurs 10am–9pm. Métro: Solférino. RER: Musée d'Orsay. FRENCH.

The designers of the Musée d'Orsay recognized the crushing fatigue that can sometimes come with a museum visit. That's why this fifth-floor cafe is something midway between a bar and a short-term rest home, where you can recuperate in front of a sweeping view that stretches as far as Notre-Dame and Sacré-Coeur, and looks over the glass-encased mechanism of a clock resembling London's Big Ben. In addition to the usual doses of caffeine and alcohol, you can order platters that are more substantial than a snack, but less filling than the main course of a conventional meal. Examples include smoked salmon with shrimp salad and rye bread, or a platter of assorted cheeses.

Fouquet's. 99 av. des Champs-Elysées, 8e. ☎ **01-47-23-70-60.** Glass of wine from 42 F ($7.15); sandwiches 45–70 F ($7.65–$11.90); main courses 160–270 F ($27.20–$45.90); fixed-price menu 265 F ($45.05). Daily 9am–2am. Restaurant noon–3pm and 7pm–1am; bar 9am–2am. Métro: George V.

Fouquet's has been collecting anecdotes and a patina since it was founded in 1901. A celebrity favorite, it has attracted Chaplin, Chevalier, Dietrich, Churchill, Roosevelt, and Jackie O. The premier cafe on the Champs-Elysées sits behind a barricade of potted flowers at the edge of the sidewalk. You can choose a table in the sunshine or retreat to the glassed-in elegance of the leather banquettes and rattan furniture of the street-level grill room. Although Fouquet's is a full-fledged restaurant, with a beautiful, very formal dining room on the second floor, most visitors come by just for a glass of wine, coffee, or a sandwich.

La Coupole. 102 bd. du Montparnasse, 14e. ☎ **01-43-20-14-20.** Breakfast buffet 89 F ($15.15); main courses 89–188 F ($15.15–$31.95) at lunch, 109–188 F ($18.55–$31.95) at dinner; fixed-price menu 132–169 F ($22.45–$28.75) at lunch, 169 F ($28.75) at dinner before 10:30pm, 132–169 F ($22.45–$28.75) after 10:30pm. Daily 7:30am–2am (breakfast buffet Mon–Fri 7:30–10:30am). Métro: Vavin.

Once a leading center of artistic life, La Coupole is now a bastion of the grand Paris brasserie style in Montparnasse. It was born in 1927 at the height of the city's jazz age. Former patrons included Josephine Baker, Henry Miller, Dalí, Calder, Hemingway, Dos Passos, Fitzgerald, and Picasso. The big, attractive cafe has grown more cosmopolitan through the years, attracting fewer locals and art-school waifs, but some of the city's most interesting foreigners show up.

The sweeping outdoor terrace is among the finest in Paris. At one of its sidewalk tables, you can sit and watch the passing scene and order a coffee or a cognac VSOP. The food is quite good, despite the fact that the dining room resembles an enormous railway station waiting room. Try such main dishes as sole meunière, cassoulet, and some of the best pepper steak in Paris. The fresh oysters and shellfish are especially popular. The waiters are as rude and inattentive as ever, and aficionados of the place wouldn't have it any other way.

La Rotonde. 105 bd. du Montparnasse, 6e. ☎ **01-43-26-68-84.** Glass of wine 20 F ($3.40); fixed-price menu 75 F ($12.75) at lunch, 180 F ($30.60) at dinner. Café daily 7am–2am, food service daily noon–2am. Métro: Vavin.

Once patronized by Hemingway, the original Rotonde faded into history but is immortalized in the pages of *The Sun Also Rises*, in which Papa wrote, "No matter what cafe in Montparnasse you ask a taxi driver to bring you to from the right bank of the river, they always take you to the Rotonde." Lavishly upgraded, its reincarnation has a paneled art-deco elegance, and shares the once-hallowed site with a motion-picture theater. If you stand at the bar, prices are lower.

Les Deux-Magots. 6 place St-Germain-des-Prés, 6e. ☎ **01-45-48-55-25.** Café au lait 25 F ($4.25); whisky soda 70 F ($11.90); plats du jour 90–140 F ($15.30–$23.80). Daily 7:30am–1:30am. Métro: St-Germain-des-Prés.

This legendary hangout for the sophisticated residents of St-Germain-des-Prés becomes a tourist favorite in summer. Visitors monopolize the few sidewalk tables as waiters rush about, seemingly oblivious to anyone's needs. Regulars from around the neighborhood reclaim it in the off-season. Deux-Magots was once a gathering place of the intellectual elite, including Sartre, Simone de Beauvoir, and Jean Giraudoux. Inside are two large statues of Confucian wise men *(magots)* that give the cafe its name. The crystal chandeliers are too brightly lit, but the regulars seem to be accustomed to the glare. After all, some of them even read their daily newspapers here.

Lizard Lounge. 18 rue du Bourg-Tibourg, 4e. ☎ **01-42-72-81-34.** Reservations not accepted. Cocktails 32–48 F ($5.45–$8.15); sandwiches, salads, and plats du jour 38–70 F ($6.45–$11.90); Sun brunch 50–95 F ($8.50–$16.15). MC, V. Daily 11:30am–2am (food service noon–10:30pm; Sat–Sun brunch 11:30am–4pm). Métro: Hôtel de Ville.

Founded by Los Angeles escapee Phil Morgan in 1994, this place resembles an Amsterdam or New York City cocktail lounge. It's an indulgently heterosexual enclave in an increasingly gay neighborhood. A rectangular space with a high ceiling, wood paneling, and bars on three different levels, it doubles as a restaurant. Looking to strike up a friendship? Order one of the margaritas, the house beer (a Dutch brew known as "Cheap Blond"), or the drink nobody can seem to get enough of, a cream-and-Kahlúa–based "Screaming

Orgasm." If you're hungry, try a New York–style deli sandwich (turkey with bacon is the best-seller), a Lizard Salad garnished with Cheddar cheese and tikka slow-cooked chicken, or any of the French-inspired plats du jour. Sunday brunch features an all-you-can-eat vegetarian buffet whose offerings are augmented with such garnishes as omelets with Canadian bacon or American-style ham and sausage.

5

Exploring Paris

*P*aris is one of those cities where taking in the street life should claim as much of your time as sightseeing in churches or museums. A gourmet picnic in the Bois de Boulogne, a sunrise pilgrimage to the Seine, an afternoon of bartering at the flea market—Paris bewitches you with these kinds of experiences. For all the Louvre's beauty, you'll probably remember the Latin Quarter's crooked alleyways better than the 370th oil painting of your visit.

SUGGESTED ITINERARIES FOR THE FIRST-TIMER

These itineraries are obviously intended for the first-time visitor, but even those making their 30th trip to Paris will want to revisit such attractions as the Louvre, where you could spend every day of your life and always see something you missed before. Use these tips as a guide, but not a bible. Paris rewards travelers with guts and independence of mind, those who will pull open the doors to a chapel or an antiquarian's shop not because they're listed on a souvenir map, but because they look intrinsically interesting. In Paris, they usually are.

If You Have 1 Day

Far too little time, but you'll have to make the most of it. Get up early and begin walking the streets in the neighborhood of your hotel. The streets of Paris are live theater. Find a little cafe; there's one on almost every block. Go in and order a typical Parisian breakfast of coffee and croissants. If you're a museum and monument junkie, and you don't dare return home without seeing the "must" sights, know that the two most popular museums are the **Louvre** and the **Musée d'Orsay.** The three most enduring monuments are the **Eiffel Tower,** the **Arc de Triomphe,** and **Notre-Dame** (which can be seen later in the day). If it's a toss-up between the Louvre and the d'Orsay, we'd make it the Louvre if you're a first-timer, because it holds a greater variety of works. If you feel the need to choose between monuments, we'd make it the Eiffel Tower just for the panoramic view of the city. If you feel your day is too short to visit museums or wait in lines for the tower, we'd suggest that instead you spend most of your time strolling the streets of Paris. The most impressive neighborhood is the **Ile St-Louis,** which we believe is the most elegant place for a walk in Paris. After exploring this island and its mansions, wander at will through such Left Bank districts as **St-Germain-des-Prés** or the area around **place St-Michel,** the heart of the student quarter. As the sun sets over Paris, head for Notre-Dame, which stands majestically along the banks of the Seine. This is a good place to watch shadows fall over Paris as the lights come on for the night. Afterward, walk along the banks of the Seine, where vendors sell books and souvenir prints. Promise yourself a return visit and have dinner in the Left Bank bistro of your choice.

If You Have 2 Days

Follow the itinerary for day 1 above. Since you've paid so much attention to the Left Bank on your first day, spend most of this day taking in the glories of the Right Bank. Begin at the Arc de Triomphe and stroll down the **Champs-Elysées,** the main boulevard of Paris, until you reach the Egyptian obelisk at the place de la Concorde (see "A Walking Tour: The Grand Promenade," in section 6). This grand promenade is one of the most famous walks in the world. The place de la Concorde affords terrific views of the Madeleine, the Palais-Bourbon, the Arc de Triomphe, and the Louvre. This is where some of France's most notable figures lost their heads on the guillotine. A nearby square, **place Vendôme,** is worth a visit, too, as it represents the Right Bank at its most elegant, with such addresses as the Ritz, and Paris's top jewelry stores. After all this walking, we'd suggest a rest stop in the **Jardin de Tuileries,** directly west and adjacent to the Louvre. After a long lunch in a Right Bank bistro, for a total contrast to monumental Paris, go for a walk in the **Marais.** Our favorite stroll is along the rue des Rosiers, a narrow street that's the heart of the Jewish community. And don't miss the **Place des Vosges.** After a rest at your hotel, select one of the restaurants down in **Montparnasse,** following in Hemingway's footsteps. This area is far livelier at night.

If You Have 3 Days

Spend days 1 and 2 as above. As you've already gotten a look at the Left Bank and the Right Bank, this day should be about following your special interests. If you're a Monet fan, you might head for the **Musée Marmottan-Claude Monet.** Or perhaps you'd rather wander the sculpture garden of the **Musée National Auguste-Rodin.** If it's the **Picasso Museum** you select, you can use part of the morning to explore a few of the art galleries of the Marais. Following in the trail of Descartes and Madame de Sévigné, select a café or restaurant here for lunch. Reserve the afternoon for **Ile de la Cité,** where you'll not only get to see Notre-Dame again, but you can visit the **Conciergerie** where Marie Antoinette and others were held captive before they were beheaded. See also the stunning stained glass of **Sainte-Chapelle** in the Palais de Justice. For dinner that night, we'd suggest a Right Bank bistro in Le Marais. Afterward, if your energy holds, you can sample Paris's nightlife—whatever you fancy, the dancers at the **Lido** or the **Folies-Bergère** or a smoky Left Bank jazz club. If you'd just like to sit and have a drink, Paris has some of the most elegant hotel bars in the world at such places as the **Hôtel Crillon** or **Plaza-Athenée.**

If You Have 4 Days

For your first 3 days, follow the itinerary above. On your fourth day, head to **Versailles,** 13 miles south of Paris, and the greatest attraction in the Ile de France. When Louis XIV decided to move to the suburbs, he created a spectacle unlike anything the world had ever seen. The good news is that most of the palace remains intact, in all its opulence and glitter. A full day here almost feels like too little time. After you return to Paris for the night, take a good rest and spend the evening wandering around the Left Bank's **Latin Quarter,** enjoying the student cafes and bars and selecting your bistro of choice for the evening. Some of the livelier streets for wandering include rue de la Huchette and rue Monsieur-le-Prince.

If You Have 5 Days

Spend days 1 to 4 as recommended above. On your fifth day, devote at least a morning to an area heretofore neglected, **Montmartre,** the community formerly known for its artists perched atop the highest of Paris's seven hills. It's like a village encircled by sprawling Paris. Although the starving artists who made it the embodiment of *la vie de bohème* have long since departed, there is much to charm and enchant you, especially if you wander the back streets. Here, away from the tacky shops and sleazy clubs, you'll see the picture-postcard lanes and staircases known to Picasso, Toulouse-Lautrec, and Utrillo. Of course, it's virtually mandatory to visit the **Basilica of Sacré-Coeur,** for the view if nothing else. Since it's your last night in Paris, let your own interests take over here. Lovers traditionally spend it clasping hands in a farewell along the Seine; less goggle-eyed visitors can still find a full agenda. We'd suggest a final evening at **Willi's Wine Bar** (see "Bars, Pubs & Clubs" in chapter 6), with more than

250 vintages and good food to go along with it. For a nightcap, we always head for the **Hemingway Bar** at the Ritz, where Garbo, Noel Coward, and F. Scott Fitzgerald once lifted their glasses. If that's too elegant, head for **Closerie des Lilas** in the 6th arrondissement, where you can rub shoulders with the movers and shakers of the film industry and fashion's "playthings." Even if you've been saving money up until now, our final suggestion is that you go all out for one really grand French meal at a fabulous restaurant. It's a memory you'll probably treasure long after you've recovered from paying the tab.

1 The Top Attractions

Arc de Triomphe. Place Charles-de-Gaulle–Etoile, 8e. ☎ **01-55-37-73-77.** Admission 40 F ($6.80) adults, 25 F ($4.25) ages 12–25, free for children 11 and under. Apr–Sept daily 9:30am–11pm; Oct–Mar daily 10am–10:30pm. Métro: Charles-de-Gaulle–Etoile.

At the western end of the Champs-Elysées, the Arc de Triomphe suggests one of those ancient Roman arches, only it's larger. Actually, it's the biggest triumphal arch in the world, about 163 feet high and 147 feet wide. To reach it, don't try to cross the square, the busiest traffic hub in Paris. With a dozen streets radiating from the "Star," the roundabout was called by one writer "vehicular roulette with more balls than numbers" (death is certain!). Take the underground passage and live a little longer.

The arch has witnessed some of France's proudest moments, and some of its more shameful and humiliating defeats, notably those of 1871 and 1940. The memory of German troops marching under the arch that had come to symbolize France's glory and prestige is still painful to the French.

Commissioned by Napoléon in 1806 to commemorate his victories, the arch wasn't ready for the entrance of his new empress, Marie-Louise, in 1810. It served its ceremonial purpose anyway, and in fact, wasn't completed until 1836, under the reign of Louis-Philippe. Four years later, the remains of Napoléon, brought from his grave at St. Helena, passed under the arch on the journey to his tomb at the Invalides. Since that time it has become the focal point for state funerals (Victor Hugo's, in 1885, was the biggest). It is also the site of the permanent tomb of the unknown soldier, in whose honor an eternal flame is kept burning.

You can take an elevator or climb the stairway to the top, where there is an exhibition hall with lithographs and photos depicting the Arc throughout its history. From the observation deck, you have the finest view of the Champs-Elysées and of such landmarks as the Louvre, the Eiffel Tower, Sacré-Coeur, and the new district of La Défense.

✪ **Cathédrale de Notre-Dame.** 6 place du parvis Notre-Dame, 4e. ☎ **01-42-34-56-10.** www.paris.org/Monuments/NDame. Free admission to the cathedral; towers and crypt 32 F ($5.45) adults, 21 F ($3.55) ages 12–25 and over 60, free for children under 12; museum and treasury 15 F ($2.55) adults, 5 F (85¢) ages 12–25 and over 60, free for children under 12. Cathedral daily 8am–6:45pm year-round. Towers and crypt Apr–Sept daily 9:30am–6pm, Oct–Mar daily 10am–4:15pm. Museum Wed and Sat–Sun 2:30–6pm. Treasury Mon–Sat 9:30–11:30am and 1–5:45pm. Métro: Cité or St-Michel. RER: St-Michel.

Notre-Dame is the heart of Paris, even of France; distances from Paris to all parts of France are calculated from its center.

Although many disagree, Notre-Dame is, in our opinion, more interesting outside than in. You'll want to walk around the entire structure to fully appreciate this "vast symphony of stone." Better yet, cross over the bridge to the Left Bank and view it from the quay.

Its setting on the banks of the Seine has always been memorable. Founded in the 12th century by Maurice de Sully, bishop of Paris, Notre-Dame grew and grew. Over the years, the cathedral has changed as Paris has, often falling victim to whims of decorative taste. Its famous flying buttresses (the external side supports, which give the massive interior a sense of weightlessness) were rebuilt in 1330.

The history of Paris and that of Notre-Dame are inseparable. Many prayed here before going off to fight in the Crusades. "Our Lady of Paris" was not spared by the revolutionaries, who destroyed the Galerie des Rois and converted the building into a secular temple. Later, Napoléon was crowned emperor here, yanking the crown out of Pius VII's hands and placing it on his own head. But carelessness, vandalism, embellishments, and wars of religion had already demolished much of the previously existing structure.

The cathedral was once scheduled for demolition, but, partly because of the popularity of Victor Hugo's *Hunchback of Notre Dame* and the revival of interest in the Gothic, a movement mushroomed to restore the cathedral to its original glory. The task was completed under Viollet-le-Duc, an architectural genius.

The houses of old Paris used to crowd in on Notre-Dame, but Haussmann ordered them torn down to show the cathedral to its best advantage from the square, known as the *parvis.* This is the best vantage for seeing the three sculpted 13th-century portals.

Paris Attractions

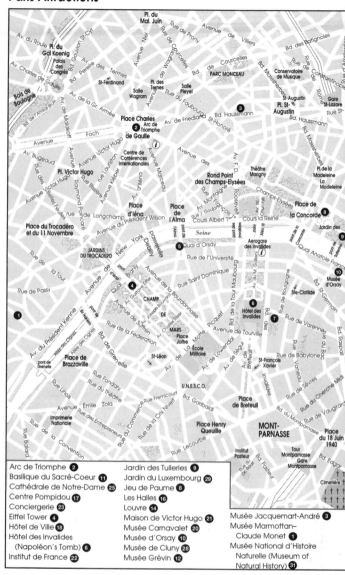

Arc de Triomphe **2**	Jardin des Tuileries **9**
Basilique du Sacré-Coeur **11**	Jardin du Luxembourg **29**
Cathédrale de Notre-Dame **25**	Jeu de Paume **8**
Centre Pompidou **17**	Les Halles **16**
Conciergerie **23**	Louvre **14**
Eiffel Tower **4**	Maison de Victor Hugo **21**
Hôtel de Ville **18**	Musée Carnavalet **20**
Hôtel des Invalides	Musée d'Orsay **10**
(Napoléon's Tomb) **6**	Musée de Cluny **28**
Institut de France **22**	Musée Grévin **12**

Musée Jacquemart-André **3**
Musée Marmottan–
   Claude Monet **1**
Musée National d'Histoire
   Naturelle (Museum of
   Natural History) **31**

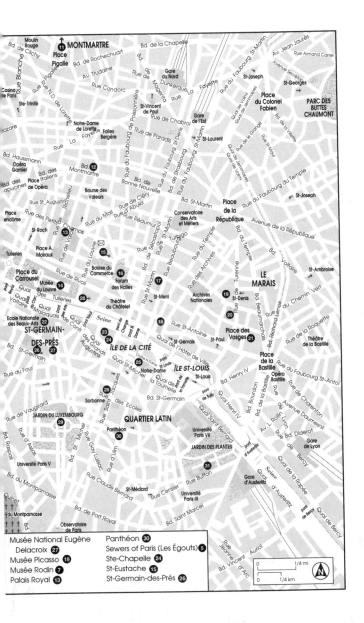

Musée National Eugène | Panthéon ③⓪
Delacroix ②⑦ | Sewers of Paris (Les Égouts) ⑤
Musée Picasso ⑲ | Ste-Chapelle ㉔
Musée Rodin ⑦ | St-Eustache ⑮
Palais Royal ⑬ | St-Germain-des-Prés ㉖

On the left, the **portal of the Virgin** depicts the signs of the zodiac and the coronation of the Virgin, an association found in dozens of medieval churches. The restored central **portal of the Last Judgment** depicts three levels: The first shows Vices and Virtues; the second, Christ and his Apostles; and above that, Christ in triumph after the Resurrection. The portal is a close illustration of the Gospel according to Matthew. Over this portal is a remarkable rose window, 31 feet wide, forming a showcase for a statue of the Virgin and Child. On the far right is the **portal of St. Anne,** depicting such scenes as the Virgin enthroned with Child. It is the best preserved and the most perfect piece of sculpture in Notre-Dame.

Equally interesting (although often missed by the scurrying visitor) is the **portal of the cloisters** (around on the left), with its dour-faced 13th-century Virgin, a survivor among the figures that originally adorned the facade. (Unfortunately, the Child she is holding is decapitated.) Finally, on the Seine side of Notre-Dame, the portal of St. Stephen traces that saint's martyrdom.

If possible, come to see Notre-Dame at sunset. Inside, of the three giant medallions that warm the austere cathedral, the **north rose window** in the transept, dating from the mid–13th century, is best. The main body of the church is typically Gothic, with slender, graceful columns. In the **choir,** a stone-carved screen from the early 14th century depicts such biblical scenes as the Last Supper. Near the altar stands the 14th-century *Virgin and Child,* highly venerated among Paris's faithful.

In the treasury are displayed vestments and gold objects, including crowns. Exhibited are a cross presented to Haile Selassie, the former emperor of Ethiopia, and a reliquary given by Napoléon. Notre-Dame is especially proud of its relic of the True Cross and the Crown of Thorns.

Finally, to visit those grimy gargoyles immortalized by Hugo, you have to scale steps leading to the twin square **towers** that rise to a height of 225 feet. Once here, you can closely inspect the devils (some giving you the raspberry), hobgoblins, and birds of prey. Look carefully and you may see the hunchback Quasimodo.

Approached through a garden behind Notre-Dame is the **Deportation Memorial,** jutting out on the very tip of the Ile de la Cité. Here, birds chirp and the Seine flows gently by, but the memories are far from pleasant. It commemorates the French citizens who were deported to such camps as Auschwitz and Buchenwald during World War II. Carved into stone in blood red are the words (in

French): "Forgive, but don't forget." The memorial is open Monday through Friday from 8:30am to 9:45pm, and Saturday and Sunday from 9am to 9:45pm. Admission is free.

Eiffel Tower (La Tour Eiffel). Champ-de-Mars, 7e. ☎ **01-44-11-23-23.** www.paris.org/Monuments/Eiffel. Admission to first landing 21 F ($3.55), second landing 43 F ($7.30), third landing 60 F ($10.20). Stairs to second floor 15 F ($2.55). Sept–May daily 9:30am–11pm; June–Aug daily 9am–midnight. In fall and winter, the stairs are open only until 6:30pm. Métro: Trocadéro, Ecole-Militaire, or Bir-Hakeim. RER: Champ-de-Mars–Tour Eiffel.

This is without a doubt the single most recognizable structure in the world. Weighing 7,000 tons but exerting about the same pressure on the ground as an average-size person sitting in a chair, the tower was never meant to be permanent. It was built for the Exhibition of 1889 by Gustave Alexandre Eiffel, the French engineer whose fame rested mainly on his iron bridges. (Incidentally, he also designed the framework for the Statue of Liberty.)

The tower, including its 55-foot television antenna, is 1,056 feet high. On a clear day you can see it some 40 miles away. An open-framework construction, the tower unlocked the almost unlimited possibilities of steel construction, paving the way for the skyscrapers of the 20th century. Skeptics said it couldn't be built, and Eiffel actually wanted to make it soar higher than it did. For years it remained the tallest man-made structure on earth, until such skyscrapers as the Empire State Building surpassed it.

We could fill an entire page with Eiffel Tower statistics. (Its plans spanned 6,000 square yards of paper, and it contains 2^{1}/$_{2}$ million rivets.) But forget the numbers. Just stand underneath the tower and look straight up. It's like a rocket of steel lacework shooting into the sky.

Initially, artists and writers vehemently denounced the tower, although later generations sang its praise. People were fond of calling it names: "a giraffe," "the world's greatest lamppost," "the iron monster." Others suggested, "Let's keep art nouveau grounded." Nature lovers feared it would interfere with the flight patterns of birds over Paris.

In the early 1890s, the tower escaped destruction when it found a new practical use: The French government installed antennae on it, thus enabling wireless communications throughout the city.

Everyone visits the landmark that has become the symbol of Paris. To see it best, however, don't sprint—approach it gradually. You can visit the tower in three stages. Taking the elevator to the **first**

landing, you have a view over the rooftops of Paris. On the first level there's a cinema museum that shows films, restaurants, and a bar open year-round. The **second landing** provides a panoramic look at the city. The **third and final stage** gives the most spectacular view. On the ground level, in the eastern and western pillars, you can visit the 1899 lift machinery when the tower is open. Eiffel's office has been re-created on the third level; wax figures depict the engineer receiving Thomas Edison.

Of course, it's the view that most people come for, and this extends for 42 miles, theoretically. In practice, weather conditions tend to limit it. Nevertheless, it's fabulous, and the best time for visibility is about an hour before sunset.

Hôtel des Invalides (Napoléon's Tomb). Place des Invalides, 7e. ☎ **01-44-42-37-72.** Admission to Musée de l'Armée, Napoléon's Tomb, and Musée des Plans-Reliefs (☎ 01-45-51-95-05) 37 F ($6.30) adults, 27 F ($4.60) ages 12–18, free for children 11 and under. Oct–Mar daily 10am–5pm; Apr–May and Sept daily 10am–6pm; June–Aug daily 10am–7pm. Closed Jan 1, May 1, Nov 1, and Dec 25. Métro: Latour-Maubourg, Varenne, or Invalides.

It was the Sun King who decided to build this "hotel" to house soldiers who'd been disabled. It wasn't entirely a benevolent gesture, since they had been injured, crippled, or blinded while fighting his battles. The massive building program was launched in 1670; when it was completed (Louis XIV was long dead by then), the corridors stretched for miles. Eventually the building was crowned by a gilded dome designed by Jules Hardouin-Mansart.

It is best to approach the Invalides by crossing over the Right Bank via the turn-of-the-century Alexander III Bridge. In the building's cobblestone forecourt, a display of massive cannons makes for a formidable welcome.

Before rushing on to Napoléon's tomb, you may want to take the time to visit the greatest military museum in the world, the **Musée de l'Armée.** If it can kill, it's enshrined here. The showcases of swords are among the finest in the world, and the mementos of World War I, including those of American and Canadian soldiers, are especially interesting.

And then there's that little Corsican general who became France's greatest soldier. The First Empire exhibit displays Napoléon's field bed with his tent. In the room devoted to the Restoration, the 100 Days, and Waterloo, you can see Napoléon's reconstituted bedroom at the time of his death at St. Helena. On the more personal side, you can view Vizir, a horse he owned (now stuffed), as well as a saddle he used mainly for state ceremonies. The Turenne Salon contains other souvenirs, including the hat Napoléon wore at Eylau, his sword from his victory at Austerlitz, and his "Flag of Farewell," which he kissed before departing for Elba.

You can gain access to the **Musée des Plans-Reliefs** through the west wing. This collection shows French towns and monuments done in scale models.

A walk across the Court of Honor delivers you to the **Eglise du Dôme** (Church of the Dome), designed by Hardouin-Mansart for Louis XIV. The great architect began work on the church in 1677, although he died before its completion. The dome is the second-tallest monument in Paris. The hearse used at the emperor's funeral on May 9, 1821, is in the Napoléon Chapel.

To accommodate the Tomb of Napoléon, the architect Visconti had to redesign the high altar in 1842. First buried at St. Helena, Napoléon's remains were returned to Paris in 1840, as Louis-Philippe had demanded of England. The triumphal funeral procession passed under the Arc de Triomphe, down the Champs-Elysées, en route to the Invalides, as snow swirled through the air.

The tomb is made of red Finnish porphyry, the base from green granite. Napoléon's remains were locked inside six coffins. Legends have abounded that some of his body parts went missing, notably his penis and his heart. According to Napoleonic scholars, the two doctors who dissected the emperor placed all his body parts in an urn positioned between his legs. Scholars deny the truth of these legends about the missing parts, although one wealthy gentleman in Connecticut frequently exhibits a penis preserved in alcohol, claiming it was once attached to the emperor. Surrounding the tomb are a dozen amazonlike figures representing his victories. Almost lampooning the smallness of the man, everything is done on a gargantuan scale. You'd think a real giant was buried here, not a symbolic one. In his coronation robes, the statue of Napoléon stands 8^1/$_2$ feet high. The grave of Napoléon's son, "the King of Rome," lies at his feet.

✪ **The Louvre (Musée du Louvre).** 34-36 quai du Louvre, 1er. Main entrance in the glass pyramid, Cour du Louvre. ☎ **01-40-20-53-17** (01-40-20-51-51 recorded message, 01-49-87-54-54 advance credit-card sales). www.louvre.fr. Admission 45 F ($7.65) before 3pm, 26 F ($4.40) after 3pm and on Sun; free for age 17 and under; free first Sun of every month. Mon and Wed 9am–9:45pm (Mon, short tour only), Thurs–Sun 9am–6pm. (Parts of the museum begin to close at 5:30pm.) 1^1/$_2$-hour English-language tours leave Mon and Wed–Sat various times of the day for 17 F ($2.90), free for children 12 and under with museum ticket. Métro: Palais-Royal–Musée-du-Louvre.

From far and wide they come—from North Dakota to Pakistan, from Nova Scotia to Japan—all bent on seeing the legendary Louvre. People on one of those "Paris-in-a-day" tours try to break track records to get a glimpse of the two most famous ladies of the Louvre: the *Mona Lisa* and the armless *Venus de Milo*. (The scene in front of the *Mona Lisa* is best described as a circus. Viewers push and shove in front of the lady's bulletproof glass as the staff looks idly on, and flashbulbs, which are forbidden, go off like popcorn on a hot stove. In all this fracas, it's hard to contemplate—or share in— her inimitable smile.) The herd then dashes on a 5-minute stampede in pursuit of *Winged Victory,* that headless statue discovered at Samothrace and dating from about 200 B.C. In defiance of the assembly-line theory of art, we head instead for David's *Portrait of Madame Récamier,* depicting Napoléon's opponent at age 23. On her comfortable sofa, she reclines agelessly in the style of classical antiquity.

Then a big question looms: Which of the rest of the other 30,000 works on display would you like to see?

The Louvre suffers from an embarrassment of riches. Here, the casual visitor often passes masterpieces blindly, simply because there are too many to behold. The Louvre is the world's largest palace and the world's largest museum (some say the greatest). As a palace, it leaves us cold, except for its old section, the **Cour Carrée.** As a museum, it's one of the greatest art collections in the world.

Between the Seine and the rue de Rivoli (Métro to Palais-Royal or Louvre, the latter the most elegant subway stop in the world), the Palace of the Louvre stretches for almost half a mile. In the days of Charles V, it was a fortress, but François I, a patron of Leonardo da Vinci, had it torn down and rebuilt as a royal residence. Less than a month after Marie Antoinette's head and body parted company, the Revolutionary Committee decided that the king's collection of paintings and sculpture should be opened to the public. At the low-est point in its history, in the 18th century, the Louvre was home for anybody who wanted to set up housekeeping there. Laundry hung out the windows, corners were literally pigpens, and familys built fires to cook their meals during the long winters. Napoléon ended that, chasing out the squatters and restoring the palace. In fact, he chose the Louvre for the site of his wedding to Marie-Louise.

So where did all these paintings come from? The kings of France, notably François I and Louis XIV, acquired many of them. Others have been willed to or purchased by the state. Many contributed by Napoléon were taken from reluctant donors: The church was one especially heavy and unwilling giver. Much of Napoléon's plunder had to be returned, although France hasn't seen its way clear to giving back all the booty.

To enter the Louvre, you'll pass through a controversial 71-foot-high **glass pyramid** in the courtyard. Commissioned by French president François Mitterrand and completed in 1989, it has received mixed reviews. Designed by I. M. Pei to allow sunlight to shine on an underground reception area, it shelters a complex of shops and restaurants. Automatic ticket machines help relieve the long lines of yesteryear.

The collections are divided into seven departments: Egyptian Antiquities; Oriental Antiquities; Greek, Etruscan, and Roman Antiquities; Sculpture; Painting; Decorative Arts; and Graphic Arts. A number of new galleries, devoted to Italian paintings, Roman glass and bronzes, Oriental antiquities, and Egyptian antiquities, were opened in 1997 and 1998. If you don't have to do Paris in a day, perhaps you can come here several times, concentrating on different collections or schools of painting. Those with little time should go on one of the **guided tours** (in English), which last about 1¹/₂ hours.

Da Vinci's much-traveled *La Gioconda* (**Mona Lisa**), has been the source of legend and lore for centuries. It was acquired by François I to hang above his bath. Note the guard and bulletproof glass: The world's most famous painting was stolen in the summer of 1911 and found in Florence in the winter of 1913. At first, both the poet Guillaume Apollinaire and Picasso were suspected as the thieves, but it was discovered in the possession of a former Louvre employee, who had apparently carried it out of the museum under his overcoat. Less well known (but to us even more enchanting) are Da Vinci's *Virgin and Child with St. Anne* and the *Virgin of the Rocks*.

After paying your respects to the enigmatically "Smiling One," allow time to see some French works stretching from the Richelieu wing through the entire **Sully wing** and even overflowing into part of the **Denon wing.** It's all here: Antoine Watteau's *Gilles* with the mysterious boy in a clown suit staring back at you; Jean-Honoré Fragonard's and François Boucher's rococo renderings of the aristocracy; and the greatest masterpieces of Jacques-Louis David, including his stellar 1785 work, *The Oath of the Horatii,* and the vast and vivid *Coronation of Napoléon.* Only the Uffizi in Florence rivals the Denon wing for its Italian Renaissance collection—everything from Raphael's *Portrait of Balthazar Castiglione* to Titian's *Man with a Glove.* Paolo Veronese's gigantic *Wedding Feast at Cana* occupies an

Some Louvre Tips

Long waiting lines outside the Louvre's pyramid entrance are notorious, but there are some tricks for avoiding them:

- Enter via the underground shopping mall, the Carrousel du Louvre, at 99 rue de Rivoli.
- Enter directly from the Palais-Royal-Musée du Louvre Métro station.
- Buy Le Pass-Musée (Museum and Monuments Pass) allowing direct entry through the priority entrance at the Passage Richelieu, 93 rue de Rivoli.
- Order tickets by phone at ☎ **01-49-87-54-54,** have them charged to your Visa or MasterCard, then pick them up at any FNAC store. This also gives you direct entry through the Passage Richelieu.

entire wall. This painting is a delight, a romp of high Viennese society of the 1500s. (That's Paolo himself playing the cello.)

Of the Greek and Roman antiquities, the most notable collections, aside from the *Venus de Milo* and *Winged Victory,* are fragments of a frieze from the Parthenon (located in the Denon wing). In Renaissance sculpture, you'll see two slaves by Michelangelo, originally intended for the tomb of Julius II but sold into other bondage. The Denon wing houses masterpieces including Ingres's *The Turkish Bath;* the Botticelli frescoes from the Villa Lemmi; Raphael's *La Belle Jardinière;* and Titian's *Open Air Concert.* The Sully wing is also filled with old masters, including Boucher's *Diana Resting after Her Bath* and Fragonard's *Bathers.*

The **Richelieu wing,** inaugurated in 1993, houses the museum's collection of northern European and French paintings, along with decorative arts, French sculpture, Oriental antiquities (a rich collection of Islamic art), and the salons of Napoléon III. First built from 1852 to 1857, the Richelieu wing was expanded to add some 230,000 square feet of exhibition space, and now shelters 12,000 works of art in 165 rooms and three covered courtyards. One of its galleries displays 21 works that Rubens painted in a space of only 2 years for Marie de Médicis's Luxembourg Palace. This wing stacks masterpiece upon masterpiece: Dürer's *Self-Portrait,* Anthony Van Dyck's *Portrait of Charles I of England,* and Holbein the Younger's *Portrait of Erasmus of Rotterdam,* with a wealth of surrounding art that includes Sumerian and Babylonian treasures, Assyrian winged bulls, and Persian friezes.

When you get tired, consider a pick-me-up at **Café Marly** in the Richelieu wing. In three grandiose rooms with high ceilings and lavish adornments, the cafe overlooks the museum's glass pyramid and offers a selection of coffees, pastries (by Paris's most legendary pastry-maker, Lenôtre), salads, sandwiches, and simple platters.

✪ **Musée d'Orsay.** 1 rue de Bellechasse or 62 rue de Lille, 7e. ☎ **01-40-49-48-14.** www.paris.org/Musees/Orsay. Admission 40 F ($6.80) adults, 30 F ($5.10) ages 18–24 and seniors, free for children 17 and under. Tues–Wed and Fri–Sat 10am–6pm, Thurs 10am–9:45pm, Sun 9am–6pm. June 20–Sept 20, museum opens 9am. Métro: Solférino. RER: Musée d'Orsay.

In the middle of Paris, architects transformed a defunct rail station, the handsome neoclassical Gare d'Orsay, into one of the greatest museums in the world. Don't skip the Louvre, but come here even if you have to miss all the other art museums of Paris. It contains one of the world's most important collections devoted to the watershed years between 1848 and 1914. Standing across the Seine from the Louvre and the Tuileries, it has a treasure trove of Van Gogh, Manet, Monet, Degas, and Renoir, but of all the less-known groups as well: the Symbolists, Pointillists, Nabis, Realists, and late Romantics.

The thousands of pieces of sculpture and painting housed here are spread across 80 different galleries, which also include belle-epoque furniture, photographs, objets d'art, and architectural models. There's even a cinema that shows classic films.

A monument to the Industrial Revolution, the Orsay station, once called "the elephant," is covered by an arching glass roof, which floods the museum with light. The museum displays works ranging from the creations of academic and historic painters such as Ingres to Romanticists such as Delacroix, to neo-Realists such as Courbet and Daumier. The Impressionists and Post-Impressionists, including Cézanne, Van Gogh, and the Fauves, share space with Matisse, the Cubists, and the Expressionists in a setting once used by Orson Welles to film a nightmarish scene in *The Trial,* based on Kafka's unfinished novel. You'll find Millet's sunny wheat fields, Barbizon landscapes, the mists of Corot, and parti-colored Tahitian Gauguins all in the same hall.

But it's the Impressionists who keep the crowds lining up. When the Louvre tripped over its traditional toes and chose not to display their works, it gave birth to a great rival. Led by Manet, Renoir, and the blessedly myopic Monet, the Impressionists shunned ecclesiastical and mythological set-pieces for a light-bathed Seine, faint figures strolling in the Tuileries, pale-faced women in hazy bars, even

Bonjour to the New Pompidou

What has been called "the most avant-garde building in the world, the **Centre Pompidou,** place Georges-Pompidou or plateau Beaubourg (☎ **01-44-78-12-33**), closed in late 1997 for extensive renovations, but parts of it remain open. The entire complex is scheduled to be fully operational again sometime in spring 2000.

The dream of former president Georges Pompidou, this center for 20th-century art, designed by Richard Rogers and Renzo Piano, opened in 1977 and immediately became the focus of loud controversy. Its bold exoskeletal architecture and the brightly painted pipes and ducts crisscrossing its transparent facade (green for water, red for heat, blue for air, and yellow for electricity) were jarring in the old Beaubourg neighborhood. Perhaps the detractors were right all along—within 20 years the building began to deteriorate so badly that a major restoration was called for.

At this writing, the areas of the complex that remain open include the South Gallery (*la galerie sud,* site of such temporary exhibitions as a retrospective of the works of British painter David Hockney) and a re-creation of the jazz-age studio of Romanian sculptor Brancusi *(l'Atelier Brancusi),* which is configured as a minimuseum separate from the rest of the center. Both areas are open Monday and Wednesday through Friday from noon to 10pm, Saturday and Sunday from 10am to 10pm. A combined ticket to both costs 30 F ($5.10) for adults, 20 F ($3.40) for persons under 18.

vulgar rail stations such as the Gare St-Lazare. And the Impressionists were the first to paint that most characteristic feature of Parisian life: the sidewalk cafe, especially in the artists' quarter of Montmartre.

The most famous painting from this era is Manet's 1863 *Déjeuner sur l'herbe (Picnic on the Grass),* whose forest setting with a nude woman and two fully clothed men sent shock waves through respectable society when it was first exhibited. Two years later, Manet's *Olympia,* also here, created another scandal. It depicts a woman lounging on her bed and wearing nothing but a flower in her hair and high-heeled shoes; she is attended by an African maid in the background. Zola called Manet "a man among eunuchs."

To provide insight into the ambitious renovation of the complex, its administrators have erected a steel-and-polyester "information teepee" adjacent to the center. It's open Sunday, Monday, and Wednesday through Friday from 12:30 to 6pm, and Saturday from 2 to 6pm.

What can you expect to see when the Pompidou is going full blast again? It encompasses four separate attractions:

The **Musée National d'Art Moderne** (National Museum of Modern Art) offers a large collection of 20th-century art. With some 40,000 works, this is the big attraction, although only some 850 works can be displayed at one time. If you want to view some real charmers, see Alexander Calder's 1926 *Josephine Baker,* one of his earliest versions of the mobile, an art form he invented. Marcel Duchamp's *Valise* is a collection of miniature reproductions of his fabled Dada sculptures and drawings, displayed in a carrying case. Every time we visit Paris, we have to see Salvador Dalí's *Portrait of Lenin Dancing on Piano Keys*—it makes our day.

The **Public Information Library** offers free access to a million French and foreign books, periodicals, films, records, slides, and microfilms. The **Center for Industrial Design** emphasizes the contributions made in the fields of architecture, visual communications, publishing, and community planning. And the **Institute for Research and Coordination of Acoustics/Music** brings together musicians and composers interested in furthering the cause of music, both contemporary and traditional.

One of Renoir's brightest, most joyous paintings is also here: the *Moulin de la Galette,* painted in 1876. Degas is represented by his paintings of racehorses and dancers; his 1876 cafe scene, *Absinthe,* also here, remains one of his most reproduced works. Paris-born Claude Monet was fascinated by the effect that changing light had on Rouen Cathedral, and in a series of five paintings displayed here, its stone bubbles to life.

One of the most celebrated works at the Orsay is by an American, Whistler's *Arrangement in Gray and Black: Portrait of the Painter's Mother,* better known as *Whistler's Mother.* It is said that this painting heralded the advent of modern art, although many critics denounced it at the time as "Whistler's Dead Mother" because of its funereal overtones. Today, the painting has been hailed as a "veritable icon of our consciousness." Whistler was content to claim he made "Mummy just as nice as possible."

2   Museums

Turn to "The Top Attractions," above, for a comprehensive look at the Louvre and the Musée d'Orsay.

Galerie Nationale du Jeu de Paume. Jardin des Tuileries/1 place de la Concorde, 1er. ☎ **01-42-60-69-69.** Admission 38 F ($6.45) adults, 28 F ($4.75) students, free for children 13 and under. Tues noon–9:30pm, Wed–Fri noon–7pm, Sat–Sun 10am–7pm. Métro: Concorde.

For years, the National Gallery in the Jeu de Paume, in the northeast corner of the Tuileries gardens, was one of the treasures of Paris, displaying some of the finest works of the Impressionists. To the regret of many, that collection was hauled off to the Musée d'Orsay in 1986. After a $12.6 million face-lift, the Second Empire building was transformed into a state-of-the-art gallery with a video screening room. No permanent collection is housed here, but every 2 or 3 months a new show is mounted. Sometimes the works of little-known contemporary artists are on display; at other times, an exhibit will feature unexplored aspects of established artists.

Originally, in this part of the gardens, Napoléon III built a ball court on which *jeu de paume,* an antecedent of tennis, was played—hence, the museum's name. The most infamous period in the National Gallery's history came during the Nazi occupation, when it served as an "evaluation center" for works of modern art. Paintings from all over France were shipped to the Jeu de Paume, and art condemned by the Nazis as "degenerate" was burned.

Maison de Victor Hugo. 6 place des Vosges, 4e. ☎ **01-42-72-10-16.** Admission 17.50 F ($3) adults, 9 F ($1.55) ages 19–25, free for age 18 and under. Tues–Sun 10am–5:40pm. Closed national holidays. Métro: St-Paul, Bastille, or Chemin-Vert.

Today, theater-goers who saw *Les Misérables,* even those who haven't read anything by Paris's great 19th-century novelist, come to place des Vosges to see where he lived and wrote. Some thought Hugo (1802 to 1885) a genius, but Cocteau called him a madman, and an American composer discovered that in his old age he was carving furniture with his teeth! From 1832 to 1848, the novelist and poet lived on the second floor of the old Hôtel Rohan Guéménée, built in 1610 on what was then the place Royale. The museum owns some of Hugo's furniture as well as pieces that once belonged to Juliette Drouet, the mistress with whom he lived in exile on Guernsey, one of the Channel Islands.

Worth the visit are Hugo's drawings, more than 450, illustrating scenes from his own works. Mementos of the great writer abound, including samples of his handwriting, his inkwell, and first editions of his works. A painting of Hugo's funeral procession at the Arc de Triomphe in 1885 is on display, as are plentiful portraits and souvenirs of his family. Of the furnishings, a chinoiserie salon stands out. The collection even contains Daumier caricatures and a bust of Hugo by David d'Angers, which, compared to Rodin's, looks saccharine.

Musée Carnavalet. 23 rue de Sévigné, 3e. ☎ **01-42-72-21-13.** Admission 35 F ($5.95) adults, 25 F ($4.25) under age 25 and over 60. Tues–Sun 10am–5:40pm. Métro: St-Paul or Chemin-Vert.

If you like history but history books bore you, spend a couple of hours here for some insight into Paris's past. The comprehensive and lifelike exhibits are great for kids too. The history of Paris comes alive in intimate detail, right down to the chessmen Louis XVI used to distract his mind while waiting to go to the guillotine. The building, a renowned Renaissance palace, was built in 1544 by Pierre Lescot and Jean Goujon and later acquired by Madame de Carnavalet. The great François Mansart transformed it between 1655 and 1661.

But it's probably best known because one of history's most famous letter writers, Madame de Sévigné, moved here in 1677. Fanatically devoted to her daughter (she ended up moving in with her because she couldn't bear their separation), she poured out nearly every detail of her life in her letters, virtually ignoring her son. A native of the Marais district, she died at her daughter's château in 1696. It wasn't until 1866 that the city of Paris acquired the mansion, eventually turning it into a museum.

Several salons cover the Revolution, with a bust of Marat, a portrait of Danton, and a model of the Bastille (one painting shows its demolition). Another salon tells the story of the captivity of the royal family at the Temple, including the bed in which Madame Elizabeth slept and the exercise book of the dauphin.

Exhibits continue at the Hôtel le Pelletier de St-Fargeau, across the courtyard. On display is furniture from the Louis XIV period to the early 20th century, including a replica of Marcel Proust's cork-lined bedroom with his actual furniture, including his brass bed.

✪ Musée Jacquemart-André. 158 bd. Hausmann, 8e. ☎ **01-42-89-04-91.** Admission 48 F ($8.15). Daily 10am–6pm. Métro: Miromesnil or St-Philippe-du-Roule.

It's the finest museum of its type in Paris, an inspired 19th-century blend of taste and money, the treasure trove of a married couple devoted to 18th-century French paintings and furnishings, 17th-century Dutch and Flemish paintings, and works from the Italian Renaissance. The collection originally belonged to the André family, prominent French Protestants who made a fortune in banking and industry in the 19th century. The family's last scion, Edouard André, spent most of his life as an officer in the French army stationed abroad, returning later in his life to marry a well-known portraitist of French governmental figures and members of the aristocracy, Nélie Jacquemart. Together, they compiled a collection of rare French 18th-century decorative art and European paintings within an 1850s town house that was continually upgraded and redecorated according to the fashions of the times.

In 1912, Mme Jacquemart willed the house and its collection to the Institut de France, which paid for an extensive renovation and enlargement that was completed in 1996. The pride of the collection are works by Bellini, Carpaccio, and Uccelo, which are complemented by Houdon busts, Gobelins tapestries, Savonnerie carpets, della Robbia terra-cottas, an awesome collection of antiques, and works by Rembrandt *(The Pilgrim of Emmaus),* Van Dyck, Tiepolo, Rubens, Watteau, Fragonard, Boucher, and Mantegna. After a major restoration, one of the most outstanding exhibits consists of three 18th-century frescoes by Giambattista Tiepolo, depicting spectators on balconies viewing Henri III's arrival in Venice in 1574. Salons drip with gilt and the ultimate in fin-de-siècle style.

Take a break from the gilded age with a cup of tea in Mme Jacquemart's high-ceilinged dining room, adorned with 18th-century tapestries. Salads, tarts, tourtes (a round pastry filled with meat or fruit), and an assortment of Viennese pastries are served during the museum's opening hours and make a perfect light lunch or pick-me-up.

A Timesaving Tip

Museums require that you check shopping bags and book bags, and sometimes lines for these can be longer than the ticket lines. Visitors who value their time should leave their bags behind: Some coat lines in Paris can take 30 minutes. Ask if a museum has more than one coat line, and if so, go to the less frequented ones.

Museum-Hopping in Paris

Museums in Paris have fairly standard hours. They are often closed on Tuesday and national holidays. Fees vary, but half-price tickets are usually provided to students, children ages 3 to 7, and extra-large families or groups. Sunday is the best day for serious museum-hopping, as most museums let you in for half price.

You can buy **Le Pass-Musée (Museum and Monuments Pass)** at any of the museums that honor it, or at any branch of the Paris Tourist office. It offers free entrance to the permanent collections of 65 monuments and museums in Paris and the Ile-de-France. A 1-day pass is 80 F ($13.60); a 3-day pass is 160 F ($27.20); a 5-day pass is 240 F ($40.80).

✪ **Musée Marmottan-Claude Monet.** 2 rue Louis-Boilly, 16e. ☎ **01-42-24-07-02.** Admission 40 F ($6.80) adults, 25 F ($4.25) ages 8–24, free for children 7 and under. Tues–Sun 10am–5:30pm. Métro: La Muette.

This collection has been hailed as "one of the great art treasures of the world," and that it is. In the past, a lone art historian would occasionally venture here to the edge of the Bois de Boulogne to see what Paul Marmottan had donated to the Académie des Beaux-Arts. Hardly anybody else did until 1966, when Michel Monet, son of Claude, died in a car crash, leaving what was then a $10 million bequest of his father's art to the little museum. The Académie des Beaux-Arts suddenly found itself with more than 130 paintings, watercolors, pastels, drawings, and a passel of Monet lovers, who can now trace the evolution of the great man's work in a single museum.

The collection includes more than 30 paintings of Monet's house at Giverny and many of water lilies, his everlasting fancy. The bequest also included *Willow* (1918), *House of Parliament* (1905), and a portrait by Renoir of the 32-year-old Monet. Ironically, the museum had always owned Monet's *Impression,* from which the movement got its name.

Paul Marmottan's original collection includes fig-leafed nudes, First Empire antiques, assorted objets d'art, bucolic paintings, and crystal chandeliers. Many tapestries date from the Renaissance, and you can also see an extensive collection of miniatures donated by Daniel Waldenstein.

Musée National du Moyen Age/Thermes de Cluny (Musée de Cluny). 6 place Paul-Painlevé, 5e. ☎ **01-53-73-78-00.** Admission 30 F ($5.10) adults, 20 F ($3.40) ages 18–25, free for age 17 and under. Wed–Mon 9:15am–5:45pm. Métro: Cluny-Sorbonne.

Along with the Hôtel de Sens in Le Marais, the Hôtel de Cluny is all that remains of domestic medieval architecture in Paris. You enter through the cobblestoned Court of Honor, where you can admire the flamboyant Gothic building with its clinging vines, turreted walls, gargoyles, and dormers with seashell motifs. Originally the Cluny was the mansion of a rich 15th-century abbot, built on top of and next to the ruins of a Roman bath. By 1515, it was the residence of Mary Tudor, teenage widow of Louis XII and daughter of Henry VII of England and Elizabeth of York.

Seized during the revolution, the Cluny was rented in 1833 to Alexandre du Sommerard, who adorned it with his collection of medieval works of art. Upon his death in 1842, both the building and the collection were bought back by the government.

The present-day collection of medieval arts and crafts is the finest in the world. Most people come primarily to see the *Unicorn Tapestries,* the most acclaimed tapestries of their kind. A beautiful princess and her handmaiden, beasts of prey, and just plain pets— all the romance of the age of chivalry lives on in these remarkable yet mysterious tapestries discovered only a century ago in Limousin's Château de Boussac. Five seem to deal with the five senses (one, for example, depicts a unicorn looking into a mirror held up by a dour-faced maiden). The sixth shows a woman under an elaborate tent with jewels, her pet dog resting on an embroidered cushion beside her, with the lovable unicorn and his friendly companion, a lion, holding back the flaps. The background in red and green forms a rich carpet of spring flowers, fruit-laden trees, birds, rabbits, donkeys, dogs, goats, lambs, and monkeys.

The other exhibits range widely, including several Flemish retables; a 14th-century Sienese (life-size) John the Baptist and other Italian sculptures; statues from Sainte-Chapelle, dating from 1243 to 1248; 12th- and 13th-century crosses, studded with gems; golden chalices, manuscripts, ivory carvings, vestments, leatherwork, jewelry, coins; a 13th-century Adam; and recently discovered heads and fragments of statues from Notre-Dame de Paris. In the fan-vaulted medieval chapel hang tapestries depicting scenes from the life of St. Stephen.

Downstairs are the ruins of the **Roman baths,** dating from around A.D. 200. Of these once-flourishing baths, the best-preserved section is seen in room X, the frigidarium. Once it measured 70 by 36 feet, rising to a height of 50 feet, with stone walls nearly 7 feet thick. The ribbed vaulting here rests on consoles that evoked ships' prows. Credit for this unusual motif goes to the builders of the baths, the boatmen of Paris. During the reign of Tiberius, a column to Jupiter was found beneath the chancel of Notre-Dame and is now on view in the court. Called "The Column of the Boatmen," it is now believed to be the oldest sculpture created in Paris.

Musée National Eugène Delacroix. 6 place de Furstenberg, 6e. ☎ **01-44-41-86-50.** Admission 22 F ($4) adults, 15 F ($2.70) ages 18–25 and over 60, free for age 17 and under. Wed–Mon 9:30am–5pm. Closed holidays. Métro: St-Germain-des-Prés.

This museum is only for serious Delacroix groupies, among whom we include ourselves. If you admire this artist and want to see where he lived, worked, and died, then this is worth at least an hour of your time. Delacroix (1798 to 1863) is something of an enigma to art historians. Even his parentage is a mystery. Many believe that Talleyrand had the privilege of fathering him. One biographer saw him "as an isolated and atypical individualist—one who respected traditional values, yet emerged as the embodiment of Romantic revolt." The poet Baudelaire called him "a volcanic crater artistically concealed beneath bouquets of flowers."

The museum is in one of the most charming squares on the Left Bank, with a highly romantic garden. A large arch on a stone courtyard leads to his studio, no poor artist's studio, but the tasteful creation of a solidly established man. Sketches, lithographs, watercolors, and oils are hung throughout, and a few mementos remain, including a lovely mahogany paint box.

✪ **Musée Picasso.** Hôtel Salé, 5 rue de Thorigny, 3e. ☎ **01-42-71-25-21.** www.paris.org/Musees/Picasso. Admission 30–38 F ($5.10–$6.45) adults, 20–28 F ($3.40–$4.75) ages 19–25 and over 60, free for age 18 and under. Apr–Sept Wed–Mon 9:30am–6pm; Oct–Mar Wed–Mon 9:30am–5pm. Métro: St-Paul, Filles-du-Calvaire, or Chemin-Vert.

When it opened at the beautifully restored **Hôtel Salé** (Salty Mansion), a state-owned property in Le Marais, the press hailed it as a "museum for Picasso's Picassos." And that's what it is. Almost overnight the museum became, and continues to be, one of the most popular attractions in Paris.

The state acquired the greatest Picasso collection in the world in lieu of a $50 million levy in inheritance taxes. The tax man claimed 203 paintings, 158 sculptures, 16 collages, 19 bas-reliefs, 88 ceramics, and more than 1,500 sketches and 1,600 engravings, along with 30 notebooks. These works span some 75 years of the artist's life and ever-changing style.

The range of paintings includes a remarkable self-portrait from 1901 and the masterpieces *Le Baiser (The Kiss), Reclining Nude,* and

Man with a Guitar, all painted at Mougins on the Riviera in 1969 and 1970. It's easy to stroll through the handsome museum seeking your own favorite work—perhaps a wicked one: *Jeune Garçon à la Langouste (Young Man with a Lobster),* painted in Paris in 1941. The Paris museum owns several intriguing studies for *Les Demoiselles d'Avignon,* the painting that shocked the establishment and launched Cubism in 1907.

Some visitors go to the Picasso Museum just to view the ribald paintings the artist turned out in his later years—perhaps just for his own erotic amusement.

Many of the major masterpieces, such as *The Crucifixion and Nude in a Red Armchair,* remain on permanent view. But because the collection is so vast, temporary exhibitions featuring such items as his studies of the Minotaur are held for the public at the rate of two each year.

In addition to Picasso's own treasure trove of art, his private collection of other masters' works is also displayed, including those of such world-class artists as Cézanne, Rousseau, Braque, André Derain, and Miró. Picasso was fascinated with African masks, many of which are on view.

Musée Rodin. In the Hôtel Biron, 77 rue de Varenne, 7e. ☎ **01-44-18-61-10.** Admission 28 F ($4.75) adults, 18 F ($3.05) ages 18–25, free for age 17 and under. Apr–Sept Tues–Sun 9:30am–5:45pm; Oct–Mar Tues–Sun 9:30am–4:45pm. Métro: Varenne.

These days Rodin is acclaimed as the father of modern sculpture, but in a different era his work was labeled obscene. The world's artistic taste changed, and in due course the government of France purchased the gray-stone 18th-century luxury residence in Faubourg St-Germain. The mansion was Rodin's studio from 1910 until his death in 1917. After the government bought the studio, it restored the rose gardens to their 18th-century splendor, making them a perfect setting for Rodin's most memorable works.

In the courtyard are three world-famous creations. Rodin's first major public commission, *The Burghers of Calais* commemorated the heroism of six citizens of the city of Calais who, in 1347, offered themselves as a ransom to Edward III in return for ending his siege of their port. Perhaps the single best-known work, *The Thinker,* in Rodin's own words, "thinks with every muscle of his arms, back, and legs, with his clenched fist and gripping toes." Not yet completed when Rodin died, *The Gate of Hell,* as he put it, is "where I lived for a whole year in Dante's *Inferno.*"

Inside the building, the sculpture, plaster casts, reproductions, originals, and sketches reveal the freshness and vitality of a remarkable artist. You can practically see many of his works emerging from marble into life. Everybody is attracted to *The Kiss,* of which one critic wrote, "the passion is timeless." Upstairs are two different versions of the celebrated and condemned nude of Balzac, his bulky torso rising from a tree trunk (Albert E. Elsen commented on the "glorious bulging" stomach). Included are many versions of his *Monument to Balzac* (a large one stands in the garden), which was Rodin's last major work and which caused a furor when it was first exhibited.

Other significant sculptures include Rodin's soaring *Prodigal Son, The Crouching Woman* (called the "embodiment of despair"), *and The Age of Bronze,* an 1876 study of a nude man, modeled by a Belgian soldier. (Rodin was falsely accused of making a cast from a living model.)

Generally overlooked is a room devoted to Camille Claudel, Rodin's mistress and a towering artist in her own right. She was his pupil, model, and lover, and created such works as *Maturity, Clotho,* and the recently donated *The Waltz* and *The Gossips.*

The little alley behind the mansion housing the Musée Rodin winds its way down to a pond with fountains and flower beds, even sandpits for children. It's one of the most idyllic hidden spots of Paris.

3 Churches

Turn to "The Top Attractions," above, for a full look at Notre-Dame.

Basilique du Sacré-Coeur. Place St-Pierre, 18e. ☎ **01-53-41-89-00.** Free admission to basilica; joint ticket to dome and crypt 30 F ($5.10) adults, 16 F ($2.70) students and children. Apr–Sept daily 9am–7pm; Oct–Mar daily 9am–6pm. Métro: Abbesses; then take the elevator to the surface and follow the signs to the funiculaire, which goes up to the church for the price of one Métro ticket.

After the Eiffel Tower, Sacré-Coeur is the most characteristic landmark of the Parisian scene. Like the tower, it has always been the subject of much controversy. One Parisian called it "a lunatic's confectionery dream." An offended Zola declared it "the basilica of the ridiculous." Sacré-Coeur has had warm supporters as well, including the poet Max Jacob and the artist Maurice Utrillo. Utrillo never tired of drawing and painting it, and he and Jacob came here regularly to pray.

Its gleaming white domes and *campanile* (bell tower) tower over Paris like a 12th-century Byzantine church. But it's not that old. After France's defeat by the Prussians in 1870, the basilica was planned as a votive offering to cure France's misfortunes. Rich and poor alike contributed money to build it. Construction was begun on the church in 1876 and it was not consecrated until 1919, but perpetual prayers of adoration have been made here day and night since 1885. The interior of the basilica is brilliantly decorated with mosaics. The stained-glass windows were shattered during the struggle for Paris in 1944, but have been well replaced. Look for the striking mosaic of Christ on the ceiling, and also the mural of his Passion at the back of the altar. The crypt contains a relic of what some of the devout believe is Christ's sacred heart—hence, the name of the church.

On a clear day you can see for 35 miles from the dome. You can also walk around the inner dome of the church, peering down like a pigeon (one is likely to be keeping you company).

St-Germain-des-Prés. 3 place St-Germain-des-Prés, 6e. ☎ **01-43-25-41-71.** Daily 8am–8pm. Métro: St-Germain-des-Prés.

Outside it's an early 17th-century town house, and handsome at that. But inside it's one of the oldest churches in Paris, dating from the 6th century when a Benedictine abbey was founded on the site by Childebert, son of Clovis, the "creator of France." Unfortunately, the marble columns in the triforium are all that remains from that period. At one time, the abbey was a pantheon for Merovingian kings. Restoration of the site of their tombs, St. Symphorien Chapel, began in 1981. During that work, unknown Romanesque paintings were discovered on the chapel's triumphal arch, making it one of the most interesting remains of old Christian Paris.

The Romanesque tower, topped by a 19th-century spire, is the most enduring landmark in the village of St-Germain-des-Prés. Its church bells, however, are hardly noticed by the patrons of Deux-Magots across the way.

The Normans nearly destroyed the abbey at least four times. The present building, the work of four centuries, has a Romanesque nave and a Gothic choir with fine capitals. Among the people interred at the church are **Descartes** (his heart at least) and **Jean-Casimir,** the king of Poland who abdicated his throne.

When you leave the church, turn right on rue de l'Abbaye and have a look at the 17th-century **Palais Abbatial,** a pink palace.

✪ **Sainte-Chapelle.** Palais de Justice, 4 bd. du Palais, 1er. ☎ **01-53-73-78-50.** Admission 35 F ($5.95) adults, 25 F ($4.25) students and ages 13–25, free for children 12 and under. Apr–Sept daily 9:30am–6:30pm; Oct–Mar daily 10am–5pm. Métro: Cité, St-Michel, or Châtelet–Les Halles. RER: St-Michel.

Countless travel writers have called this tiny chapel a jewel box. That hardly suffices. Nor will it do to call it "a light show." Go when the sun is shining and you'll need no one else's words to describe the remarkable effects of natural light on Sainte-Chapelle.

The church is approached through the Cour de la Sainte-Chapelle of the Palais de Justice. If it weren't for the chapel's 247-foot spire, the law courts here would almost swallow it up.

Built in 5 to 7 years, beginning in 1246, the chapel has two levels. It was constructed to house relics of the True Cross, including the Crown of Thorns acquired by St. Louis (the Crusader king, Louis IX) from the emperor of Constantinople. (In those days, cathedrals throughout Europe were busy acquiring relics for their treasuries, regardless of their authenticity. It was a seller's, perhaps a sucker's, market.) Louis IX is said to have paid heavily for his relics, raising the money through unscrupulous means. He died of the plague on a crusade and was canonized in 1297.

You enter through the lower chapel, supported by flying buttresses and ornamented with fleur-de-lys designs. The lower chapel was used by the servants of the palace, the upper chamber by the king and his courtiers. The latter is reached by ascending narrow spiral stairs.

Viewed on a bright day, the 15 stained-glass windows seem to glow with Chartres blue, and reds that have inspired the Parisian saying, "Wine the color of Sainte-Chapelle's windows." The walls consist almost entirely of the glass, which had to be removed for safe-keeping during the Revolution and again during both world wars. In their biblical designs are embodied the hopes and dreams—and the pretensions—of the kings who ordered their construction.

Sainte-Chapelle stages concerts most nights in summer, with tickets ranging from 120 F to 150 F ($20.40 to $25.50). Call ☎ **01-42-77-65-65** for more details (daily from 11am to 6pm).

St-Eustache. 2 rue du Jour, 1er. ☎ **01-42-36-31-05.** Apr–Sept daily 8am–8pm; Oct–Mar daily 9am–7pm. Sun mass 9:30am, 11am, and 6pm; Sun organ recitals 5:30pm. Métro: Les Halles.

In our opinion, this mixed Gothic and Renaissance church completed in 1637 is rivaled only by Notre-Dame. It took nearly a century to build. Madame de Pompadour and Richelieu were baptized here, and Molière's funeral was held here in 1673. The church has been known for organ recitals ever since Liszt played here in 1866. Inside rests the black-marble tomb of Jean-Baptiste Colbert, the minister of state under Louis XIV. On top of his tomb is his marble effigy flanked by statues of *Abundance* by Coysevox and *Fidelity* by J. B. Tuby. The church's most famous painting is Rembrandt's *The Pilgrimage to Emmaus.* There's a side entrance to the church on rue Rambuteau.

4   Architectural & Historical Highlights

Conciergerie. 1 quai de l'Horloge, 1er. ☎ **01-53-73-78-50.** www.paris. org/Monuments/Conciergerie. Admission 35 F ($5.95) adults, 23 F ($3.90) ages 12–25 and over 60, free for children under 12. Apr–Sept daily 9:30am–6:30pm; Oct–Mar daily 10am–5pm. Métro: Cité, Châtelet, or St-Michel. RER: St-Michel.

London has its Tower, Paris its Conciergerie. Although the Conciergerie had a long and regal history before the Revolution, it was forever stained by the Reign of Terror and other horrors. It lives as an infamous symbol of the days when carts pulled up daily to haul off a fresh supply of victims to the guillotine.

On the Seine, the Conciergerie is approached through its land-mark twin towers, the **Tour d'Argent** and the **Tour de César.** The vaulted 14th-century **Guard Room,** which dates from when the Capets made the Palace of the Cité a royal residence, is the actual entrance to the building. Also dating from the 14th century, and even more interesting, is the vast, dark, and foreboding Gothic *Salle des Gens d'Armes* (Room of People at Arms), utterly changed from the days when the king used it as a banquet hall.

But architecture plays a secondary role to the list of famous pris-oners who spent their last miserable days here. Few in its history endured tortures as severe as Ravaillac's, who assassinated Henry IV in 1610. He got the full treatment—pincers in the flesh, and hot lead and boiling oil poured on him like bath water.

During the Revolution, the Conciergerie became a symbol of ter-ror to the nobility and enemies of the State. Just a short walk from the prison, the Revolutionary Tribunal dispensed a skewed, hurried justice to the beat of the guillotine. If it's any consolation, the jurists of the Revolution did not believe in torturing their victims, only in decapitating them.

In failing health and shocked beyond grief, Marie Antoinette was brought here to await her trial. Only a small screen (and sometimes not even that) protected her modesty from the gaze of guards sta-tioned in her cell. The Affair of the Carnation failed in its attempt to abduct her and secure her freedom. By accounts of the day, she was shy and stupid, although the evidence is that upon her death she displayed the nobility of a true queen. (What's more, the famous "Let them eat cake" she supposedly uttered when told the peasants had no bread is probably apocryphal.) It was shortly before noon on the morning of October 16, 1793, when her executioners came for her, grabbing her and cutting her hair, as was the custom for victims marked for the guillotine.

Hôtel de Ville. 29 rue de Rivoli, 4e. ☎ **01-42-76-43-43.** Free admission. Information center open Mon–Sat 9am–6:30pm. Métro: Hôtel de Ville.

The Hôtel de Ville isn't a hotel at all, but the grandiose city hall of Paris. On a large square with fountains and turn-of-the-century lampposts, it is a 19th-century Cinderella's Palace. The medieval structure it replaced had witnessed countless municipally ordered executions. Henry IV's assassin, Ravaillac, was quartered alive on the square in 1610, his body tied to four horses that bolted in opposite directions. On May 24, 1871, the communards doused the city hall with petrol, creating a blaze that lasted for 8 days. The Third Republic ordered the structure rebuilt, with many changes, even creating a Hall of Mirrors evocative of Versailles. For security reasons, the major splendor of this building is closed to the general public. However, there is an on-site Information Center sponsoring exhibits on Paris in the main lobby.

Institut de France. 23 quai de Conti, 6e. ☎ **01-44-41-44-41.** Métro: Pont-Neuf or Odéon.

Designed by Louis Le Vau, this dramatic baroque building with an enormous cupola is the seat of all five Academies—Académie Francaise, des Sciences, des Inscriptions et Belles Lettres, des Beaux Arts, and des Sciences Morales et Politiques—which dominate the intellectual life of the country. The members of the Academy (limited to 40), the guardians of the French language who are referred to as "the immortals," gather here. Many of them are unfamiliar figures (though Jacques Cousteau and Marshall Pétain were members), and indeed, the Academy is remarkable for the great writers and philosophers who have not been invited to join—Balzac, Baudelaire, Diderot, Flaubert, Descartes, Proust, Molière, Pascal, Rousseau, and Zola, to name only a few. The cenotaph was designed by Coysevox for Mazarin.

Palais-Royal. Rue St-Honoré, 1er. Daily 8am–7pm. Métro: Palais-Royal–Musée-du-Louvre.

The Palais-Royal was originally known as the Palais-Cardinal, for it was the residence of Cardinal Richelieu, Louis XIII's prime minister. Richelieu had it built, and after his death it was inherited by the king, who died soon after. Louis XIV spent part of his childhood here with his mother, Anne of Austria, but later resided at the Louvre and Versailles. The palace was later owned by the duc de Chartres et Orléans, who encouraged the opening of cafes, gambling dens, and other public entertainments.

Although government offices occupy the Palais-Royal and they're not open to the public, do visit the **Jardin du Palais-Royal,** an enclosure bordered by arcades. Don't miss the main courtyard, with the controversial 1986 sculpture by Buren: 280 prison-striped columns, oddly placed.

The Panthéon. Place du Panthéon, 5e. ☎ **01-44-32-18-00.** Admission 35 F ($5.95) adults, 23 F ($3.90) ages 12–25, free for children 11 and under. Apr–Sept daily 9:30am–6:30pm; Oct–Mar daily 10am–6:15pm (last entrance 45 minutes before closing). Métro: Cardinal-Lemoine or Maubert-Mutualité.

Some of the most famous men in the history of France are buried here in austere grandeur, on the crest of the mount of St. Geneviève. The former church was converted after the revolution into a "Temple of Fame"—ultimately a pantheon for the great men (and one woman: Marie Curie) of France. In the 19th century, the building changed roles so many times—first a church, then a pantheon, then a church—that it was hard to keep its function straight. After Victor Hugo was buried here, it became a pantheon for good. Other notables entombed within include Jean-Jacques Rousseau, Soufflot, Emile Zola, and Louis Braille.

5 Neighborhood Highlights

In Paris, the neighborhoods often turn out to be attractions unto themselves. Following are some of our favorites. (See also "A Walking Tour: The Grand Promenade," in section 6.)

ISLANDS IN THE STREAM: ILE DE LA CITÉ & ILE ST-LOUIS

ILE DE LA CITÉ: WHERE PARIS WAS BORN Medieval Paris, that blend of grotesquerie and Gothic beauty, bloomed on this island in the Seine (Métro: Cité). Ile de la Cité, which the Seine protects like a surrounding moat, has been known as "the cradle" of Paris ever since. As Sauval once observed, "The Island of the City is shaped like a great ship, sunk in the mud, lengthwise in the stream, in about the middle of the Seine."

Medieval Paris was not only a city of legends and lovers, but also of blood-curdling tortures and brutalities. No story illustrates this better than the affair of Abélard and his charge Héloïse, whose jealous and unsettled uncle hired ruffians to castrate her lover. (The attack predictably quelled their ardor, and he became a monk, she an abbess.)

Don't miss the **Pont-Neuf,** or "New Bridge," at the opposite tip of the island from Notre-Dame. The span isn't new, of course; it's actually the oldest bridge in Paris, erected in 1604. In its day the bridge had two unique features: It was not flanked with houses and shops, and it was paved.

At the **Musée Carnavalet** in the Marais (see "Museums," above), a painting called *Spectacle of Buffoons* shows what the bridge was like between 1665 and 1669. Duels were fought on the bridge; the nobility's great coaches crossed it; peddlers sold their wares on it; and entertainers such as Tabarin came here to seek a few coins from the gawkers. As public facilities were lacking, the bridge also served as a de facto outhouse.

Just past the Pont-Neuf is the "prow" of the island, the **Square du Vert Galant.** Pause to look at the equestrian statue of the beloved Henri IV, who was killed by an assassin. A true king of his people, Henry was also (to judge from accounts) regal in the boudoir—hence the nickname "Vert Galant," or old spark. Gabrielle d'Estrées and Henriette d'Entragues were his best-known mistresses, but they had to share him with countless others, some of whom would casually catch his eye as he was riding along the streets of Paris.

In fond memory of the king, the little triangular park continues to attract lovers. If at first it appears to be a sunken garden, that's because it remains at its natural level; the rest of the Cité has been built up during the centuries.

ILE ST-LOUIS   The little iron footbridge from the rear of Notre-Dame to the Ile St-Louis exposes visitors to a world of tree-shaded quays, aristocratic town houses with courtyards, restaurants, and antique shops. (You can also take the Métro to Sully-Morland or Pont-Marie.) The fraternal twin of Ile de la Cité, Ile St-Louis is primarily residential; plaques on the facades of houses identify the former residences of the famous. **Marie Curie** lived at 36 quai de Béthune, near Pont de la Tournelle.

The most exciting mansion is the **Hôtel de Lauzun,** at 17 quai d'Anjou. It was the home of the duc de Lauzun, a favorite of Louis XIV, until his secret marriage angered the king, who had him tossed into the Bastille. Baudelaire lived here in the 19th century, squandering his family fortune and penning poetry that would be banned in France until 1949. Now the house belongs to the City of Paris and is used to house official guests.

Voltaire lived with his mistress in the **Hôtel Lambert,** at 2 quai d'Anjou, where their quarrels were legendary. The mansion also housed the Polish royal family for over a century.

Farther along, at **no. 9 quai d'Anjou,** stands the house where Honoré Daumier, the painter, sculptor, and lithographer, lived between 1846 and 1863. Here he produced hundreds of lithographs satirizing the bourgeoisie and attacking government corruption. His caricature of Louis-Philippe landed him in jail for 6 months.

RIGHT BANK HIGHLIGHTS

LES HALLES   In the 19th century, Zola called it "the underbelly of Paris." For 8 centuries, **Les Halles** (Métro: Les Halles; RER: Châtelet–Les Halles) was the major wholesale fruit, meat, and vegetable market of the city. The smock-clad vendors, the carcasses of beef, the baskets of the best fresh vegetables in the world—all belong to the past. Today, the action has moved to a steel-and-glass edifice at Rungis, a suburb near Orly Airport. The original market, Baltard's old zinc-roofed Second Empire "iron umbrellas," has been torn down.

Replacing these so-called umbrellas is **Les Forum des Halles,** which opened in 1979. This large complex, much of it underground, contains dozens of shops, plus several restaurants and movie theaters. Many of these shops are unattractive, but others contain a wide display of merchandise that has made the complex popular with both residents and visitors alike.

For many tourists a night on the town still ends in the wee hours with a bowl of onion soup at Les Halles, usually at **Au Pied de Cochon** (The Pig's Foot) or at **Au Chien Qui Fume** (The Smoking Dog). One of the most classic scenes of Paris was elegantly dressed Parisians (many fresh from Maxim's) standing at a bar drinking cognac with blood-smeared butchers. Some writers have suggested that one Gérard de Nerval introduced the custom of frequenting Les Halles at such an unearthly hour. (De Nerval was a 19th-century poet whose life was considered "irregular." He hanged himself in 1855.)

A newspaper correspondent described today's scene this way: "Les Halles is trying to stay alive as one of the few places in Paris where one can eat at any hour of the night."

LEFT BANK HIGHLIGHTS

ST-GERMAIN-DES-PRÉS   This neighborhood in the 6th arrondissement (Métro: St-Germain-des-Prés) was the postwar home of existentialism, associated with Jean-Paul Sartre, Simone de Beauvoir, Albert Camus, and an intellectual, bohemian crowd that gathered at the **Café de Flore,** the **Brasserie Lipp,** and **Les Deux-Magots.** Among them, the black-clad poet and singer Juliette Greco was known as *la muse de St-Germain-des-Prés,* and to Sartre she was the woman who had "millions of poems in her throat." Her long hair, black slacks, black sweater, and black sandals launched a fashion trend adopted by young women from Paris to California.

In the 1950s, new names appeared, like Françoise Sagan, Gore Vidal, and James Baldwin, but by the 1960s the tourists were just as firmly entrenched. Today, St-Germain-des-Prés retains a bohemian and intellectually stimulating street life, full of many interesting bookshops, art galleries, cave (basement) nightclubs, and bistros and coffeehouses, as well as two historic churches.

Just a short walk from the Delacroix museum, **rue Visconti** was designed for pushcarts and is worth visiting today. At **no. 17** is the house where Balzac established his printing press in 1825. (The venture ended in bankruptcy, forcing the author back to his writing desk.) In the 17th century, the French dramatist Jean-Baptiste Racine lived across the street. Such celebrated actresses as Champmeslé and Clairon also lived here.

MONTPARNASSE   For the "lost generation," life centered around the literary cafes of Montparnasse, at the border of the 6th and 14th arrondissements (Métro: Montparnasse-Bienvenue). Hangouts such as the **Dôme,** the **Coupole,** the **Rotonde,** and the **Sélect** became legendary, as artists—especially American expatriates—turned their backs on Montmartre, dismissing it as too touristy.

Picasso, Modigliani, and Man Ray came this way, and Hemingway was also a popular figure. So was Fitzgerald when he was poor (when he wasn't, you'd find him at the Ritz). William Faulkner, Archibald MacLeish, Isadora Duncan, Miró, James Joyce, Ford Madox Ford, even Trotsky—all spent time here.

The most notable exception was Gertrude Stein, who never frequented the cafes. To see her, you would have to wait for an invitation to her salon at **27 rue de Fleurus.** She bestowed this favor on Sherwood Anderson, Elliot Paul, Ezra Pound, and, for a time, Hemingway. When Pound launched himself into a beloved chair and broke it, he incurred Stein's wrath, and Hemingway decided there wasn't "much future in men being friends with great women."

When not receiving guests, Stein was busy buying the paintings of Cézanne, Renoir, Matisse, and Picasso. One writer said that her salon was engaged in an international conspiracy to promote modern art.

The grand salon of Natalie Barney is still at **20 rue Jacob.** This American expatriate and writer from Ohio conducted a salon here every Friday that attracted the literati of her day, including Djuna Barnes, Colette, Janet Flanner, Gertrude Stein, William Carlos Williams, and Sylvia Beach. The salon met on and off for half a century, interrupted only by two world wars. Near the place Furstenburg, Barney's former residence is landmarked but not open to the public. In the garden you can see a small Doric temple bearing the inscription *A l'Amitié,* "to friendship."

Aside from the literary legends, one of the most notable characters of the sector was Kiki de Montparnasse. Actually she was an artist's model and prostitute named Alice Prin. She sang at **Le Jockey** at 127 boulevard du Montparnasse, which no longer exists, although Hemingway called it the best nightclub "that ever was." In her black hose and garters, she captivated dozens of men, among them Frederick Kohner, who went so far as to entitle his memoirs *Kiki of Montparnasse.* Kiki would later write her own memoirs, with an introduction by Hemingway. Papa called her "a Queen," noting that that was "very different from being a lady."

Towering over the entire arrondissement is the **Tour Montparnasse** (☎ **01-45-38-52-56**), rising 688 feet above the Paris skyline. Like the Eiffel Tower, it's an instantly recognizable landmark. Completed in 1973, it was immediately denounced by some critics as "bringing Manhattan to Paris." The city soon passed an ordinance outlawing any further structures of this size in the heart of Paris. Today, the tower houses a mammoth underground shopping mall, as well as much of the infrastructure for the Gare de Montparnasse railway station, one of the city's biggest. You can ride an elevator up to the 56th floor, then climb three flights of stairs to the rooftop terrace. From the top, your view will include virtually every important monument of Paris, including Sacré-Coeur, Notre-Dame, and the hypermodern La Défense district along Paris's northwestern fringe. A bar and restaurant are on the 56th floor. Admission to the tower costs 46 F ($7.80) for adults, 38 F ($6.45) for seniors, 35 F ($5.95) for students, and 30 F ($5.10) for children

5 to 14 (children 4 and under enter free). From April through September, it's open daily from 9:30am to 11:30pm; October through March, Monday to Friday from 9:30am to 10:30pm. Metro: Montparnasse-Bienvenue.

The life of Montparnasse still centers around its cafes and exotic nightclubs, many only a shadow of what they used to be. Its heart is at the crossroads of the boulevard Raspail and the boulevard du Montparnasse, one of the settings of *The Sun Also Rises*. Hemingway wrote that "the boulevard Raspail always made dull riding." Rodin's controversial statue of Balzac swathed in a large cape stands guard over the prostitutes who cluster around the pedestal. Balzac seems to be the only one in Montparnasse who doesn't feel the weight of time.

6 A Walking Tour: The Grand Promenade

Start: Arc de Triomphe.
Finish: Place Vendôme.
Time: 3 leisurely hours; the distance is 2 miles.
Best Time: Sunday morning.
Worst Time: Rush hour.

This is a lengthy walking tour, but it's the most popular walk in Paris. Start at the:

1. **Arc de Triomphe** (Métro: Charles-de-Gaulle–Etoile). To reach it, don't try to cross the square, the busiest traffic hub in Paris. Take the underground passage and live a little longer. For more on the Arc, turn to "The Top Attractions," in section 1.
Stand here a moment (somewhere safe from traffic) and gaze down the long:

2. **Champs-Elysées,** which has been called "the highway of French grandeur." Louis XIV ordered construction of the 1.1-mile avenue in 1667. Since then, it has witnessed some of the greatest moments in French history and some of the worst, such as when Hitler's army paraded down the street in 1940.

Stroll along the avenue. Along one stretch, it's a chestnut-lined park; on the other, a commercial avenue of sidewalk cafés, automobile showrooms, airline offices, cinemas, lingerie stores, and hamburger joints. Even if the avenue has lost some of its turn-of-the-century elegance, it still hums like a hive.

🌣 **TAKE A BREAK**   Make it **Fouquet's,** 99 av. des Champs-Elysées (☎ 01-47-23-70-60). Founded in 1901 and still serving

A Walking Tour: The Grand Promenade

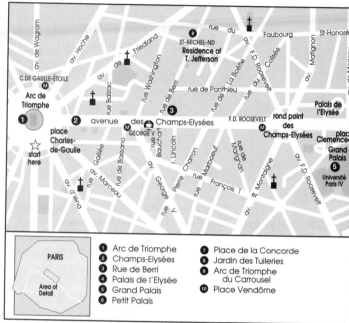

❶ Arc de Triomphe	❼ Place de la Concorde
❷ Champs-Elysées	❽ Jardin des Tuileries
❸ Rue de Berri	❾ Arc de Triomphe
❹ Palais de l'Elysée	du Carrousel
❺ Grand Palais	❿ Place Vendôme
❻ Petit Palais	

coffee, wine, and food, this is an institution. In summer, you can enjoy the flowers, and in winter the large glass windows will shelter you from the winds. Take plenty of money.

Head down the avenue toward place de la Concorde, staying on the left-hand side. When you reach:

3. Rue de Berri, turn left to no. 20, site of Thomas Jefferson's residence from 1785 to 1789, when he was fledgling America's Minister to France. In its place today is a large apartment building. Back on the avenue again, continue to the Rond-Pont des Champs-Elysées, the dividing point between the avenue's park and commercial sections. Close by is a philatelist's delight, the best-known open-air stamp market in Europe, held Thursday and Sunday.

Continue down the avenue until you reach avenue Winston-Churchill on your right (from here there's a good panorama looking toward the Invalides). Ducking traffic and pausing for a view, cross back over to the other side of the Champs and turn down the avenue de Marigny. On your right will be the:

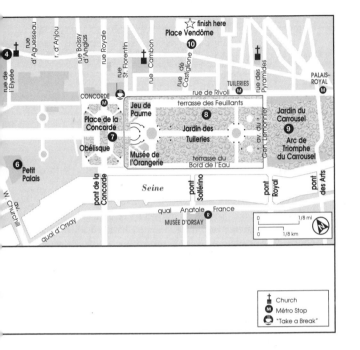

4. **Palais de l'Elysée,** France's presidential palace, whose main entrance is along fashionable Faubourg St-Honoré. Now occupied by the president of France, it cannot be visited without an invitation.

   Now backtrack to the meeting of the Champs-Elysée and avenue Winston-Churchill, where you'll find the:

5. **Grand Palais,** which was constructed for the World Exhibition of 1900. When it's restored, the Grand Palais will be devoted to special exhibitions concerning Paris at the millennium. Also constructed for the 1900 World Exhibition was the:

6. **Petit Palais** (☎ 01-42-65-12-73), which contains a hodgepodge of works of art belonging to the city of Paris.

   Continue along the Champs-Elysées until you come to the landmark:

7. **Place de la Concorde,** an octagonal traffic hub built in 1757 to honor Louis XV. Floodlit at night, it is dominated nowadays by an Egyptian obelisk from Luxor, the oldest man-made object in Paris. It was carved circa 1200 B.C. and spirited out of French-dominated Egypt in 1829.

In the Reign of Terror, the dreaded guillotine was erected on this spot, where it claimed the lives of thousands, everybody from Louis XVI, who died bravely, to Madame du Barry, who went screaming and kicking all the way. Marie Antoinette, Robespierre, Danton, Madame Roland, and Charlotte Corday were executed here in front of leering crowds. (You can still lose your life on the place de la Concorde if you chance the traffic and cross over.)

For a spectacular sight, look down the Champs-Elysées, where the Marly horses frame the view.

☕ **TAKE A BREAK** The **Bar of the Hôtel de Crillon,** 10 place de la Concorde (☎ **01-44-71-15-00**), is one of the best places in the world to have a drink. Fashion designer Sonia Rykiel and sculptor "César" have given it new luster, and the drinks, the setting, the ambience, and the atmosphere have remained undiminished over the decades.

From place de la Concorde, you can enter the:

8. **Jardin des Tuileries** (☎ **01-40-20-90-43**), as much a part of Paris as the Seine. These statue-studded gardens were designed by Le Nôtre, the gardener to Louis XIV. About 100 years before that, a palace was built here by Catherine de Médicis. Connected to the Louvre, it was occupied by Louis XVI after he left Versailles; after the Revolution, Napoléon I called it home. Twice attacked by the people of Paris, it was burnt to the ground in 1871 and never rebuilt. But the gardens remain, the trees arranged geometrically along arrow-straight paths. Bubbling fountains soften the sense of order and formality.

You'll find half of Paris in the Tuileries on a warm spring day, listening to the chirping birds and watching the daffodils and red tulips bloom. Fountains gurgle, and parents roll carriages over the grounds where 18th-century revolutionaries killed the king's Swiss guards.

At the other end of the Tuileries, pause at the:

9. **Arc de Triomphe du Carrousel,** at the Cour du Carrousel. Pierced with three walkways and supported by marble columns, the monument celebrates Napoléon and the Grand Armée's victory at Austerlitz on December 5, 1805. Surmounting the arch are statuary, a chariot, and four bronze horses. "Paris needs more monuments," Napoléon once proclaimed. He got his wish.

At this point, take avenue du Gal. Lemonnier to rue de Rivoli, away from the Seine. Take a left, then walk to the rue de

Castiglione and turn right. You've reached the last stop on our tour, the:

10. **Place Vendôme.** Always aristocratic, sometimes royal, place Vendôme enjoyed its golden age in the heyday of the Second Empire. It has attracted such tenants as Chopin, who lived at no. 12 until his death in 1849. Louis Napoléon lived here, wooing his future empress, Eugénie de Montijo, at the Hôtel du Rhin. In its halcyon days, Strauss waltzes echoed across the plaza, before they were replaced by cannon fire.

To get to the nearest Métro stop, walk through the other end of Place Vendôme on rue de la Paix until you reach rue Daunou and the Opéra station.

7   A Park & a Celebrity Cemetery

JARDIN DU LUXEMBOURG

Hemingway told a friend that these gardens (Métro: Odéon, RER: Luxembourg) "kept us from starvation." He related that in his poverty-stricken days in Paris, he wheeled a baby carriage (the vehicle was considered luxurious) and child through the gardens because it was known "for the classiness of its pigeons." When the gendarme went across the street for a glass of wine, the writer would eye his victim, preferably a plump one, then lure him with corn and "snatch him, wring his neck," and hide him under Bumby's blanket. "We got a little tired of pigeon that year," he confessed, "but they filled many a void."

Before it became a feeding ground for famished artists of the 1920s, Luxembourg knew greater days. Marie de Médicis, the much-neglected wife and later widow of the roving Henri IV, ordered a palace built on the site in 1612. The queen didn't get to enjoy the palace for very long, as she was forced into exile by her son, Louis XIII, after it was discovered that she was plotting to overthrow him.

But you don't come to the Luxembourg to visit the palace—not really. The gardens are the attraction. For the most part, they are in the classic French tradition: well groomed and formally laid out, the trees planted in patterns. Come here to soak in the atmosphere. It's a good place for kids: You can sail a toy boat, ride a pony, or attend an occasional grand guignol puppet show. Or even better, you can play boules with a group of elderly men who aren't ashamed to wear black berets and have Gauloises dangling from the corner of their mouths.

✪ CIMETIÈRE DU PÈRE-LACHAISE

Père-Lachaise Cemetery. 16 rue du Repos, 20e. ☎ **01-43-70-70-33.** Free admission. Mon–Fri 8am–6pm, Sat 8:30am–6pm, Sun 9am–6pm; closes at 5:30pm from early Nov to early Mar. Métro: Père-Lachaise.

The cemeteries of Paris are often viewed by sightseers as being somewhat like parks, suitable places for strolling and for contemplating the graves of celebrities from the past. When it comes to name-dropping, Père-Lachaise knows no peer; it's been called the "grandest address in Paris." Everybody from Sarah Bernhardt to Oscar Wilde was buried here. So were Balzac, Delacroix, and Bizet. The body of Colette was taken here in 1954, and in time the little sparrow, Piaf, would follow. The lover of George Sand, the poet Alfred de Musset, was buried here under a weeping willow. Napoléon's marshals, Ney and Masséna, lie here, as do Chopin and Molière. Marcel Proust's black tombstone rarely lacks a tiny bunch of violets. Colette's black granite slab always sports flowers, and legend has it that cats replenish the red roses.

Some tombs are sentimental favorites: Lovetorn graffiti radiates a half-mile from the tomb of singer Jim Morrison. The great dancer Isadora Duncan came to rest in the columbarium where bodies have been cremated and "filed" away. If you search hard enough, you can find the tombs of that star-crossed pair Abélard and Héloïse, the ill-fated lovers of the 12th century. Other famous lovers also rest here: A stone is marked "Alice B. Toklas" on one side, "Gertrude Stein" on the other. One grave site that attracted attention recently was that of entertainer Yves Montand. His corpse was exhumed in the middle of the night for DNA testing in a paternity lawsuit.

Spreading over more than 110 acres, Père-Lachaise was acquired by the city of Paris in 1804. Nineteenth-century sculpture abounds, each family trying to outdo the other in ornamentation and cherubic ostentation. Frenchmen who died in the Resistance or in Nazi concentration camps are also honored by monuments here. Some French Socialists still pay tribute at the **Mur des Fédérés,** the anonymous grave site of the Communards who were executed in the cemetery on May 28, 1871. When these last-ditch fighters of the Paris Commune, the world's first anarchist republic, made their final desperate stand against the troops of the French government, they were overwhelmed, lined up against the wall, and shot in groups. A handful survived and lived hidden in the cemetery for years like wild animals, venturing into Paris at night to forage for food.

A free map of Père-Lachaise is available at the newsstand across from the main entrance.

8   Shopping

Shopping is a favorite pastime of the Parisians; some would even say it reflects the city's soul. The City of Light is one of the rare places in the world where you don't have to go anywhere to shop—shopping surrounds you instead. Each walk you take immerses you in uniquely French styles. The windows, stores, and people (even their dogs) brim with energy, creativity, and a sense of visual expression found in few other cities.

You don't have to buy anything to appreciate shopping in Paris—just soak up the art form the French have made of rampant consumerism. Peer in the *vitrines* (display windows), absorb cutting-edge ideas, witness new trends, and take home with you a whole new education in style.

When you walk into a French store, it's traditional to greet the owner or sales clerk with a direct address, not a fey smile or even a weak bonjour. Only "Bonjour, madame" (or monsieur) will do.

BEST BUYS

PERFUMES, MAKEUP & BEAUTY TREATMENTS   A flat discount of 20% to 30% makes these items a great buy; qualify for a VAT refund (see below) and you'll save 40% to 45% off the Paris retail price, allowing you to bring home goods at half the U.S. price. Duty-free shops abound in Paris and are always less expensive than the ones at the airport.

For bargain cosmetics, try out French dime store and drugstore brands such as **Bourjois** (made in the Chanel factories), **Lierac,** and **Galenic. Vichy,** famous for its water, has a complete skin care and makeup line. The newest retail trend in Paris is the *parapharmacie,* a type of discount drugstore loaded with inexpensive brands, health cures, French beauty regimes, and diet plans. These usually offer a 20% discount.

FOODSTUFF   Nothing makes a better souvenir than a product of France brought home to savor later. Supermarkets are located in prime tourist neighborhoods; stock up on coffee, designer chocolates, mustards (try the Maille brand), and for the kids, perhaps American products in French packages.

FUN FASHION　Sure you can spend on couture or *prêt-à-porter,* but French teens and trendsetters have their own stores where the latest looks are affordable. Even the dime stores in Paris sell designer copies and hotshot styles.

In the stalls in front of the department stores on bd. Haussmann, you'll find some of the latest fashion accessories, guaranteed for a week's worth of small talk once you get home.

VALUE-ADDED TAX (VAT) REFUNDS

French tax is now a hefty 20.6%, but you can get most of that back if you spend 2,000 F ($340) or more in any store that participates in the VAT refund program. (Most stores participate.)

Once you meet your required minimum purchase amount, you qualify for a tax refund. The amount of the refund varies with the way the refund is handled and the fee some stores charge you for processing it. So the refund at a department store may be 13%, whereas at a small shop it will be 15% or even 18%.

You will receive **VAT refund papers** in the shop; some stores, like Hermès, have their own; others provide a government form. Fill in the forms before you arrive at the airport, and expect to stand in line at the Customs desk for as long as half an hour. You are required by law to show the goods at the airport, so have them on you or visit the Customs office before you check your luggage. Once the papers have been mailed to the authorities, a credit will appear, often months later, on your credit-card bill.

All refunds are processed at the final point of departure from the **European Union (EU),** so if you are going to another EU country, don't apply for the refund in France.

Be sure to mark the paperwork to request that your refund be applied to your credit card so you aren't stuck with a check in francs that is hard to cash. This also ensures the best rate of exchange. In some airports you are offered the opportunity to get your refund back in cash, which is tempting. But if you accept cash in any currency other than francs, you will be losing money on the conversion rate. You'll do far better with a credit-card conversion.

DUTY-FREE BOUTIQUES

The advantage of duty-free shops is that you never have to pay the VAT tax, so you avoid the red tape of getting a refund. Both airports have shopping galore, but prices are often equal or better in the city. You'll find lots of duty-free shops on the avenues that branch out from the Opéra Garnier, in the 1e and 2e arrondissements. **Charles**

de Gaulle Airport has a virtual shopping mall with crystal, cutlery, chocolates, luggage, wine, whisky, pipes and lighters, lingerie, silk scarves, perfume, knitwear, jewelry, cameras and equipment, cheeses, and even antiques.

BUSINESS HOURS

Shops are *usually* open Monday through Saturday from 10am to 7pm, but the hours vary greatly and Monday mornings in Paris do not run at full throttle. Small shops sometimes close for a 2-hour lunch break and may not even open until after lunch on Monday. Thursday is the best day for late-night shopping, with stores open until 9 or 10pm.

Sunday shopping is currently limited to tourist areas and flea markets, although there is growing demand for full-scale Sunday hours, as in the United States and the United Kingdom. The big department stores are now open on the five Sundays before Christmas. **Carrousel du Louvre,** a mall adjacent to the Louvre, is open and hopping on Sunday, but closed on Monday. The tourist shops that line the rue Rivoli across from the Louvre are all open on Sunday, as are the antiques villages, assorted flea markets, and specialty events. There are several good food markets in the streets on Sunday. **Virgin Megastore** on the Champs-Elysées, a big teen hangout, pays a fine to stay open on Sunday.

SHIPPING IT HOME

Shipping charges will possibly double your cost on goods and you may have to pay duties on the items (see above). The good news: The VAT refund is automatically applied to all shipped items; no need to worry about the 2,000 F ($340) minimum. Some stores do have a $100 minimum for shipping, though. You can also walk into any post office and mail home a jiffy bag or small box of goodies. French do-it-yourself boxes cannot be reopened once closed, so pack carefully. The clerk at the post office will help you assemble the box (it's tricky), seal it, and send it off.

GREAT SHOPPING NEIGHBORHOODS

1st & 8th Arrondissements These two *quartiers* adjoin each other (invisibly) and form the heart of Paris's best Right Bank shopping strip—together they're one big hunting ground. This area includes the famed **rue du Faubourg-St-Honoré,** where the big designer houses are, and the **Champs-Elysées,** where the mass market and teen scene are hot. At one end of the 1er is the **Palais-Royal,** one of the best shopping secrets in Paris, where an arcade of boutiques flanks each side of the garden of the former palace.

The 1er also contains the **avenue Montaigne,** the most glamorous shopping street in Paris, boasting 2 blocks of the fanciest shops in the world, where you simply float from big name to big name and in a few hours can see everything from Louis Vuitton to Ines de la Fressange, the model turned retailer. Avenue Montaigne is also the address of **Joseph,** a British design firm, and **Porthault,** makers of the fanciest sheets in the world.

2nd Arrondissement Right behind the Palais Royal is the **Garment District** (Sentier), as well as a few very sophisticated shopping secrets such as **place des Victoires.** This area also hosts a few old-fashioned passageways, alleys filled with tiny stores, such as **Galerie Vivienne,** on rue Vivienne.

3rd & 4th Arrondissements The border between these two arrondissements gets fuzzy, especially around the **place des Vosges,** center stage of the Marais. No matter. The districts offer several dramatically different shopping experiences.

On the surface, the shopping includes the "real people stretch" (where all the nonmillionaires shop) of the **rue Rivoli** and **rue St-Antoine,** featuring everything from The Gap and a branch of Marks and Spencer, to local discount stores and mass merchants. Two "real people" department stores are in this area: **Samaritaine** and **BHV;** there's also **Les Halles** and the **Beaubourg** neighborhood, which is anchored by the Centre Georges Pompidou.

Meanwhile, hidden away in the Marais is a medieval warren of tiny twisting streets chockablock with cutting-edge designers and up-to-the-minute fashions and trends. Start by walking around the place des Vosges for art galleries, designer shops, and special little finds, then dive in and lose yourself in the area leading to the Picasso Museum.

Finally, the 4e is also the home of the **Bastille,** an up-and-coming area for artists and galleries where the newest entry on the retail scene, **Viaduc des Arts** (which actually stretches into the 12e), is situated. It's a collection of about 30 stores occupying a series of narrow valuted niches under what used to be railroad tracks. They run parallel to the avenue Daumesnil, centered around the boulevard Diderot.

6th & 7th Arrondissements Whereas the 6e is one of the most famous shopping districts in Paris—it is the soul of the Left Bank—a lot of the really good stuff is hidden in the zone that turns into the wealthy residential district of the seventh. **Rue du Bac,** stretching from the 6e to the 7e in a few blocks, stands for all that wealth and glamor can buy.

8th Arrondissement   See above, "1st & 8th Arrondissements."

9th Arrondissement   To add to the fun of shopping the Right Bank, the 9e sneaks in behind the 1er, so if you choose not to walk toward the Champs-Elysées and the 8e, you can instead head to the city's big department stores, all built in a row along the **boulevard Haussmann** in the 9e Department stores here include not only the two big French icons, **Au Printemps** and **Galeries Lafayette,** but a large branch of Britain's **Marks and Spencer** and a branch of the Dutch answer to K-mart, the low-priced **C&A.**

9 Especially for Kids

Boasting playgrounds with tiny merry-go-rounds and gondola-style swings, the large parks of Paris are always a treat for kids.

If you're staying on the Right Bank, take the children for a stroll through the **Tuileries** (see "A Walking Tour: The Grand Promenade" in section 6), where there are donkey rides, ice-cream stands, and a marionette show; at the circular pond, you can rent a toy sailboat. On the Left Bank, similar delights exist in the **Jardin du Luxembourg** (see "A Park & a Celebrity Cemetery," in section 7). After a visit to the Eiffel Tower, you can take the kids for a donkey ride in the nearby gardens of the **Champ-de-Mars.**

A great Paris tradition, **puppet shows** are worth seeing for their enthusiastic, colorful productions—they're a genuine French child's experience. At the Jardin du Luxembourg, puppets reenact sinister plots set in Gothic castles and Oriental palaces; many young critics say the best puppet shows are held in the Champ-de-Mars.

On Sunday afternoon, French families head up to the **Butte Montmartre** to bask in the fiesta atmosphere. You can join in the fun: Take the Métro to Anvers and walk to the Funiculaire de Montmartre (the silver cable car that carries you up to Sacré-Coeur). Once up top, follow the crowds to place du Tertre, where a Sergeant Pepper–style band will usually be blasting off-key and you can have the kids' pictures sketched by local artists. You can take in the views of Paris from the various vantage points and treat your children to ice cream.

MUSEUMS

Cité des Sciences et de l'Industrie. La Villette, 30 av. Corentine-Cariou, 19e. ☎ **01-40-05-70-48.** Cité Pass (entrance to all exhibits) 50 F ($8.50) adults, free to children 7 and under; Géode 25 F ($4.25). Tues–Sun 10am–6pm. Métro: Porte de la Villette.

This place is so vast, with so many exhibits, that a single visit gives only an idea of the scope of the Cité. Busts of Plato, Hippocrates, and a double-faced Janus gaze silently at a tube-filled, space-age riot of high-tech girders, glass, and lights—something like the way you might imagine the inside of an atomic generator or a futuristic airplane hangar. The sheer dimensions of the place pose a challenge to the curators of its constantly changing exhibits. Some exhibits are couched in Gallic humor—imagine using the comic-strip adventures of a jungle explorer to explain seismographic activity. **Explora,** a permanent exhibit, occupies the three upper levels of the building, examining four themes: the universe, life, matter, and communication.

The Cité also has a multimedia library, a planetarium, and an "inventorium" for children. The silver-skinned **geodesic dome** called the *Géode*—a 112-foot-high sphere with a 370-seat theater—projects the closest thing to a 3-D cinema in Europe.

The Cité is in **Parc de la Villette,** the city's largest park, with 136 acres of greenery—twice the size of the Tuileries. Here you'll find a belvedere, a video workshop for children, and information about exhibitions and events, along with a cafe and restaurant.

Musée Grévin. 10 bd. Montmartre, 9e. ☎ **01-47-70-85-05.** Admission 55 F ($9.35) adults, 36 F ($6.10) children 14 and under. Apr–Aug daily 1–7pm; Sept–Mar daily 1–6:30pm; school holidays daily 10am–7pm. Ticket office closes 1 hour before museum. Métro: rue Montmartre.

Grévin is the number-one waxworks of Paris. Comparisons to Madame Tussaud's of London are almost irresistible. It isn't all blood and gore, and doesn't shock as much as Tussaud's might. It presents a panorama of French history in a series of tableaux.

Depicted are the consecration of Charles VII in 1429 in the Cathedral of Reims (Joan of Arc, dressed in armor and carrying her standard, stands behind the king); Marguerite de Valois, first wife of Henri IV, meeting on a secret stairway with La Molle, who was soon to be decapitated; Catherine de Médicis with the Florentine alchemist Ruggieri; Louis XV and Mozart at the home of the marquise de Pompadour; and Napoléon on a rock at St. Helena, reviewing his victories and defeats.

There are also displays of contemporary sports and political figures, as well as 50 of the world's best-loved film stars. Two shows are staged frequently throughout the day. The first, called the **Palais des Mirages,** starts off as a sort of Temple of Brahma, and through magically distorting mirrors changes into an enchanted forest, then a fete at the Alhambra at Granada. A magician is the star of the second show, **Le Cabinet Fantastique;** he entertains children of all ages.

Musée National d'Histoire Naturelle (Museum of Natural History). 57 rue Cuvier, 5e. ☎ **01-40-79-30-00.** Admission 30 F ($5.10) adults, 20 F ($3.40) children 4–16, free for children 3 and under. Apr–Sept Wed–Mon 10am–6pm; off-season Wed–Mon 10am–5pm. Métro: Jussieu or Gare d'Austerlitz.

This museum in the Jardin des Plantes has a wide range of science and nature exhibits that draw the children of Paris. It was founded in 1635 as a scientific research center by Guy de la Brosse, physician to Louis XIII. The museum's Grande Gallery of Evolution recently received a $90 million restoration. At the entrance, an 85-foot-long skeleton of a whale greets visitors. One display containing the skeletons of dinosaurs and mastodons is dedicated to endangered and vanished species. The museum also houses galleries that specialize in the fields of paleontology, anatomy, mineralogy, and botany. Within the museum's grounds are tropical hothouses containing thousands of species of unusual plant life and a menagerie with small animal life in simulated natural habitats.

A ZOO

Parc Zoologique de Paris. Bois de Vincennes, 53 av. de St-Maurice, 12e. ☎ **01-44-75-20-00.** Admission 40 F ($6.80) adults; 30 F ($5.10) children 4–15, students 16–25, and over 60; free for chidren 3 and under. Daily 9am–6pm (until 5:30pm Dec–Mar). Métro: Porte Dorée or Château de Vincennes.

There's a modest zoo in the **Jardin des Plantes,** but without a doubt, the best zoo this city has to offer is in the Bois de Vincennes on the southeastern outskirts of Paris, quickly reachable by Métro. Many of this modern zoo's animals live in settings similar to their natural habitat, hemmed in by rock barriers, not bars or cages. Here you'll never see an animal in a cage too small for it. The lion has an entire veldt to himself, and you can lock eyes comfortably across a deep protective moat. On a cement mountain reminiscent of Disneyland's Matterhorn, exotic breeds of mountain goats and sheep leap from ledge to ledge or pose gracefully for hours watching the penguins in their pools at the mountain's foot. The animals seem happy and are playful. Keep well back from the bear pools or you might get wet.

10 Paris Underground

Les Catacombs. 1 place Denfert-Rochereau, 14e. ☎ **01-43-22-47-63.**
Admission 27 F ($4.60) adults, 19 F ($3.25) ages 7–25 and students, free for
children 6 and under. Tues–Fri 2–4pm, Sat–Sun 9–11am and 2–4pm. Métro:
Denfert-Rochereau.

Every year an estimated 50,000 tourists explore some 1,000 yards
of tunnel in these dank Catacombs to look at six million ghoulishly
arranged skull-and-crossbones skeletons. First opened to the public
in 1810, this "empire of the dead" is now illuminated with overhead
electric lights over its entire length.

In the Middle Ages, the Catacombs were quarries, but by the end
of the 18th century, overcrowded Parisian cemeteries were becoming a menace to the public health. City officials decided to use the
Catacombs as a burial ground, and the bones of several million persons were transferred here. In 1830, the prefect of Paris closed the
Catacombs to the viewing public, considering them obscene and
indecent. He maintained that he could not understand the morbid
curiosity of civilized people who wanted to gaze upon the bones of
the dead. In World War II, the Catacombs were the headquarters
of the French Resistance.

Les Egouts (The Sewers of Paris). Pont de l'Alma, 7e. ☎ **01-53-68-
27-81.** Admission 25 F ($4.25) adults, 20 F ($3.40) students and seniors, 15 F
($2.55) children 5–12, free for children under 5. May–Oct Sat–Wed 11am–5pm;
Nov–Apr Sat–Wed 11am–4pm. Closed 3 weeks in Jan for maintenance. Métro:
Alma-Marceau. RER: Pont de l'Alma.

Some sociologists assert that the sophistication of a society can be
judged by the way it disposes of waste. If that's the case, Paris re-
ceives good marks for its mostly invisible network of sewers. Victor
Hugo is credited with making these sewers famous in *Les Misérables.*

Today, the network of sewers is 1,300 miles long. Within its cavi-
ties, it contains freshwater mains, compressed air pipes, telephone
cables, and pneumatic tubes. Every day, 1.2 million cubic meters of
wastewater are collected and processed by a plant in the Parisian suburb of Achères. One of the largest in Europe, it's capable of treat-
ing more than two million cubic meters of sewage per day.

The *égouts* of the city are constructed around four principal
tunnels, one 18 feet wide and 15 feet high. As Hugo observed, it's
like an underground city, with the street names clearly labeled.
Further, each branch pipe bears the number of the building
to which it is connected. These underground passages are truly
mammoth.

Tours of the sewers begin at Pont de l'Alma on the Left Bank. A stairway here leads into the bowels of the city. However, you often have to wait in line as much as half an hour. Visiting times might change during bad weather, as a storm can make the sewers dangerous. The tour consists of a film on sewer history, a small museum visit, and then a short trip through the maze. Be warned that the smell is pretty bad, especially in the summer.

11 Organized Tours

BY BUS Get-acquainted tours of Paris are offered by **Cityrama,** 147-149 rue Saint-Honoré, 1er (☎ **01-44-55-61-00;** Métro: Palais-Royal or Musée-du-Louvre). The company operates a fleet of double-decker red-and-yellow buses, each with oversized windows and a series of multilingual recorded commentaries that recite an overview of Paris's history and monuments. The most popular is a 2-hour tour that departs from the Place des Pyramides, adjacent to the rue de Rivoli and the Tuileries Gardens, every day at 9:30am, 10:30am, 1:30pm, and 2:30pm. There are additional tours every Saturday and Sunday at 11:30am, and between March and October at 3:30 and 4:30pm daily. The price is 150 F ($25.50) per person. Other, more detailed tours are also available. They include a 3¹/₂-hour morning tour (Monday, Wednesday, Friday, and Saturday) to the interiors of Notre-Dame and the Louvre, priced at 295 F ($50.15) per person. There are 3¹/₂-hour morning tours to Versailles at 320 F ($54.40) per person and 3¹/₂-hour afternoon tours to Chartres at 275 F ($46.75) per person. You can buy tickets for both Versailles and Chartres for 500 F ($85). And if you're interested in a night tour of Paris to see how the City of Light got its name, tours depart every evening at 10pm in summer and at 7pm in winter, for 150 F ($25.50) per person.

CRUISES ON THE SEINE A boat tour on the Seine provides sweeping vistas of the riverbanks and some of the best views of Notre-Dame. Many of the boats have open sundecks, bars, and restaurants. **Bateau-Mouche** cruises (☎ **01-42-25-96-10** for reservations, 01-40-76-99-99 for schedules; Métro: Alma-Marceau) depart from the Right Bank of the Seine, next to the Pont de l'Alma, and last about 75 minutes each. Tours leave every day at 20- to 30-minute intervals between May and October, beginning at 10am and ending at 11:30pm. Between November and April, there are at least nine departures every day between 11am and 9pm, with a schedule that changes frequently according to demand and the weather. Fares cost 40 F ($6.80) for adults and 20 F ($3.40) for children 5 to 15. Three-hour **dinner cruises** depart every evening at 8:30pm and cost between 500 F and 700 F ($85 and $119), depending on which of the set-price menus you order. Jackets and ties are required for men.

Some visitors prefer longer excursions along the Seine and its network of canals. The **Seine et le Canal Saint Martin** tour, offered by **Paris Canal, S.A.R.L.** (☎ 01-42-40-96-97), requires advance reservations for 3-hour tours that begin at 9:30am at the quays in front of the Musée d'Orsay (Métro: Solférino) and at 2:30pm in front of the Cité des Sciences et de l'Industrie at Parc de la Villette (Métro: Porte de la Villette). Excursions negotiate the waterways and canals of Paris, including the Seine, an underground tunnel below the place de la Bastille, and the Canal St-Martin. The cost is 100 F ($17) for adults, and free for children under 4. With the exception of excursions on Sunday and holidays, prices are usually reduced to 75 F ($12.75) for passengers ages 12 to 25 and over 60, and to 55 F ($9.35) for children 4 to 11. Tours are offered twice daily from mid-March to mid-November. The rest of the year, tours are offerd only on Sunday.

12 A Side Trip to Versailles

For centuries, the name of this Parisian suburb resounded through the consciousness of every aristocratic family in Europe. The palace at Versailles outdazzled every other kingly residence in Europe; it was a horrendously expensive scandal and a symbol to later generations of a regime obsessed with prestige above all else.

Back in the *grand* (17th) *siécle,* all you needed to enter was a sword, a hat, and a bribe for the guard at the gate. Providing you didn't have smallpox, you'd be admitted to the precincts of the château, to stroll through salon after glittering salon—to watch the Sun King at his banqueting table, to dance or flirt or even do something far more personal. Louis XIV had all the privacy of a bus station.

ESSENTIALS

GETTING THERE   To get to Versailles, 13 miles southwest of Paris, catch the RER line C at the Gare d'Austerlitz, St-Michel, Musée d'Orsay, Invalides, Ponte-de-l'Alma, Champ-de-Mars, or Javel station and take it to the Versailles Rive Gauche station, from which there's a shuttle bus to the château. The 35 F ($5.95) trip takes about 35 to 40 minutes; Eurailpass holders travel free on the train, but pay 20 F ($3.40) for a ride on the shuttle bus.

Regular SNCF trains also make the run from central Paris to Versailles: One train departs from the Gare St-Lazare for the Versailles Rive Droite RER station, a 15-minute walk from the château. If you can't or don't want to walk, you can take bus B from Versailles Chantiers to the château for 8 F ($1.35) each way.

As a last resort, you can get to Versailles using a combination of Métro and city bus. Travel to the Pont-de-Sèvres stop by Métro, then transfer to bus 171 for a westward trek that will take from 20 to 45 minutes, depending on traffic. The bus will cost you three Métro tickets and will deposit you near the gates of the château.

If you're driving, take route N-10, following the signs to Versailles, then along avenue de Géneral Leclerc. Park on the Place d'Armes in front of the château.

ORIENTATION   The palace dominates the town. Three main avenues radiate from place d'Armes in front of the palace. The **tourist office** is at 7 rue des Réservoirs (☎ **01-39-50-36-22**).

✪ THE CHÂTEAU

The **Château de Versailles,** place d'Armes (☎ **01-30-84-74-00**), was conceived of as a glittering private world, far from the grime and noise and bustle of Paris. Seeing all of the château's rooms would take several days, although most visitors in a rush devote only a morning to the château. You should probably skip some of the rooms and save your energy for the park, which is the ultimate in French landscaping. Its makers disciplined every tree, shrub, flower, and hedge into a frozen ballet pattern and spread them among soaring fountains, sparkling pools, grandiose stairways, and hundreds of marble statues. It's like a colossal stage setting—even the view of the blue horizon seems like an ornately embroidered backdrop. The garden is an Eden for puppet people, a place where you expect the birds to sing coloratura soprano.

Inside, the **Grand Apartments,** the **Royal Chapel,** and the **Hall of Mirrors** (where the Treaty of Versailles was signed) can be visited without a guide. Other sections of the château may be visited only at specific hours or on special days. Some sections are temporarily closed as they undergo restoration. Try to save time to visit the **Grand Trianon,** which is a good walk across the park. In pink-and-white marble, it was designed by Hardouin-Mansart for Louis XIV in 1687 but is now mostly furnished with Empire pieces. You can also visit the **Petit Trianon,** built by Gabriel in 1768. This was the favorite residence of Marie Antoinette, who could escape the rigors of court here, and a retreat for Louis XV and his mistress, Madame du Barry.

The château is open May 2 through September 30, Tuesday through Sunday from 9am to 6:30pm; until 5:30pm the rest of the year. The grounds are open daily from 7am to dusk, which can be anytime between 5:30 and 9:30pm, depending on the time of year. The Trianons maintain the same hours as the château, but they open 1 hour later. Admission to the château is 45 F ($7.65) for adults, 35 F ($5.95) for ages 18 to 25, and free for under age 18 and over 60. Admission to the Grand Trianon is 25 F ($4.25) for adults, 15 F ($2.55) for ages 18 to 25, and free for under age 18. Admission to the Petit Trianon is 15 F ($2.55) for adults, 10 F ($1.70) for ages 18 to 25, and free for under age 18. Admission to both Trianons is 30 F ($5.10) for adults, 20 F ($3.40) for ages 18 to 25, and free for under age 18. Adults pay the reduced rates for all attractions after 3:30pm.

EVENING SPECTACLES   The French government offers a program of evening fireworks and illuminated fountains throughout the summer called **Les Fêtes de Nuit de Versailles (Rêve de Roi).** These always capture the heightened sense of the glory of France's *ancien régime.* At scattered dates throughout the summer, 200 actors in period costume portray Louis XVI and members of his court. Between April and October, shows begin at 10:30pm (9:30pm during August and September). Spectators sit on bleachers clustered at the château's boulevard de la Reine entrance, adjacent to the Fountain (Bassin) of Neptune. The most desirable seats cost 250 F ($42.50), and standing room sells for 70 F ($11.90), with no discounts offered for either children or students. Gates that admit you into the bleacher area open 90 minutes before showtime, and the show itself lasts 90 minutes.

Tickets can be purchased in advance at the tourist office in Versailles—inquire by phone, fax, or mail—or in central Paris at any of the FNAC stores (☎ 02-49-87-50-50). You can also take your chances and buy tickets an hour prior to the event from a kiosk adjacent to the boulevard de la Reine entrance. Call ☎ 01-30-83-78-88 for general information about any of the nighttime or Sunday afternoon spectacles on the grounds surrounding the château.

SUNDAY AFTERNOON PROMENADES IN THE PARK   Every Sunday between early April and mid-October, and every Saturday between early July and late August, between 11am and noon, and again between 3:30 and 5:30pm, classical music is broadcast throughout the park, and every fountain is turned on. The effect of these Grandes Eaux Musicales is to duplicate the landscaping vision of the 18th-century architects who designed Versailles. They even allow you to walk freely around the park, enjoying the juxtapositions of grand architecture and lavish waterworks. The cost of admission to the park during these events is 25 F ($4.25) per person.

DINING

Le Potager du Roy. 1 rue du Maréchal Joffre. ☎ **01-39-50-35-34.** Reservations required. Fixed-price menu 130 F ($22.10) at lunch, 175 F ($29.75) at dinner. AE, V. Tues–Sat noon–2:30pm; Tues–Sun 7–10:30pm. FRENCH.

Philippe Letourneur cooks from the heart, preparing food one Parisian critic called soulful. He specializes in uncomplicated cuisine with robust flavors, adding a breath of novelty to Versailles's jaded and world-weary dining scene. His attractive restaurant occupies an 18th-century building in a neighborhood known during the days of the French monarchs as the *Parc des Cerfs* ("Stag Park"). Here any bored courtier could find paid companionship with B- and C-list courtesans. The skillfully prepared menu is reinvented with the seasons. Examples include foie gras served with a vegetable-flavored vinaigrette; a ragout of macaroni with a persillade of snails; roasted duck with a navarin of vegetables; and roasted codfish served with roasted peppers in the style of Provence. Looking for something earthy and unusual? Try the fondant of pork jowls with a confit of fresh vegetables. If at all possible, save room for the chocolate cake, flavored with orange and served with coconut ice cream—it's oozing and intensely chocolatey.

Le Quai No. 1. 1 av. de St-Cloud. ☎ **01-39-50-42-26.** Reservations required. Main courses 85 F ($14.45); fixed-price menu 110 F ($18.70) at lunch, 140–185 F ($23.80–$31.45) at dinner. MC, V. Tues–Sat noon–2:30pm and 7:30–11pm; Sun noon–2:30pm. FRENCH.

This relatively informal seafood bistro is in an 18th-century building overlooking the western facade of France's most famous château. Lithographs and wood paneling spangle the dining room, and outside there's a terrace. Though the cuisine isn't as opulent, esoteric, or expensive as what's served within chef Gérard Vié's grander main restaurant, **Les Trois Marches** (see below), it's charming, very French, and dependable in presentation. The fixed-price menus make Le Quai a dining bargain in high-priced Versailles. Specialties include seafood sauerkraut, seafood paella, bouillabaisse, home-smoked salmon, and an enduringly popular upscale version of North American surf and turf, with grilled Breton lobster and sizzling sirloin. The chef recommends the seafood platter. Care and imagination go into the cuisine, and the service is both professional and polite.

✪ **Les Trois Marches.** In the Hôtel Trianon Palace, 1 bd. de la Reine. ☎ **01-30-84-38-40.** Reservations required. Fixed-price menu 350 F ($59.50) at lunch Mon–Fri, 610–750 F ($103.70–$127.50) at lunch Sat–Sun and at dinner. AE, DC, MC, V. Daily noon–2pm and 7:30–10pm. FRENCH.

Situated in a 5-acre garden, the Trianon hotel became world-famous in 1919 when it served as headquarters for signatories to the Treaty of Versailles. The dining room still retains an old-world splendor in its crystal chandeliers and fluted columns. Gérard Vié is the most talented and creative chef in Versailles these days, attracting a discerning clientele that doesn't mind paying the high prices. His *cuisine moderne* is subtle, often daringly conceived and inventive, and the service is smooth. Begin with a lobster salad flavored with fresh herbs and served with an onion soufflé, a galette of potatoes with bacon, chardonnay, and sevruga caviar, or perhaps the citrus-flavored bisque of scallops. You'll understand why the chef is considered such an innovator when you taste his main courses, especially his pigeon roasted and flavored with rosé and accompanied by celeriac and truffles. If you arrive in late autumn, you might encounter penne-like pasta, tossed with morels, mushrooms, and Parmesan, and blended in a butter sauce deeply infused with the flavor of white Alba truffles. One dish that is absolutely deserving of a culinary prize is celeriac fashioned into ravioli, filled with foie gras, and topped with a thick slice of black truffle. It's too hard to choose a dessert, so opt for the signature assortment.

6

Paris After Dark

After a long sleep, Paris nightlife has awakened. Late-night bars fill like gaudy aquariums, and French rap has flourished as a kind of hybrid of British, American, and North African influences. In this chapter we describe after-dark diversions that range from cafe concerts to "where the boys are."

Parisians start the serious part of their evenings just as Anglos stretch, yawn, and announce it's time for bed. Once a Paris workday is over, many people go straight to the cafe to meet up with friends; after a time, they proceed to a restaurant, bar, or theater; and much later, they grace a nightclub or late-night bar.

For the cafe scene, see chapter 4.

1 The Performing Arts

Announcements of shows, concerts, and operas are plastered on kiosks all over town. Listings can be found in *Pariscope,* a weekly entertainment guide with a section in English, or the English-language *Boulevard,* a bimonthly magazine. Performances start later in Paris than in London or New York—anywhere from 8 to 9pm—and Parisians tend to dine after the theater. You may not want to do the same, since many of the less-expensive restaurants close as early as 9pm.

A STATESIDE TICKET AGENCY   For tickets and information to just about any show and entertainment in Paris, **Globaltickets,** from Edwards and Edwards, has a New York office if you'd like to arrange your schedule before you go. It's at 1270 Ave. of the Americas, Suite 2414, New York, NY 10020 (☎ **800/223-6108** or 914/328-2150). They also have an office in Paris for assistance while you are there: 19 rue des Mathurins, 9e (☎ **01-42-65-39-21;** Métro: Havre-Caumartin). A personal visit isn't necessary. Edwards and Edwards will mail tickets to your home, fax confirmation, or leave tickets at the box office in Paris. There is a markup of 10% to 20% (excluding opera and ballet) over box-office price plus a U.S. handling charge of $8. Hotel/theater packages are also available.

DISCOUNTS Several agencies sell tickets for cultural events and plays at discounts of up to 50%. One is the **Kiosque Théâtre,** 15 place de la Madeleine, 8e (no phone; Métro: Madeleine), offering leftover tickets for about half price on the day of the performance. Tickets for evening performances are sold Tuesday through Friday from 12:30 to 8pm and Saturday from 2 to 8pm. If you'd like to attend a matinee, buy your ticket Saturday from 12:30 to 2pm or Sunday from 12:30 to 4pm. Other, possibly less crowded, branches are in the basement of the Châtelet–Les Halles Métro station and in front of the Gare Montparnasse.

Students with ID can often get last-minute tickets by trying at the box office an hour before curtain time.

For easy availability of tickets for festivals, concerts, and the theater, try one of two locations of the **FNAC** record store chain: 136 rue de Rennes, 6e (☎ **01-49-54-30-00;** Métro: Montparnasse-Bienvenue), or in the Forum des Halles, 1-7 rue Pierre-Lescot, 1er (☎ **01-40-41-40-00;** Métro: Châtelet–Les-Halles).

THEATER

Comédie-Française. 2 rue de Richelieu, 1er. ☎ **01-44-58-15-15.** Tickets 70–190 F ($11.90–$32.30). Métro: Palais-Royal or Musée-du-Louvre.

Those with a modest understanding of French can still delight in a sparkling production of Molière at this national theater, established to keep the classics alive and promote the most important contemporary authors. Nowhere else will you see the works of Molière and Racine so beautifully staged. The box office is open daily from 11am to 6pm, but the hall is dark from July 21 to September 5. In 1993, a Left Bank annex was launched, **Comédie Française–Théâtre du Vieux Colombier,** 21 rue du Vieux-Colombier, 4e (☎ **01-44-39-87-00**). Although its repertoire varies, it's known for presenting some of the most serious French dramas in town. Tickets are 160 F ($27.20), 65 F ($11.05) for age 26 and under.

OPERA, DANCE & CLASSICAL CONCERTS

Cité de la Musique. 221 av. Jean-Jaurès, 19e. ☎ **01-44-84-45-00,** or 01-44-84-44-84 for tickets and information. Tickets 80–200 F ($13.60–$34) for 4:30pm and 8pm concerts.

Of the half-dozen *grands travaux* (great projects) conceived by the Mitterrand administration, this testimony to the power of music has been the most widely applauded, the least criticized, and the most innovative. At the city's northeastern edge in what used to be a run-down and depressing neighborhood, this $120 million stone-and-glass structure incorporates a network of concert halls, a library and research center for the study of all kinds of music from around the world, and a museum. The complex hosts a rich variety of concerts, ranging from Renaissance through the 19th and 20th centuries, including jazz and traditional music from different nations around the world.

Maison de Radio France. 116 av. Président-Kennedy, 16e. ☎ **01-42-30-15-16.** Tickets 50–100 F ($8.50–$17). Métro: Passy-Ranelagh.

This is the site of many of the performances of the Orchestre Philharmonique de Radio-France and the somewhat more conservative Orchestre National de France. The concert hall's box office is open Monday through Saturday from 11am to 6pm.

✪ **Opéra Bastille.** Opera National de Paris. Place de la Bastille, 120 rue de Lyon, 75012 Paris. ☎ **01-43-43-96-96.** Tickets 60–660 F ($10.20–$112.20) opera, 60–650 F ($10.20–$110.50) dance. Métro: Bastille.

This controversial building—it's been called a "beached whale"—was designed by Canadian architect Carlos Ott, with curtains created by Japanese fashion designer Issey Miyake. Since its much-publicized opening in July 1989 (for the French Revolution's bicentennial), the opera house has presented masterworks such as Mozart's *Marriage of Figaro* and Tchaikovsky's *Queen of Spades.* The main hall is the largest of any French opera house, with 2,700 seats, but music critics have lambasted the acoustics. The building contains two additional concert halls, including an intimate 250-seat room that usually hosts chamber music. Both traditional opera performances and symphony concerts are presented here.

Several concerts are given for free in honor of certain French holidays. Write ahead for tickets.

Opéra-Comique. 5 rue Favart, 2e. ☎ **01-42-44-45-45.** Tickets 50–610 F ($8.50–$103.70). Métro: Richelieu-Drouot.

This is a particularly charming venue for light opera, on a smaller scale than Paris's major opera houses. Built in the late 1890s in an ornate style that might remind you of the Palais Garnier, it's the site of small productions of such operas as *Carmen, Don Giovanni, Tosca,* and *Palleas & Melisande.* There are no performances between mid-July and late August. The box office, however, is open year-round, every Monday through Saturday from 11am to 7pm.

✪ **Opéra Garnier (Palais Garnier).** Place de l'Opéra, 9e. ☎ **01-40-01-17-89.** Tickets 60–650 F ($10.20–$110.50) opera, 30–405 F ($5.10–$68.85) dance. Métro: Opéra.

Opéra Garnier is the premier stage for dance and, once again, for opera. Because of the competition from the Opéra Bastille, the original opera has made great efforts to present more up-to-date works, including choreography by Jerome Robbins, Twyla Tharp, Agnes de Mille, and George Balanchine. This rococo wonder was designed in a contest by young architect Charles Garnier at the heyday of the French Empire. The facade is adorned with marble and sculpture, including *The Dance* by Carpeaux. The world's great orchestral, operatic, and ballet companies have performed here. Now months of painstaking restorations have burnished the Garnier's former glory: In mid-1995, it reopened grandly with Mozart's *Cosí fan tutte*, its boxes and walls lined with flowing red and blue damask, gilt gleaming abundantly, its Chagall ceiling cleaned and air-conditioning added. The box office is open Monday through Saturday from 11am to 6:30pm.

Théâtre National de Chaillot. 1 place du Trocadéro, 16e. ☎ **01-53-65-30-00.** Tickets 180 F ($30.60) adults, 120 F ($20.40) under age 25 and over 60. Métro: Trocadéro.

Designed as part of the architectural complex facing the Eiffel Tower, this is one of the city's largest concert halls, hosting a variety of cultural events that are announced on billboards in front. Sometimes (rarely) dance is staged here, or else you might see a brilliantly performed play by the great Marguerite Duras. The box office is open Monday through Saturday from 11am to 7pm and Sunday from 11am to 5pm.

2 The Club & Music Scene

Paris is still a late-night mecca, though some of the once-unique attractions now glut the market. The fame of Parisian nights was established in those distant days when the British and Americans still gasped at the sight of a bare bosom in a chorus line. The fact is that contemporary Paris has less vice than London, Hamburg, or San Francisco.

Nevertheless, both the quantity and the variety of Paris nightlife still exceed that of other cities. Nowhere else will you find such a huge and mixed array of nightclubs, bars, dance clubs, cabarets, jazz dives, music halls, and honky-tonks.

Paris's bar scene is hopping, though bars here aren't as clearly defined as in other cities—they can be cafes and cafes can be bars, restaurants can be bars, and bars can also be clubs. It can get confusing. The best way to think about it is not to let the name give you any preconceived notions of what the place might be like. (Café Marly, for example, is much more than just a cafe, and Buddha-bar is known more for its food than its cocktails.)

The trendiest new area is the **rue Oberkampf,** where you'll find lots of bars lining the street starting from Métro Ménilmontant. Some of the new spots seem intentionally dilapidated, while others evoke the elegance of 19th-century watering holes. The walls often exhibit the work of local artists, and the music is kept fairly low-key to avoid attracting the troublemakers often drawn by aggressive music.

A MUSIC HALL

Olympia. 28 bd. des Capucines, 9e. ☎ **01-47-42-25-49.** Tickets 150–300 F ($25.50–$51). Métro: Opéra or Madeleine.

Charles Aznavour and other big names make frequent appearances in this cavernous hall. The late Yves Montand appeared once, and the performance was sold out 4 months in advance. Today, you are more likely to catch Gloria Estefan. A typical lineup might include an English rock group, showy Italian acrobats, a well-known French singer, a dance troupe, juggling American comedians (doing much of their work in English), plus the featured star. A witty emcee and an on-stage band provide a smooth transition. Performances usually begin at 8:30pm Tuesday through Sunday; Saturday matinees start at 5pm.

CHANSONNIERS

Chansonniers (literally "songwriters") provide a bombastic musical satire of the day's events. This combination of parody and burlesque is a time-honored Gallic amusement and a Parisian institution. Songs are often created on the spot, inspired by the "disaster of the day."

Au Caveau de la Bolée. 25 rue de l'Hirondelle, 6e. ☎ **01-43-54-62-20.** Fixed-price dinner 260 F ($44.20) Mon–Fri, 300 F ($51) Sat. Cover 150 F ($25.50) Mon–Sat if you don't order dinner. Drinks 30–65 F ($5.10–$11.05) each. Dinner Mon–Sat 8:30pm; cabaret 10:30pm. Métro: St-Michel.

To enter this bawdy boîte, you descend into the catacombs of the early 14th-century Abbey of St-André, once a famous cafe that attracted such personages as Verlaine and Oscar Wilde, who slowly snuffed out his life in absinthe here. The singing is loud and smutty, just the way the predominantly student audience likes it. Occasionally, the audience sings along. Frankly, you'll enjoy this place a lot more if you can follow the thread of the French-language jokes and satire, but even if you don't, there are enough visuals (magic acts and performances by singers) to amuse.

The fixed-price dinner is followed by a series of at least four entertainers, usually comedians. In lieu of paying admission for the cabaret, you can order dinner. If you've already had dinner, you can just order a drink.

✪ **Au Lapin Agile.** 22 rue des Saules, 18e. ☎ **01-46-06-85-87.** Cover (including the first drink) 130 F ($22.10). Tues–Sun 9:15pm–2am. No meals are served; drinks cost 30–40 F ($5.10–$6.80). Métro: Lamarck.

Picasso and Utrillo patronized this little cottage near the top of Montmartre, then known as the Cabaret des Assassins. It has been painted by numerous artists, including Utrillo. For many decades, the heart of French folk music has beat here. You'll sit at carved wooden tables in a dimly lit room with walls covered by bohemian memorabilia and listen to French folk tunes, love ballads, army songs, sea chanteys, and music-hall ditties. You're encouraged to sing along, even if it's only the "oui, oui, oui—non, non, non" refrain of "Les Chevaliers de la Table Ronde." The best sing-alongs are on weeknights after tourist season ends.

NIGHTCLUBS & CABARETS

Decidedly expensive, these places do provide some of the most lavishly spectacular floor shows anywhere.

✪ **Folies-Bergère.** 32 rue Richer, 9e. ☎ **01-44-79-98-98.** Cover 160–320 F ($27.20–$54.40); dinner and show 660–740 F ($112.20–$125.80). Tues–Sat at 9pm, Sun at 3pm. Métro: Rue-Montmartre or Cadet.

The Folies-Bergère has been a Paris institution for foreigners since 1886. Josephine Baker, the African-American singer who used to throw bananas into the audience, became "the toast of Paris" here. According to legend, the first GI to reach Paris at the 1944 Liberation asked for directions to the club.

Don't expect the naughty and slyly permissive skin-and-glitter revue that used to be the trademark of this place. In 1993, all of that ended with a radical restoration and reopening under new management. Today, the site is configured as a conventional 1,600-seat theater that focuses on musical revues permeated with a sense of nostalgia for old Paris. You're likely to witness an intriguing, often charming, but not particularly erotic repertoire of mostly French songs, interspersed with the banter of a master/mistress of ceremonies. A restaurant serves set-price dinners in an anteroom to the theater. Latecomers are not admitted.

✪ **Lido de Paris.** 116 bis av. des Champs-Elysées, 8e. ☎ **800/227-4884** or 01-40-76-56-10. Cover for 10pm or midnight show 450–660 F ($76.50–$112.20) including a half bottle of champagne; or 8pm dinner-dance, including a half bottle of champagne, and 10pm show 815–1,015 F ($138.55–$172.55). Métro: George V.

As it heads for the millennium, the Lido has changed its feathers and modernized. Its $15 million current production, *C'est Magique*, is a dramatic reworking of the classic Parisian cabaret show, with eye-popping special effects and bold new themes, both nostalgic and contemporary, including aerial and aquatic ballets that use more than 60,000 gallons of water per minute. The show, the most expensive ever produced in Europe, uses 80 performers, $4 million in costumes, and a $2 million lighting design with lasers. There's even an ice rink and swimming pool that magically appear and disappear. The Bluebell Girls, those legendary sensual showgirls, are still here, however. Now that the celebrated chef Paul Bocuse is a consultant, the cuisine is better than ever. The quality of the shows and the professionalism of the entertainers seem to justify the high prices charged.

LE COOL JAZZ

The great jazz revival that long ago swept America is still going strong here, with Dixieland or Chicago rhythms being pounded out in dozens of jazz cellars, mostly called caveaux. Most clubs are between rue Bonaparte and rue St-Jacques on the Left Bank, which makes things easy for seekers of syncopation.

Le Bilboquet/Club St-Germain. 13 rue St-Benoît, 6e. ☎ **01-45-48-81-84.** No cover. Le Bilboquet nightly 8pm–2:45am; jazz music 10:30pm–2:45am. Club St-Germain Tues–Sun 11pm–5am. Métro: St-Germain-des-Prés.

This restaurant/jazz club/piano bar, where the film *Paris Blues* was shot, offers some of the best music in Paris. Jazz is played on the upper level in the restaurant, Le Bilboquet, a wood-paneled room with a copper ceiling, brass-trimmed sunken bar, and Victorian candelabra. The menu is limited but classic French, specializing in lamb, fish, and beef. Dinner costs 180 F to 300 F ($30.60 to $51).

Under separate management is the downstairs Club St-Germain disco, where entrance is free but drinks cost 100 F ($17). You can walk from one club to the other but have to buy a new drink each time you change venues.

New Morning. 7-9 rue des Petites-Ecuries, 10e. ☎ **01-45-23-51-41.** Cover 100–180 F ($17–$30.60). Call ahead, but the hours are generally Mon–Sat 8pm–1:30am. Métro: Château-d'Eau.

Jazz maniacs come to drink, talk, and dance at this long-enduring club, which is now in the same league as the Village Vanguard in New York's Greenwich Village. The club remains on the see-and-be-seen circuit, as exemplified by recent guests: Spike Lee and the artist formerly known as Prince. The high-ceilinged loft, previously a newspaper office, was turned into a nightclub in 1981. Many styles of music are played and performed. The club is especially popular with jazz groups from Central and South Africa. A phone call will let you know what's going on the night you plan to visit. Sometimes they're open on Sunday. No food is served.

DANCE CLUBS

The nightspots below are among hundreds of places where people go chiefly to dance—distinct from others where the main attraction is the music. The area around the **Eglise St-Germain-des-Prés** is full of dance clubs. They come and go so quickly that you could arrive in your club clothes to find a hardware store in the place of last year's disco—but, like all things in nature, the new springs up to take the place of the old. Check out *Time Out: Paris* or *Pariscope* to get a sense of current trends.

Club Zed. 2 rue des Anglais, 5e. ☎ **01-43-54-93-78.** Cover 50–100 F ($8.50–$17) including the first drink. Wed–Thurs 10:30pm–3am, Fri–Sat 10:30pm–5am. Métro: Maubert-Mutualité.

This popular nightspot in a former bakery with a vaulted masonry ceiling may surprise you with its mix of musical offerings, including samba, rock-and-roll, 1960s pop, and jazz.

La Balajo. 9 rue de Lappe, 11e. ☎ **01-47-00-07-87.** Cover 50 F ($8.50) including first drink on Sun afternoon, 100 F ($17) evenings. Thurs–Sat 11:30pm–5am, Sun 1–11pm. Métro: Bastille.

Established in 1936, this dance club is best remembered as the venue where Edith Piaf first won the hearts of thousands of Parisian music lovers. Today, Le Balajo is hardly as fashionable, although it continues its big-band tradition on Sunday afternoon when patrons dance to World War II–era swing. Thursday to Saturday nights, they bring out the disco ball, or play reggae, salsa, rock-and-roll, and rap.

La Chapelle des Lombards. 19 rue de Lappe, 11e. ☎ **01-43-57-24-24.** Cover 100 F ($16.95) Thurs, 120 F ($20.30) Fri–Sat. Métro: Bastille.

A festive tropical ambience and diverse music—everything from salsa to raggae—attract a lively mixed crowd to this hip club near the Bastille. To really enjoy this place, you have to dress the part, which means no sneakers or jeans, but rather your sophisticated best.

Le Saint. 7 rue St-Severin, 5e. ☎ **01-43-25-50-04.** Cover 60–90 F ($10.20–$15.30) including first drink. Daily 11pm–6am. Métro: St-Michel.

Set in three medieval cellars deep within Paris's university area, this place lures 20- and 30-somethings who dance and drink and generally feel happy to be in a Left Bank student dive. The music melds New York, Los Angeles, and Europe, and often leads to episodes of "Young Love Beside the Seine" that many visitors remember in a kind of shameful reverie for months afterward.

Les Bains. 7 rue du Bourg-l'Abbé, 3e. ☎ **01-48-87-01-80.** Cover 100 F ($17) including first drink. Nightly midnight–6am. Métro: Réaumur.

This chic enclave has been pronounced "in" and "out," but lately it's very "in," attracting model types and growing a bit gayer, especially on Monday night. Customers dress more for show than for comfort. The name Les Bains comes from the place's old function as a Turkish bath attracting gay clients, none more notable than Marcel Proust. It may be hard to get in if the bouncer doesn't like your looks. A restaurant has been added.

ROCK & ROLL

Bus Palladium. 6 rue Fontaine, 9e. ☎ **01-53-21-07-33.** Cover 100 F ($17) for men, 100 F ($17) for women Fri–Sat only. Tues–Sat 11pm–6am. Métro: Blanche or Pigalle.

Set in a single room with a very long bar, this rock-and-roll temple has varnished hardwoods and fabric-covered walls that barely absorb the reverberations of nonstop recorded music. You won't find techno, punk-rock, jazz, blues, or soul here. It's rock-and-roll and nothing but rock-and-roll, for hard-core, mostly heterosexual, rock wannabes ages 25 to 35. Alcoholic drinks of any kind cost 80 F ($13.60), except for women on Tuesday, when they drink as much as they want for free.

SALSA

Les Étoiles. 61 rue du Château d'Eau, 10e. ☎ **01-47-70-60-56.** Cover 150 F ($25.50) including first drink. Métro: Château d'Eau.

Since 1856, this red-swabbed old-fashioned music hall has shaken with the sound of performers at work and patrons at play. Its newest incarnation is as a restaurant discothèque where the music is exclusively salsa and the food Cubano. Expect simple but hearty portions of fried fish, shredded pork or beef, white rice, beans, and flan as bands from Venezuela play salsa to a crowd that already knows or quickly learns how to dance to South American rhythms.

3 Bars, Pubs & Clubs

WINE BARS

Many Parisians now prefer the wine bar to the traditional cafe or bistro. The food is often better and the ambience more inviting. For cafes, see chapter 4.

✪ **Au Sauvignon.** 80 rue des Sts-Pères, 7e. ☎ **01-45-48-49-02.** Mon–Sat 8:30am–10:30pm. Métro: Sèvres-Babylone.

This tiny place has tables overflowing onto a covered terrace where wines range from the cheapest Beaujolais to the most expensive Saint Émilion Grand Cru. A glass of wine is 21 F to 30 F ($3.55 to $5.10), and it costs an additional 2 F (35¢) to consume it at a table. To accompany your wine, choose an Auvergne specialty, including goat cheese and terrines. The fresh Poilâne bread is ideal with ham, pâté, or goat cheese. The place is decorated with old ceramic tiles and frescoes done by Left Bank artists.

Aux Négociants. 27 rue Lambert, 18e. ☎ **01-46-06-15-11.** Mon and Fri noon–8pm, Tues–Thurs noon–10:30pm. Métro: Lamarck-Caulincourt or Château-Rouge.

Ten minutes downhill from the north facade of Sacré-Coeur, this bistro à vins has flourished since it was founded in 1980 as an outlet for wines produced in the Loire Valley. Artists, street vendors, and office workers all come here, linked only by an appreciation of wine and the allure of the simple but hearty plats du jour priced from 60 F to 70 F ($10.20 to $11.90). It's hearty and unpretentious, the kind of place you'd expect to find in the countryside. Wines range from 16 F to 28 F ($2.70 to $4.75) for a glass.

✪ **Willi's Wine Bar.** 13 rue des Petits-Champs, 1er. ☎ **01-42-61-05-09.** Mon–Sat noon–11pm. Métro: Bourse, Louvre, or Palais-Royal.

Journalists and stockbrokers patronize this increasingly popular wine bar in the center of the financial district, run by an Englishman, Mark Williamson. About 250 kinds of wine are offered, including a dozen wine specials you can taste by the glass for 20 F to 83 F ($3.40 to $14.10). Lunch is the busiest time—on quiet evenings you can better enjoy the warm ambience and 16th-century beams. Daily specials are likely to include lamb brochette with cumin or lyonnaise sausage in truffled vinaigrette, plus spectacular desserts such as chocolate terrine. Platters of food, each priced at 90 F ($15.30), include Scottish salmon baked in a salt crust, served with a fricassée of artichoke hearts, and fillet of beef roasted with ginger.

BARS & PUBS

These "imported" establishments try to imitate American cocktail bars or masquerade as British pubs—most strike an alien chord. But that doesn't prevent fashionable Parisians from barhopping (not to be confused with cafe-sitting). In general, bars and pubs are open daily between 11am and 1:30am, though of course there are exceptions to the rule.

Bars and Salons of the Plaza Athénée. 25 av. Montaigne, 8e. ☎ **01-53-67-66-65.** Métro: Alma-Marceau.

Residents of the surrounding neighborhood have always enjoyed dropping into this hotel for a drink in cosseted, supremely well-upholstered circumstances. The drinking venue is set to move from the Bar Anglais, on the hotel's lower level, to one of the street-level salons. A pianist and singer usually perform between 10:30pm and 1:30am, and a prosperous, polyglot crowd of hotel guests and upscale locals amuse and entertain one another.

China Club. 50 rue de Charenton, 12e. ☎ **01-43-43-82-02.** Métro: Bastille.

Designed to recall France's 19th-century colonies in Asia or a bordello in 1930s Shanghai (on the ground floor) and England's empire-building zeal in India (upstairs), the China Club will allow you to chitchat or flirt with the singles who crowd into the street-level bar, then escape to calmer, more contemplative climes upstairs. You'll see regulars from Paris's worlds of fashion and the arts, along with a pack of postshow celebrants from the nearby Opéra de la Bastille. There's a Chinese restaurant on the street level serving dinner every night from 7pm to 12:30am, a scattering of books, newspapers, and chess boards upstairs, and a more animated (and occasionally raucous) bar in the cellar, where live music is presented every Friday and Saturday between 10pm and 3am. There's never a cover charge. Beer costs 25 F ($4.25).

L'Académie de la Bière. 88 bis bd. du Port-Royal, 5e. ☎ **01-43-54-66-65.** Métro: Port-Royal.

The decor is paneled, woodsy, and rustic, an appropriate foil for an "academy" whose curriculum includes more than 150 kinds of beer, each from a microbrewery. Stella Artois, the best-selling beer in Belgium, isn't available, although more than half of the dozen on tap are from small-scale, not particularly famous breweries in Belgium that deserve to be better known. Mugs or bottles cost from 29 F to 43 F ($4.95 to $7.30) each, depending on how esoteric they are.

Snack-style food is available, including platters of mussels, assorted cheeses, and sausages with mustard.

Le Bar l'Hôtel. In L'Hôtel, 13 rue des Beaux-Arts, 6e. ☎ **01-44-41-99-00.** Métro: St-Germain-des-Prés.

This is the hyper-artsy and theatrically overdecorated bar of a hotel that has wooed film-industry types who want to avoid the more mainstream luxury of Paris's palatial hotels. The rose-filter cheeriness is deceptive: This is the hotel where Oscar Wilde died, disgraced and impoverished, after his self-imposed exile from England. The staff is conscientiously straitlaced, but you'd expect a musical comedy to break out at any moment.

Le Web Bar. 32 rue de Picardie, 3e. ☎ **01-42-72-57-47.** Métro: Temple.

Few other nightclubs seem to tap as gleefully into the computer age as Le Web Bar. It occupies a three-story space at the eastern edge of the Marais that echoes with the sound of people talking and schmoozing with each other and with silent computer-transmitted partners many thousands of miles away. The site consists of a restaurant on the street level, a battery of at least 25 computers one floor upstairs, and a top-floor art gallery. And to keep things perking, there's live music every night beginning around 7pm. Beer costs 18 F ($3.05); a plat du jour averages 50 F ($8.50), and use of the somewhat battered computers is free. Menu items stress comfort food, which in this case refers to such conservative French specialties as boeuf bourguignonne. If you want to check out the place ahead of time, it has a Web page at **www.ethernite.com**. It's open daily from 8am to 2am.

Pub St-Germain-des-Prés. 17 rue de l'Ancienne-Comédie, 6e. ☎ **01-43-29-38-70.** Métro: Odéon.

With 9 different rooms and 650 seats, this is the largest pub in France, offering 450 brands of beer, 26 of which are on draft. The deliberately tacky decor, which has seen a lot of beer swilled and spilled since its installation, consists of faded gilt-framed mirrors, hanging lamps, and a stuffed parrot in a gilded cage. Leather booths let you drink discreetly in an atmosphere that is usually quiet, relaxed, and posh. Featured beers change frequently, but usually include Amstel, many different Belgian brews (including both blonde and brunet versions of Belforth), Whitbread, and Pimm's No. 1. If frat houses turn you on, it gets really fun between 10:30pm and 4am, when above the chatter of live rock everything becomes loud, raucous, and sudsy.

4   Gay & Lesbian Bars & Clubs

Gay life is centered around Les Halles and Le Marais, with the greatest concentration of gay and lesbian clubs, restaurants, bars, and shops between the Hôtel-de-Ville and Rambuteau Métro stops. Gay dance clubs come and go so fast that even the magazines devoted to their pursuit—*e.m@ale* and *Illico,* both distributed free in the gay bars and bookstores—have a hard time keeping up. For lesbians, the guide *Exes Femmes* publishes a free seasonal listing of bars and clubs. Also look for Gai Pied's *Guide Gai,* available at kiosks for 69 F ($11.75) and *Pariscope's* regularly featured English-language section, "A Week of Gay Outings."

Amnesia Café. 42 rue Vieille-du-Temple, 4e. ☎ **01-42-72-16-94.** Métro: Hôtel-de-Ville.

Its function and clientele changes throughout the course of the day, despite the constant presence of a local cadre of gay men. Combining aspects of a cafe, tearoom, bistro, and bar, it includes two beige bar and dining areas, a mezzanine, and a cellar-level bar that opens later in the evening. Beer and cocktails are the drinks of choice, with a specialty coffee (café amnesia) that combines caffeine with cognac and Chantilly cream. Deep armchairs and soft pillows combine with 1930s accents here, creating an ambience that's conducive to talk and a cheerfulness that's not always apparent in the more sexually charged bars nearby. Plats du jour cost 60 F to 80 F ($10.20 to $13.60) each and include surprisingly conservative food like Basque chicken and beef bourguignonne.

Banana Café. 13 rue de la Ferronnerie, 1er. ☎ **01-42-33-35-31.** Métro: Châtelet or Les-Halles.

This popular gay bar is a ritualized stopover for anyone visiting or doing business in Paris. Occupying two floors of a 19th-century building, it has walls the color of an overripe banana, dim lighting, and a well-publicized policy of raising the price of drinks after 10pm, when things become really interesting. On theme nights such as Valentine's Day, expect the entire premises to be plastered with pink crepe paper. There's a street-level bar and a dance floor in the cellar that features a live pianist and recorded music—sometimes with dancing. On many nights, go-go dancers from all over perform from spotlit platforms in the cellar.

La Champmeslé. 4 rue Chabanais, 2e. ☎ **01-42-96-85-20.** Métro: Pyramides or Bourse.

The leading lesbian bar in Paris. With dim lighting, background music, and comfortable banquettes, La Champmeslé offers a cozy meeting place for women, and to a much, much lesser extent for "well-behaved" men. The club is housed in a 300-year-old building heavy on exposed stone and ceiling beams, with retro 1950s-style furnishings. Every Thursday night, one of the premier lesbian events of Paris, a cabaret, begins at 10pm (but the price of cover and drinks doesn't rise); and every month there is a well-attended exhibition of paintings by mostly lesbian artists. The bar is named in honor of a celebrated 17th-century actress, La Champmeslé, who was instrumental in interpreting the then-fledgling dramatic efforts of the celebrated playwright Racine.

Le Queen. 102 av. des Champs-Elysées, 8e. ☎ **01-53-89-08-90.** Cover 50 F ($8.50) Mon, 100 F ($17) Fri–Sat. Métro: F. D. Roosevelt.

Should you miss gay life à la New York, follow the flashing purple sign on the "main street" of Paris, near the corner of avenue George-V. The place is often mobbed, primarily with gay men and, to a lesser degree, models, actresses, and the like. Look for go-go boys, drag shows, muscle shows, and everything from 1970s-style disco nights (Monday) to Tuesday-night foam parties (only in summer), when cascades of mousse descend onto the dance floor. Go very, very late, as the place is open daily from midnight to 6 or 7am.

5 A Literary Haunt

✪ **Harry's New York Bar.** 5 rue Daunou, 2e. ☎ **01-42-61-71-14.** Métro: Opéra or Pyramides.

"Sank roo doe Noo," as the ads tell you to instruct your cab driver, is the most famous bar in Europe—quite possibly in the world. Opened Thanksgiving Day 1911, by a bearded Hemingway precursor by the name of MacElhone, it's sacred to Papa disciples as the spot where members of ambulance corps drank themselves silly during World War I, and as the master's favorite place to snuff brain cells in Paris. The site is legendary for other reasons too: White Lady and Sidecar cocktails were invented here in 1919 and 1931, respectively. It's also the alleged birthplace of the Bloody Mary and the headquarters of a loosely organized fraternity of drinkers known as the International Bar Flies (IBF). Harry's New York Bar has stayed in the family: Duncan, MacElhone's bilingual grandson now owns and runs it.

The place's core is the street-level bar, where CEOs and office workers loosen their neckties on more or less equal footing. Daytime crowds draw from the neighborhood's insurance, banking, and travel industries; evening crowds include pre- and post-theater groupies and night owls who aren't bothered by the gritty setting and deliberately unflattering lighting. A softer ambience reigns in the cellar, where a pianist provides highly drinkable music every night from 10pm to 2am, accompanied by whatever patron feels uninhibited enough to join in.

Index

See also separate Accommodations and Restaurant indexes, below.

ACCOMMODATIONS

RESTAURANTS

FROMMER'S® COMPLETE TRAVEL GUIDES

FROMMER'S® DOLLAR-A-DAY GUIDES

Australia from $50 a Day
California from $60 a Day
Caribbean from $70 a Day
England from $70 a Day
Europe from $60 a Day
Florida from $60 a Day

Hawaii from $70 a Day
Ireland from $50 a Day
Israel from $45 a Day
Italy from $70 a Day
London from $85 a Day
New York from $80 a Day

New Zealand from $50 a Day
Paris from $85 a Day
San Francisco from $60 a Day
Washington, D.C.,
    from $60 a Day

FROMMER'S® PORTABLE GUIDES

Acapulco, Ixtapa &
    Zihuatanejo
Alaska Cruises & Ports of Call
Bahamas
Baja & Los Cabos
Berlin
California Wine Country
Charleston & Savannah
Chicago

Dublin
Hawaii: The Big Island
Las Vegas
London
Maine Coast
Maui
New Orleans
New York City
Paris

Puerto Vallarta, Manzanillo
    & Guadalajara
San Diego
San Francisco
Sydney
Tampa & St. Petersburg
Venice
Washington, D.C.

FROMMER'S® NATIONAL PARK GUIDES

Family Vacations in the
    National Parks
Grand Canyon

National Parks of the
    American West
Rocky Mountain

Yellowstone & Grand Teton
Yosemite & Sequoia/
    Kings Canyon
Zion & Bryce Canyon

FROMMER'S® GREAT OUTDOOR GUIDES

New England
Northern California

Southern California & Baja
Washington & Oregon

FROMMER'S® MEMORABLE WALKS

Chicago
London

New York
Paris

San Francisco
Washington D.C.

FROMMER'S® IRREVERENT GUIDES

Amsterdam
Boston
Chicago
Las Vegas

London
Los Angeles
Manhattan

New Orleans
Paris
San Francisco

Seattle & Portland
Vancouver
Walt Disney World
Washington, D.C.

FROMMER'S® BEST-LOVED DRIVING TOURS

America
Britain
California

Florida
France
Germany

Ireland
Italy
New England

Scotland
Spain
Western Europe

THE UNOFFICIAL GUIDES®

Bed & Breakfast in New England
Bed & Breakfast in the Northwest
Beyond Disney
Branson, Missouri
California with Kids
Chicago
Cruises
Florida with Kids
The Great Smoky & Blue Ridge Mountains
Inside Disney
Las Vegas
London
Miami & the Keys
Mini Las Vegas
Mini-Mickey
New Orleans
New York City
Paris
San Francisco
Skiing in the West
Walt Disney World
Walt Disney World for Grown-ups
Walt Disney World for Kids
Washington, D.C.

SPECIAL-INTEREST TITLES

Born to Shop: France
Born to Shop: Hong Kong
Born to Shop: Italy
Born to Shop: New York
Born to Shop: Paris
Frommer's Britain's Best Bike Rides
The Civil War Trust's Official Guide to the Civil War Discovery Trail
Frommer's Caribbean Hideaways
Frommer's Europe's Greatest Driving Tours
Frommer's Food Lover's Companion to France
Frommer's Food Lover's Companion to Italy
Frommer's Gay & Lesbian Europe
Israel Past & Present
Monks' Guide to California
Monks' Guide to New York City
The Moon
New York City with Kids
Unforgettable Weekends
Outside Magazine's Guide to Family Vacations
Places Rated Almanac
Retirement Places Rated
Road Atlas Britain
Road Atlas Europe
Washington, D.C., with Kids
Wonderful Weekends from Boston
Wonderful Weekends from New York City
Wonderful Weekends from San Francisco
Wonderful Weekends from Los Angeles